Social Work and
Drug Use

'This is the most important book on illicit drug use and social work to be published for a long time ... Whilst it may inspire some to become "drug specialists", its most important purpose is in dealing with drug issues which are apparent in all social work settings. Just as importantly, this book should be read by those responsible for redesigning social work and social work education in order that substance use forms part of the curriculum.'

Ken Barrie, Alcohol and Drug Studies, University of West Scotland, UK

'This comprehensive, well written book will be essential reading for social work students and practitioners who need a clear, useful and relevant overview of the issues involved in working constructively with drug using service users. Its emphasis on working in partnership, while also attending to issues of risk and vulnerability, is realistic and practical, and being resolutely "social" in its outlook, the book will appeal to and inspire novice and experienced practitioners alike.'

Dr Mark Hardy, Department of Social Policy and Social Work,
University of York, UK

Social Work and Drug Use

Ian Paylor, Fiona Measham and Hugh Asher

 Open University Press

Open University Press
McGraw-Hill Education
McGraw-Hill House
Shoppenhangers Road
Maidenhead
Berkshire
England
SL6 2QL

email: enquiries@openup.co.uk
world wide web: www.openup.co.uk

and Two Penn Plaza, New York, NY 10121-2289, USA

First published 2012

A catalogue record of this book is available from the British Library

ISBN-13: 978-0-33-523455-4 (pb)
ISBN-10: 0-33-523455-0 (pb)
eISBN: 978-0-33-524023-4

Library of Congress Cataloging-in-Publication Data
CIP data applied for

Typesetting and e-book compilations by
RefineCatch Limited, Bungay, Suffolk
Printed and bound in the UK by Bell & Bain Ltd, Glasgow

The McGraw·Hill Companies

Contents

Abbreviations

AA   Alcoholics Anonymous
ACMD   Advisory Council on the Misuse of Drugs
ACPO   Association of Chief Police Officers
ADP   Antidiscriminatory practice
AIDS   Acquired immune deficiency syndrome
BBV(s)   Blood-borne virus(es)
BCS   British Crime Survey
BMJ   British Medical Journal
CBM   Cognitive behavioural model
CBT   Cognitive Behavioural Therapy
CDT   Community Drug Team
CFI   Central Funding Initiative
DAAT   Drug and Alcohol Action Team
DANOS   Drugs and Alcohol National Occupational Standards
DAT   Drug Action Team
DDUs   Drug Dependency Units
DfEE   Department of Education and Employment
DIP   Drug Intervention Programme (*renamed* – was Criminal Justice Interventions Programme (CJIP))
DoH   Department of Health
DPAS   Drug Prevention Advisory Service
DRR(s)   Drug Rehabilitation Requirement(s)
DSM   Diagnostic and Statistical Manual of Mental Disorders
DTTO(s)   Drug Treatment and Testing Order(s)
EBP   Evidence-based practice
EMCDDA   European Monitoring Centre for Drugs and Drug Addiction
ESPAD   European School Survey Project on Alcohol and Other Drugs
GSCC   General Social Care Council
HBV   Hepatitis B virus
HCV   Hepatitis C virus
HIV   Human Immunodeficiency Virus
HO   Home Office
HPA   Health Protection Agency
HR   Harm reduction
IDU(s)   Injecting drug user(s)
LSCBR   Local Safeguarding Children Boards Regulations

MDA   Misuse of Drugs Act 1971
NA   Narcotics Anonymous
NGO(s)   Non governmental organization(s)
NHS   National Health Service
NICE   National Institute for Health and Clinical Excellence
NTA   National Treatment Agency
NTORS   National Treatment Outcome Research Study
ONS   Office of National Statistics
OTC   Over The Counter
PDU(s)   Problem Drug User(s)
PND(s)   Penalty Notices for Disorder
QUADS   Quality in Alcohol and Drugs Services
RCGP   Royal College of General Practitioners
RCT   Randomized control trial
RSA   Royal Society of Arts
SCIE   Social Care Institute for Excellence
SCR   Serious case reviews
THC   Tetrahydrocannabinol
UKATT   United Kingdom Alcohol Treatment Trial
UKDPC   United Kingdom Drug Policy Committee
UKHRA   United Kingdom Harm Reduction Alliance
UNODC   United Nations Office on Drugs and Crime
VBP   Values-based practice
WHO   World Health Organization

Introduction: the challenge for social work

At Lancaster University we invite all prospective social work students for an individual interview. One of the many questions we ask in an interview is: What do you think social work is? Invariably the first nervous answer is 'it is about helping people'. When asked to elaborate we get a variety of replies but usually the answer is something along the lines of: Social workers enable children, adults, families, groups and communities to participate, function and develop in society. When pushed candidates will acknowledge that social work interventions may be resisted and resented and invoke feelings of hostility and suspicion. Getting students to appreciate the complexity of social work begins at that very first interview.

There are a host of divergent views as to the function of social workers. Social workers practise in a society of complexity, uncertainty, risk, change and diversity and the majority of people to whom they provide services are among the most disadvantaged and vulnerable in society (Adams *et al.*, 2009). Social work invariably encounters problems whose origins lie in inequality, discrimination and disadvantage. Social work typically engages with service users whose background and experiences often reflect a history of social exclusion,[1] and that forms the context for any intervention (Higham, 2006).

Whatever the form or type of social work intervention,[2] ever since the early days of the profession, social workers have been confronted with personal and social problems caused by service users' use of drugs and alcohol.[3] Substance misuse is a key feature in social work with children and families. Parental substance misuse is a common factor in social work cases especially in the more serious cases; for example, where children are on the child protection register and/or are involved in court proceedings. In particular parental alcohol misuse is the most important contributory factor in the reception of children into local authority care. Dealing with parental use of drugs and alcohol is one of the most important challenges facing social workers (Forrester and Harwin, 2011).

There are high rates of overlap between domestic violence and substance use (Cleaver *et al.*, 2007) with the evidence being particularly strong for women seeking formal help for alcohol or other drug problems (Galvani, 2009; Bennett and O'Brien, 2007). Social workers are on the front line supporting individuals and families living with these issues (Humphreys *et al.*, 2005; Galvani, 2006).

In addition there is evidence of high rates of substance use among people experiencing mental health problems (Crome *et al.*, 2009), and continuing concern about drug use by young people (Roberts, 2010; Paylor, 2009), the homeless (Bonner and Luscombe, 2009), female sex workers (Greater London Authority (GLA), 2005) and a growing concern about substance use among older people (Simmill-Binning *et al.*, 2009) and people with disabilities (McLaughlin *et al.*, 2007).

While some social workers specialize in substance use, most do not; however, alcohol and drug use are cross-cutting issues in all areas of social work practice (Galvani and Forrester, 2008; Bien *et al.*, 1993). There is overwhelming evidence of high rates of substance use among people who receive social work interventions and support, yet this evidence is thought to underestimate the actual extent due to service users' unwillingness to disclose or report substance use.

The National Occupational Standards for Social Work in England (Training Organisation for the Personal Social Services (TOPSS), 2002) identify alcohol and drug users as one of the main groups of social work service users.[4] The National Treatment Agency for Substance Misuse (NTA), a special health authority within the National Health Service (NHS) established by the government in 2001 to improve the availability, capacity and effectiveness of drug treatment in England, also acknowledges that social workers are on the front line in terms of identifying and intervening with people with substance-use problems (Department for Children, Schools and Families (DCSF), Department of Health (DoH and NTA 2009).

Current changes in the pipeline for social work following the Social Work Task Force (2009) report and the Munro Review (Department for Education, 2011) and the fact that in recent Serious case reviews[5] it was stated that all agencies were failing to address overlapping issues of substance use, domestic violence and parental mental ill health make it clear that good social work practice should include identifying and responding to alcohol and drug problems.

Social workers can and should be equipped to provide it. They don't need to be specialists but need to know enough to offer the right help. If nothing else there is a need to address this gap in social work education for the sake of service users. Service users have the right to a confident and informed social work response.

Although there is a long history of social work involvement with substance users, many social workers report feeling ill-equipped to work with service users who are experiencing problems associated with alcohol and drugs (McCarthy and Galvani, 2004) particularly in key skill areas such as how to talk to service users about alcohol and drug issues and how to assess substance use (Galvani and Forrester, 2008). Additional training and support in identifying problem substance use, and in assessing and providing interventions or referral is a necessary area for professional development for social workers who do not feel confident in these areas, and will provide a higher level of credibility for those working with substance-using service users.

Yet there is still a lack of training in such things like the basic skills in making the links between a child's difficulties and the nature and severity of parental substance misuse. Despite this we still have a situation where social work degree courses are not required to teach about substance misuse when the evidence presented makes a strong case for compulsion. Martin Barnes, Chief Executive of DrugScope, recently stated that he was surprised that there is not a requirement for social workers to have training or experience of working with substance use (Watson, 2010).

We have a situation in the UK[6] that many newly qualified social workers are still finding themselves regularly, if not daily, having to deal with alcohol and drug issues, without adequate (or indeed any) substance-use knowledge, nor any reflection on the appropriateness of their skills or values in relation to substance use (Galvani and Forrester, 2011).

In actual fact social workers are 'ideally placed' to deal with substance use problems due to their education, training and experience (Collins and Keene, 2000). Social workers have expertise in social care, housing liaison work, welfare rights, assisting with financial problems and in linking service users with a wide range of other agencies. This point also sits comfortably with the ethical standpoint of social work in which a holistic approach is emphasized (Hugman, 2008). What is more, social workers are trained in assessment skills (Parker, 2008), which are identified by service users as essential to the development of an effective and needs-led aftercare package (Croft and Beresford, 2008). Many social workers will also have experience of working with service users under stress and at periods of crisis in their lives (Dominelli, 2009). This is obviously extremely beneficial when working with drug users.

However, social work and drug use continues to present the profession with a series of ethical dilemmas. Social workers have to make choices, and these are subject to a number of influences, including their own values and working assumptions, as well as the structural and agency context and external rules, constraints and incentives which apply to them.

There is an inherent perception within social work which locates drug problems as problems concerning health and this has resulted in a lack of understanding from social workers as to how drug use relates to social work (Galvani, 2007). This is partly due to the lack of effective supervision of social workers working with drug users and the fact that there is no sustained pressure on social work educators to include drug use modules within social work degrees (Galvani, 2007). The result of such bureaucratic lunacy is that many social workers are actually missing a relevant knowledge base that concerns drug users, leaving many social workers feeling ill-equipped in working with, for example, injecting drug users (IDUs) (McCarthy and Galvani, 2004; Galvani, 2007) and thus, ill-equipped in preventing blood-borne viruses (BBV) (Paylor and Mack, 2010).

Effective and progressive social work also has to cope with institutional expectations regarding the capability to deal with increasing case loads, institutional constraints and organizational protocols and procedures as well as maintaining good relations with work colleagues against a background of a number of professional uncertainties, especially for those working in the statutory sector (Carey, 2009).

Social work is not a neutral activity, devoid of values and an ethical base. It is not simply a technical activity, but depends on the appreciation and application of a number of core values. Social workers have tasks to fulfil; they develop skills for their work. The skills have a technical aspect, but are a means to an end, that of ethical practice (Stern with Clough, 1996).

The form of intervention with drug users will depend very much on the starting point (i.e. the beliefs and assumptions) of individual practitioners with the nature of that intervention dependent on the prevailing perspective held by practitioners and their agencies. The approach undertaken will depend on the relative influence of competing views as to the source of the 'problem' and the most appropriate way of dealing with it. The approach taken by social workers will also depend on their understanding of the proper scope, principles, functions and methods of social work itself (Galvani, 2008).

Effective social work practice with drug users depends on negotiating a series of complex and interlocking questions, both about drugs and the reasons people use them and about the nature of the professional task.

In the specific context of social work with drug users, there are particular issues which social work encounters and which practitioners must address in order to intervene effectively; this can perhaps be summarized in terms of the processes of stigmatizing to which drug users are peculiarly susceptible. Drug users and their behaviour are seen as fundamentally problematic, and this is accentuated by the specific impact of wider causes such as 'marginalization'.

In particular, research suggests that stigma, exclusion and discrimination continue to be features in the lives of those who use drugs in daily, dependent and potentially harmful ways such as injecting. Furthermore, if recreational drug use comes to the attention of criminal justice agencies, social services or child protection agencies, then the extent to which drug use can be considered a 'tolerable deviance' (Hathaway, 1997) becomes seriously compromised (Gilman, 1991). This can be illustrated in the circumstances surrounding the death of Isobel Reilly, a 15-year-old who took two ecstasy tablets at her friend's house party in April 2011. The ecstasy tablets were allegedly the property of her friend's father who had left his 14-year-old daughter alone for the night while he visited friends in another city. His daughter and her friends held a party at the house and consumed ecstasy and ketamine which they had found hidden in her father's bedroom wardrobe. When Reilly died and three other children were hospitalized having taken ecstasy tablets after drinking heavily, the father was arrested and charged with possession of controlled drugs and child abandonment, received an eight month prison sentence suspended for two years, as well as being suspended from his job as a university researcher. It is difficult to imagine the same legal and social admonishment if it had been the alcohol rather than the ecstasy pills that had been implicated in Reilly's death.

While it is unrealistic to expect the total elimination of all stigma against social groups, practical steps can be taken towards reducing the discrimination that disadvantaged and marginalized groups face, and challenging the stereotypes underpinning them. To this end campaigning groups such as Transform and Release attempt to advance the rights of drug users as citizens and human beings. For social workers who have to make assessments and decisions regarding drug users' lives, this is an area of particular importance which links to the general professional standards of good practice in the field (General Social Care Council (GSCC), 2002).

While Newcombe (2007) has constructed a charter of rights for drug users, Walsh (2010) has argued for the utilization of human rights law to protect the interests of drug users and their right to 'cognitive liberty'. In particular Walsh identifies the 'untapped potential' of the European Convention on Human Rights, which was incorporated into UK law in the form of the Human Rights Act 1998, as a tool to challenge drug prohibition and reform UK drug policy. She suggests that the Human Rights Act could be utilized to advocate first, the right to self-medicate (e.g., if an individual believes that cannabis helps alleviate pain or anxiety); second, the right to practise religions such as Rastafarianism freely, and third (and most contentiously), the right to use psychoactive drugs to explore one's own consciousness, a sort of 'individual sovereignty over one's interior environment' (Walsh, 2010: 433). Furthermore, Walsh notes the legal ambiguities between the state allowing self-regulation by the population in their consumption of legal drugs such as alcohol and tobacco which together kill approximately 160 000 people in the UK each year, by comparison with the state prohibition of illegal drugs which kill less than 1 per cent of this number.

However, as noted by Lloyd, legal protection may have only limited use in the context of the stigmatization and discrimination experienced by drug users. In Peay's (2004) review of legislation relevant to mental illness (including the Mental Health Act 2007, the Disability Discrimination Act 1995 and the Human Rights Act 1998) he concluded that 'legal protection may be of limited use in the context of the stigmatisation' and warned that:

> Whilst the law might encourage people to be fair in their treatment of others, and may provide redress for those subject to unfair discrimination, the fundamentals of fair treatment lie in our attitudes to others. Law may overtly attempt to rectify any imbalance, but its very presence may be as much counterproductive as beneficial.
>
> (Peay, 2004: 372)

Lloyd (2010 : 63) concurs, suggesting that for drug users:

> While legal changes may be important for symbolic reasons, they may be of limited practical value. Ultimately, the complex, interactional nature of stigma may mean that the law is too much of a blunt tool where one is ultimately looking to change people's attitudes towards others.

For practitioners, these tensions are intensified by the requirement to 'see both sides', and to respond equally to concerns about problematic behaviour, and drug users' rights and occasional sense of injustice. In order for social workers to understand and address these challenges, and develop creative and empowering interventions, there is a need to locate the specifics of practice within a broad analysis of the complex interplay between differing perspectives, interests and cultural and structural influences. This book seeks to draw out the implications for practice in light of this analysis. In sum, the aim is to provide a comprehensive basis for social workers to develop a rounded and considered approach to their practice with drug and alcohol users, in light of a clear understanding of the competing pressures that impact on drug and alcohol users' lives.

1 Prevalence, patterns and policy

Introduction

Before considering the role that drugs play in the remit of social workers, it is first necessary to map out the contemporary drugs landscape in the UK. This chapter provides an overview of the prevalence and patterns of drug use in the UK, alongside some of the key features of current drug policy and recent legislative change. Specific patterns of drug use and groups of drug users identified in this chapter – including the socially excluded, young people, older people, women, minority ethnic groups, and lesbians and gay men – highlight the significance of the circumstances affecting different socio-demographic groups, thereby providing evidence of the compound effects of these experiences, which will illustrate the complex nature of the challenges facing social workers in the field of drugs.

Drug use in the general population

The most robust information on levels and patterns of contemporary drug use is provided by surveys, primarily of the general population but also of school-children, and adolescents. Regarding general population surveys, the annual national British Crime Survey (BCS) available from the Home Office website provides the best data on the use of different drugs by different socio-demographic groups. While its strengths lie in the large annual random sampling which produces robust indicators of changing trends in self-reported drug use, the private household sampling means that groups which may have higher than average drug-using rates (including the homeless, those living in hostels, prisons and transient populations) are excluded. Along with some anticipated underreporting within the home, we can envisage, therefore, that figures will be an underestimate of the scale of drug use in the UK (Aldridge *et al.*, 2011).

The most recent BCS for 2009/10 estimates that over one in three adults aged 16–59 (36 per cent) report ever having used illicit drugs; that is, almost 12 million people out of over 32 million of the population aged 16–59 in England and Wales. It is estimated that nearly three million people (9 per cent) have used drugs in the past year and one in 20 adults had drugs in the last month (Hoare and Moon, 2010: 6). Each year the most popular reported drug is cannabis although use has been falling in the UK and across Europe in recent years, with 16 per cent of young adults aged 16–24 reporting having used it in the last year (Hoare and Moon, 2010: 13). The use of cocaine and ecstasy, the second and third most popular drugs, has fluctuated throughout the noughties with just under 6 per cent of young adults reporting using cocaine in the last year and over 4 per cent reporting using ecstasy. In relation to heroin use in the UK, indicators suggest that the heroin-using population has risen rapidly throughout the 25-year period from 1975 to 2000 (Reuter and Stevens, 2008) and is now stable. In terms of general BCS trends over the last 15 years, while there has been a statistically significant increase in the past year use of crack and cocaine reported by adults; the use of amphetamines, LSD, 'magic' mushrooms and cannabis have all fallen since the mid-1990s; and there has been no change in the use of heroin, ecstasy, amyl nitrite or glue (Hoare and Moon, 2010: 10).

The value of the BCS through its sampling and year-on-year data bank lies in its identification of such trends in drug use, as well as regional and socio-demographic differences; it does not provide data, however, on mobile, transient or institutionalized populations. Also up to now, only young people over 16 were included. Surveys of school pupils and other institutionalized groups are therefore an essential complement to national adult household surveys such as the BCS, providing data on initiation into drug use, prevalence and patterns of use in the early teens, and the development of problem drug use with specific sub-samples. A key survey of drinking, smoking and illegal drug use is conducted each year by the National Health Service Information Centre (The NHS Information Centre, 2009; see also Aldridge, 2008), providing annual comparisons for school pupils aged 11–16. For international comparisons of teenage drinking, smoking and drug use, the European School Survey Project on Alcohol and Other Drugs (ESPAD) is collected every fourth year in 35 countries among 15–16-year-olds (Hibell *et al.*, 2009). These ongoing ESPAD surveys confirm the findings from British secondary school surveys that while self-reported experiences of illegal drug use, frequent drinking, drunkenness and binge drinking remain among the highest in Europe, there is evidence of stability or a recent decrease in the UK.

These cultural distinctions of British consumption have also been identified with older cohorts. For example, in a focus group study of 16–25-year-olds (Martinic and Measham, 2008), young Italians strongly criticized drunkenness, stating that intoxication was an undesirable consequence of consumption whereas for young people from the UK, by contrast, drunkenness was one of the main goals from social drinking (see also Measham and Brain, 2005). Qualitative studies have endorsed this strong desire among adolescents and young adults in the UK to achieve altered states of intoxication, whether with legal or illicit intoxicants (Griffin *et al.*, 2009; Measham *et al.*, 2010; Szmigin *et al.*, 2008). Such intoxication is built into the cultural fabric of British 'intoxicated weekends' (Parker and Williams, 2004) within both alcohol-oriented (Chatterton and Hollands, 2003) and illegal drug-infused leisure space (Measham and Moore, 2009).

Also of use are longitudinal or times series studies which follow up a cohort of people for an extended period of time in order to explore changing patterns of drug use. While resource-intensive, longitudinal studies can be particularly useful in understanding patterns of adolescent drug use, risk factors in relation to initiation, as well as resistance and desistance from drug use, and from a developmental or life-stage perspective, understanding how drug careers can develop and the factors which influence young people's drug-taking decisions along their drug pathways. Four recent longitudinal studies in the UK in recent years have been the *North West England Longitudinal Study* (Parker *et al.*, 1998; Aldridge *et al.*, 2011) which began in 1991; the *DPAS Study* (Aldridge *et al.*, 1999) which began in 1996; the *Belfast Youth Development Study* (McCrystal, 2009) which began in 2000 and the *Edinburgh Study of Youth Transitions and Crime* (McVie and Bradshaw, 2005) which began in 1998. These various studies differ in their estimates of the overall level of drug use in the UK population but concur that experimentation and use of illegal drugs increased throughout the 1990s with widespread availability of a growing range of drugs, peaked just after the millennium and has remained stable or fallen slightly in recent years. Longitudinal studies are also able to track the large minority of young people (e.g., up to one-third in the *DPAS Study*, Aldridge *et al.*, 1999) who may try drugs just a handful of times, without undue negative consequences, as part of adolescent experimentation, but who do not progress to become regular users, and thus distinguish between drug triers and drug users. Conversely, when tracked across adolescence and into adulthood, youthful abstainers who initially profess no intention of trying illegal drugs may come to experiment in their late teens and early twenties when they leave the parental home, attend higher education institutions or become regular pub/club-goers (Aldridge *et al.*, 2011).

It is estimated that between one-third and half of young people try illegal drugs at some point in their lives with about one in twenty going on to become regular or monthly users, and a significant minority continue to take illegal drugs at least on an occasional basis, interwoven into their adult lives and leisure time. Of further significance here is that longitudinal studies have shown how structural factors such as gender, ethnicity and socio-economic class are no longer predictors of, or protectors from, adolescent experimentation with so-called 'recreational' drugs (Parker *et al.*, 1998).

Key patterns and drug user groups

There are various types of problems associated with drug use. First, 'problem drug use' is most usually identified in the UK by drug type; that is, the use of heroin and other opiates, crack cocaine and benzodiazepines. A second cluster of definitions relate to motivations for drug use (e.g., occasional, recreational, dependent) and the problems arising particularly from dependent drug use, compulsion or 'addiction'. The third way to define drug problems relates to the outcomes or consequences of drug use; that is, to the severity of the harms for the user, their family, community and wider society resulting from their drug use. The fourth and final group of typologies of drug problems focus on patterns of use and user groups rather than the types of drugs consumed or motivations for consumption. In this model, drug use may well be a problem for a user's family, whether or not they could be considered a daily or dependent user, whether or not their use fits the classic disease model of addiction (see Chapter 5) and whether or not the user sees their drug use (or drug use in general) as problematic.

A complex relationship exists between poverty, offending, homelessness and drug use which many social workers will face in their working lives. The 'drug problem' has been characterized as a problem of poverty or social exclusion (Pearson, 1999; Seddon, 2000) and a strong association exists between heroin, crack, income and unemployment (Buchanan, 2006). A wide literature explores the complexities of this relationship between drugs, poverty and crime (for over-views see Bean, 2004 and Hammersley, 2008), with a particular emphasis on the relationship between addiction and acquisitive crime which draws upon the economic-compulsive model of drug-related crime (Goldstein, 1985) whereby addicts steal to feed their 'habit'. While it seems that offending careers for many users start before their drugs careers and therefore there is not a simple causal explanation, nevertheless there is a strong association between these multiple indicators of social exclusion, disadvantage and marginalization. It should be noted that this is a relatively recent development in the UK, however. Heroin was not always associated with poverty and crime: the historical reviews of Berridge (1984) and Seddon (2007) show that opiates were drugs taken by small numbers of middle-class professionals in the UK from Victorian times up to the 1960s, as well as by the rural and urban masses before the Pharmacy Act 1868.

Gender remains a key issue in relation to drug use. While in general women's overall levels of drug use are lower than men's, there was a substantial rise in young women's drug use and women's heavy drinking in the 1990s in the UK so that levels are only slightly lower than men's for certain drugs and in some cultural scenes such as ecstasy use in the dance scene (Henderson, 1999; Hutton, 2006). For women, however, there may be differential access to drugs in an illegal trade which in some ways mirrors the gender discrimination of legal markets

(Maher, 1997). Furthermore, for female drug users, the ways in which drugs affect their bodies link to broader gender issues of body image and identity, tied to female reproductive capacity and the consequential formal and informal processes of control which operate over the female body (Ettorre, 2007). The harms from drug use affect not only drug users themselves but also their families and communities, and for mothers, the issue of child welfare and child safety may mean greater surveillance of their lives and child-rearing habits than for non-drug users (Harbin, 2006), leading to a potential 'vicious circle' for women (Raine, 2001), seen as doubly deviant for criminal activities which break both the law and the boundaries of acceptable feminine behaviour. The report 'Hidden Harm: the children of problem drug users' (Advisory Council for the Misuse of Drugs (ACMD), 2003) revealed the extent and scale to which drug use can impact upon users' children and the development and welfare of them. This is a key issue for social work practice and is explored further throughout this book.

While stereotypes have prevailed regarding ethnic, religious and national identities and drugs,[7] the realities are more complex and challenge such misconceptions. In terms of the BCS, mixed ethnic groups and then white people have the highest levels of self-reported drug use, particularly cannabis, while Asian groups have the lowest levels of use. More recently, however, there have been studies suggesting both increased drug use by young Asians (Patel, 2000) and also an increase in Asian drug supply in recent years, facilitated by friendship and kinship networks (Akhatar and South, 2000), set alongside growing alarm at the perceived emergence of organized criminality among south Asians in the noughties (Ruggiero, 2010).

Particular concerns relate to the disproportionate policing of the Misuse of Drugs Act 1971 (MDA) in relation to young people, minority ethnic communities and marginalized groups in urban areas. Formal cannabis warnings were introduced in 2004 within the framework of broader policing reforms in order to reduce 'stop and search' and improve relations between the police and young people from disadvantaged and minority ethnic communities (MORI Social Research Institute and Police Foundation, 2002; Reuter and Stevens, 2007).

Concerns remain, however, regarding the disproportionate policing of minority ethnic drug use, particularly of young men in urban areas (Miah *et al.*, 2010).

Alcohol and older people

The population is ageing. There were 20 million people aged 50 and over in the UK in 2003. This was a 45 per cent increase over five decades, from 13.8 million in 1951. The projected increase is a 36 per cent rise by 2031, when there will be 27.2 million people aged 50 and over.

Over the last 50 years there has also been a substantial change in the age composition of older people. In 1951, those aged 50–59 represented 43 per cent, and those aged 85 and over made up just 1.6 per cent of the 50 and over population. In 2003 the two age groups represented 37.8 per cent and 5.5 per cent, respectively, of the older population. Projections indicate these proportions will be respectively 28.6 and 7.9 per cent by 2031 (Office of National Statistics (ONS), 2008).

There is some evidence that today's population of older people may be relatively heavier drinkers than previous generations. Drinking surveys suggest that since 1984, in both men and women aged 45–65 and over, the proportions of those exceeding the 'sensible limits' have been rising steadily.

General household surveys show an increasing proportion of older (age 65+) people in Britain drinking above recommended levels. In 1984, 12 per cent of men and 3 per cent of women aged 65 or over were drinking above 21 and 14 units, respectively. By 1996 this figure had risen to 18 per cent of men and 7 per cent of women. The ONS (2008) statistics show that around a quarter of men aged 65–74 and around one in twenty women aged 65–74 had exceeded the daily benchmark.

Media attention and public health initiatives tend to focus on younger age groups while research on problems associated with alcohol use in older people is scant and contradictory. The subject of problematic alcohol use in late life has received relatively little attention in the literature. This is despite the fact that elderly people are particularly vulnerable to the adverse effects of alcohol (Johnson, 2000). Demographic data predicts that in the first half of the next century there will be an increase in the absolute number of elderly people with alcohol problems. The recognition and treatment of alcohol problems are likely therefore to become more important as this population expands. High rates of co-morbidity with physical and psychiatric illness mean that elderly problematic alcohol users are liable to be frequent users of health facilities (Snyder, 1977).

Source: Simmill-Binning, C., Paylor, I. and Wilson, A. (2009). Alcohol and older people, *Drug and Alcohol Today*, 9(2): 13–18.

Studies of lesbian, gay and bisexual groups also find higher levels of heavy drinking and drug use than the general population, for recent and lifetime use, for individual drugs and also for polydrug use. For example, one in three gay or bisexual adults compared with one in ten heterosexual adults report having taken a drug in the last year, and 11 per cent of gay/bisexual adults compared with 4 per cent of heterosexual adults report having taken a Class A drug in the last year (Hoare and Moon, 2010: 93). In part this relates to a leisure lifestyle, age and disposable income linked to the night-time economy and higher levels of drug use associated with these 'going-out' groups (Deehan and Saville,

2003; Measham *et al.*, 2001) and specifically gay male urban culture (Stall *et al.*, 2001).

The core of British drug policy: from the Defence of the Realm to the Misuse of Drugs Act

The increasing regulation of drugs, medicines and poisons in the UK began in the nineteenth century, with the expansion of the medical profession and associated pharmaceutical supplies. Sales of opiates and cocaine were increasingly restricted after the Pharmacy Act 1868, and, after Harrods had been fined in 1916 for infringing the Pharmacy Act and selling cocaine and morphine at its London store (Berridge, 1984: 20), these drugs were banned first for military personnel with the Defence of the Realm Act 1916, and then extended to civilians with the Dangerous Drugs Act 1920. The period from 1926 to 1968 has come to be known as the '40-year calm' in UK drug policy due to the equilibrium achieved by the Rolleston Report of 1926 which characterized addiction as an illness in need of medical treatment rather than a moral failing requiring criminal sanction. The introduction of maintenance prescriptions of heroin by ordinary family GPs to the small numbers of heroin users who existed in the early and mid-twentieth century consolidated a long-standing alliance between doctors and the state (Berridge, 1979).

A heroin epidemic in the late 1960s and the development of drug subcultures (Young, 1971), along with increased restrictions on prescribing, increased importation of heroin from the Golden Triangle and then the Golden Crescent,[8] combined to result in an increase in heroin use throughout the last quarter of the last century, with two further peaks or 'epidemics' identified in the 1980s and 1990s (Parker *et al.*, 1988; Parker *et al.*, 2001). As Berridge (1984) has noted, however, the medical humanitarian model of heroin prescribing in the UK from the 1920s to the 1960s was possible only because there was such a limited number of mostly middle-class heroin addicts in that period. Once a much larger and more diverse drug user base developed from the late 1960s onwards, heroin and cocaine prescribing was taken away from ordinary GPs and drug policy increasingly moved from medical to Home Office control.

Some have suggested that the tension between treatment and control was a key driver of UK drug policy (Edwards, 1989), emphasizing the *discontinuities* in the policy pendulum swinging from a medical or treatment agenda during the '40-year calm' towards a 'law and order' agenda after the late 1980s (Hunt and Stevens, 2004; Stimson, 2001), and further exacerbated by the shift to coercive drug treatment from the late 1990s discussed below. Others by contrast have emphasized instead the *continuities* with a focus on 'risk' populations and the drug 'problem' within public health/harm reduction[9] models (Berridge, 1979; Seddon, 2007).

At the heart of understanding the impact of drugs, are the consequences for individual users, their family and community, and for wider society. In terms of the 'drug problem', the central issue is the illegality of many psychoactive drugs discussed in this book, alongside the harm that may be caused by drugs to users and society. A wide range of psychoactive drugs are consumed on an occasional or regular basis with both desired and undesired effects, many of which are controlled by legislation.

In some societies (Ruggiero, 1999), a distinction is made between legitimate use of *medicines* and illicit use of *drugs* whereas in others (including the United States, where pharmacies are called drugstores) the term 'drug' may refer to any psychoactive substance regardless of its legal status. Others have argued that 'the puzzling dual socio-legal status of heroin as a therapeutic medicine and as dangerous drug' illustrates that there is nothing 'inevitable' in our contemporary control system (Seddon, 2007: 152). Given the value-laden associations surrounding the term 'drugs', some researchers (e.g., Ettorre, 1992) have suggested that the more neural term *substance* is preferable to *drug*.[10]

For others, a distinction is made between *use, misuse* and *abuse* with use relating to the act of consumption, misuse relating to inappropriate use (e.g., usage or dosage not sanctioned by a medical practitioner) and abuse relating to inappropriate use which then results in significant problems for the user such as dependence. As Manderson (1995: 171) has noted, however, in terms of the MDA, simply by consuming a controlled drug without medical sanction, one is defined as misusing it.

In the UK, a distinction is usually drawn between drug use, which most usually relates to illegal drugs and substance use which also includes popular legal drugs such as alcohol and tobacco. Regarding which drugs are illegal, the cornerstone of legislation is the MDA 1971, although cocaine, heroin and cannabis were outlawed in the Dangerous Drugs Acts of 1920 and 1928. The MDA and its subsequent amendments establish which drugs are currently controlled within the UK, the various drug-related criminal offences on the statute book such as possession and supply, the level of restrictions imposed and the penalties for the various offences. At the core of the MDA is a classification system which proscribes which category each drug is placed into, with the availability and consequent scale of penalties relating to the schedule and class of each drug, respectively.

In the 40 years since the law was passed, a series of amendments has led to the range of drugs covered by the MDA widening and in practice the law has encompassed ever-more psychoactive substances as they are discovered, move into general usage and are perceived by the authorities to be in some way problematic. In theory there is the potential, although rarely utilized (with the notable exception of the brief depenalization of cannabis from Class B down to C in 2004–7, Warburton *et al.*, 2005a), for drugs to move towards either higher or lower classifications as the severity of their harm becomes known to the scientific community. In recent years the list of drugs included within the MDA has grown ever longer with some commentators suggesting that this is tantamount to a new wave of criminalization of intoxication before the harm from a specific drug is established, characterized as 'proactive prohibition' by Measham and Moore (2008). This new wave of criminalization includes drugs such as ketamine, anabolic steroids, 'fresh' magic mushrooms, gamma-hydroxybutyrate (GHB) and its successor gamma-butyrolactone (GBL). This is not necessarily a new feature of British drug policy, however, with ecstasy controlled in 1977, more than 10 years before it became widely available and popularized in the acid house and rave scene (Shapiro, 1999).

In terms of the operation of the act, 235 000 drugs offences were recorded by the police in 2009/10, of which 163 000 (69 per cent) were for the personal possession of cannabis (Flatley *et al.*, 2010: 161). Nevertheless, there is considerable police discretion in the disposal of those caught in possession of drugs (Association of Chief Police Officers (ACPO), 2009) in the UK, compared with other developed countries such as Portugal, Denmark or Australia (Stevens, 2011). For example, Penalty Notices for Disorder (PNDs) were introduced nationally in 2004/5, at the same time as Cannabis Warnings for possession of cannabis. From January 2009, PNDs could also be given for an offence of cannabis possession. The most recent figures show that there were 103 000 PNDs and 87 000 Cannabis Warnings given in 2009/10.

Revision of the MDA

There have been various criticisms of the MDA in recent years, including issues around accuracy of classification of individual drugs, concerns about the impact and efficacy of drug policy, and on a broader philosophical level, the human right to take drugs. These three issues, considered below, broadly correlate with the three perspectives on drug policy raised by Reuter and Stevens (2007, 2008) in their recent analysis of trends in UK drug policy.

1 Reclassification of individual drugs
First, regarding amendments to the classification of individual drugs, this is a perspective which considers that there are significant errors or inconsistencies in the current classification system which need rectification or refinement. Proponents of the refinement view include Nutt and colleagues (Nutt, 2009a, 2009b; Nutt *et al.*, 2007, 2010), who have questioned the relative ranking of harm represented in the current classification of drugs and have proposed an alternative model to calculate relative harm in order to refine the current system. Significantly, legal drugs such as alcohol and tobacco are also included in their model, suggesting the need for a more consistent regulatory approach to the whole range of psychoactive drugs currently consumed in the UK.

A House of Commons Science and Technology Committee review concurred that 'a more scientifically based scale of harm would have greater credibility than the current system where the placing of drugs in particular categories is ultimately a political decision' (House of Commons Science and Technology Committee, 2006: 46). This need for revision of the MDA classification system was also recognized within the Home Office, with a consultation process started and then stalling in 2006 (Home Office, 2006).

This refinement model is not without its critics. McKeganey (2007) suggests that the logical inference of a more careful assessment of the relative harms of different drugs, rather than a move towards reduced restrictions on illegal drugs, is to increase the regulation of legal ones instead. Given the power of the alcohol industry lobby this seems unlikely. A key concern of Rolles and Measham (2011) in their critique of Nutt *et al.*'s (2010) model of relative harm is that it is essential for any model of harm to disaggregate the harm from prohibitionist drug policy from the harms caused by the substances themselves. In Nutt *et al.*'s model this is not the case, resulting in illegal drugs such as heroin being inappropriately highly ranked and considered to cause major harms with legal drugs ranked considerably lower; as much as a consequence of their legal status as the innate pharmacological properties of each substance *per se*.

2 Substantial review of UK drug policy

Two substantial reviews of the MDA, the Runciman Report (Police Foundation, 2000) and the Royal Society of Arts (RSA) review (Royal Society of Arts Drugs Commission, 2007) both called for a comprehensive overhaul of the MDA and expressed concerns about the harms which result from drug policy as well as from drug use and the drug trade. The RSA, endorsing the earlier STC report, concluded that the MDA is 'no longer fit for purpose. It should be scrapped and replaced with a new Misuse of Substances Act' which would include alcohol, tobacco and other psychoactive substances (2007: 20). On cannabis, the Runciman Report stated their 'conclusion is that the present law on cannabis produces more harm than it prevents'.

The extent to which drug policy influences drug-related attitudes and behaviours is an ongoing area of debate. Current prohibitionist drug policy is based on the premise that the threat of punishment deters the supply and demand for drugs, thereby reducing drug use and drug-related harms. Thus the removal of this deterrent threat would increase the demand and supply of drugs, increase drug use and lead to increased drug-related harms for users and wider society. In the UK this assumption of a deterrence value to the MDA has been questioned both inside and outside parliament. While the government repeats the *en vogue* mantra of 'evidence-based' policy making, it is not clear what evidence exists of the role the MDA plays in motivations for drug use and the extent to which it operates as a deterrent to usage. With the classification of cannabis, for example, there is no evidence that its reclassification to Class B (for deterrent purposes in light of the emergence of higher Tetrahydrocannabinol (THC)-strength skunk and its possible association with psychosis) would lead to a greater deterrent effect with users than as Class C; increase the confusion surrounding its legal status (with the government spending one million pounds in 2004 on a public information campaign to remind the general public that cannabis was still illegal); or whether cannabis classification had little impact on motivations to use or desist, given that prevalence of cannabis use has been declining across Europe across the noughties anyway (European Monitoring Centre for Drugs and Drug Addiction (EMCDDA), 2011). In relation to ketamine, a study of 90 ketamine users found little evidence to suggest that the criminalization of ketamine impacted on either the supply or use of the drug, with only one user noticing any appreciable difference to their usual ketamine supply (Morgan *et al.*, 2011).

An alternative analysis is that the MDA results in a displacement rather than a deterrent effect. This was evident among the small numbers of GHB users. Once criminalized in 2003, the small body of users (predominantly gay and clubbing groups) switched from GHB to GBL, a legal drug (until also subsequently controlled in 2009) with similar effects, yet given its greater potency, increasing the possibility of overdose, hospitalization and dependency (Wood *et al.*, 2008).

Non-governmental organizations (NGOs) such as the drug reform organization Transform and the drug charity Lifeline have also argued that if a complete reform of the prohibitionist drug system is not achievable, then substantial revision and impact assessment of the MDA is essential. Such calls have recently been echoed by a range of influential professionals in the field, from Tim Hollis (drug lead at ACPO) to Professor Ian Gilmore when standing down from his position as President at the Royal College of Physicians as well as editorials in the *British Medical Journal* (BMJ) (Wood, 2010), *The Lancet* (Horton and Das, 2010) and *The Observer* (2010).

At the international level, studies suggest that prohibition and enforcement do not have the deterrent effects on the use of drugs that are intended by national legislation or international anti-drugs agreements – neither demand nor supply was reduced, nor have they been able to prevent the 'normalisation of cannabis throughout the world' (Levine, 2003: 145). Morin and Collins (2000) also consider that law enforcement and drug interdiction policies are ineffective in reducing drug use. The Netherlands effectively decriminalized cannabis in the 1970s, yet cannabis prevalence in the Netherlands has remained similar to France and Germany. In the USA, 11 states effectively decriminalized cannabis controls yet cannabis use did not rise in these states compared to comparable states which retained prohibition (Wodak *et al.*, 2002). An interesting study by Reinarman *et al.* (2004) compared two similar samples of experienced cannabis users in two similar port cities known for their cosmopolitan, liberal and diverse populations, in order to compare the relative influence of the contexts of criminalization (San Francisco) and decriminalization (Amsterdam). Of significance to policy-makers, the study suggested that 'if drug policies are a potent influence on user behaviour, there should not be such strong similarities across such different drug control regimes'. In fact Reinarman *et al.* (2004: 840–41) concluded that there was no evidence that either criminalization reduced use or decriminalization increased use and therefore the policy context to drug use has only 'limited relevance'.

The lack of significance of legal status is also relevant to non-drug users as well as drug users. A study of non-ecstasy-using adults by Vervaeke *et al.* (2008) found that the illegal status of ecstasy was not an issue for respondents, with only 3 per cent mentioning it as a reason not to take the drug. A study by McIntosh *et al.* (2005) found that young adolescents rarely mentioned illegality as a reason not to take drugs. Similarly, studies with adolescents who do use drugs also show that illegal status is not a concern, when discussing the negative aspects of their drug use. Health, personal relationships and parental discovery concern adolescent drug users more than the illegality of their use (Parker *et al.*, 1998). This is perhaps not surprising given that evidence is limited on the deterrent effect of legal sanctions for offending more generally, despite it being a cornerstone of criminal justice policies around the world (Akers, 2000; Inciardi, 1999; Paternoster, 1989).

Perhaps the most interesting international example, though, is Portugal. In July 2001, the country decriminalized the possession of less than 10 days' supply of any illicit drug. In the 10 years since, drug problems have declined, HIV infection rates have fallen and surveys report that drug use has not increased, suggesting that the removal of the deterrent principle does not impact on prevalence, while the removal of criminal penalties for users can be beneficial to the population in terms of public health and treatment impact. By contrast, a harshly repressive drug policy in the USA has not prevented a major increase in drug-related deaths and levels of problematic use which are high by comparison with other developed countries (Stevens, 2011).

3 Overthrow of MDA

Third, on a philosophical level, the MDA has been challenged as a breach of human rights under the European Convention on Human Rights, with Walsh (2010; see also van Ree, 1999) making a novel argument that the criminalization of psychoactive drug use contained in the MDA restricts British citizens' right to self-medicate, to practice their religion (e.g., Rastafarianism) and to explore their consciousness (discussed earlier). For social work, this line of thinking moves our attention away from the *motivations* of why people choose to take psychoactive drugs, to focus instead on the *consequences* of such drug use, regardless of legal status, and specifically whether or not there is a negative impact on those around them – such as children, extended families and communities – that might require medical or social intervention.

The 'legal highs' debate

A key challenge for social workers is the desirability of being informed of such a rapidly changing regulatory and legal landscape while also recognizing that legislation alone may not determine the degree of harm or otherwise involved in the use of specific drugs. Therefore prescription, over the counter (OTC) and novel psychoactive drugs or so-called 'legal highs' can also impact upon health, personal relations and families in equally significant ways as those drugs controlled by the MDA which might more usually be associated with drug problems.

While the emergence and rapid growth in popularity of so-called 'legal highs' such as mephedrone in 2009 can be seen as an illustration of the popularity of psychoactive drug use in the UK, the appeal was at least in part due to the perceived higher purity, easier access and avoidance of the street trade in illegal drugs (Measham *et al.*, 2010; Winstock *et al.*, 2011), which suggests that legal status is not totally irrelevant to drug-taking decisions. The challenge which emerged alongside the second generation of legal highs in the summer of 2010 was that test purchases showed many products to contain the recently controlled methcathinones or first-generation legal highs such as mephedrone (Brandt *et al.*, 2010; Ramsey *et al.*, 2010). It could be argued that legal highs – because of the growing diversity of substances consumed, combined with a growing tendency to polydrug use (EMCDDA, 2009), a decreased awareness of which psychoactive drugs a branded product may contain and what its effects might be – lead us away from twentieth-century policy responses based on individual drugs, and towards a new approach to policy and practice which emphasizes instead the wider context of use, (the 'drug, set and setting', Zinberg, 1984), and the harm-reduction implications of the social context of use, as advocated by Erickson and Cheung (1999).

McKeganey (2007) has argued against this line of thinking, however, and against the shift in UK drug policy in recent years from its long-standing commitment to education, prevention, treatment and enforcement to a focus on harm reduction, for example, reflected in the reports of the RSA and the UK Drug Policy Commission. In contrast to the growing body of criticism of the MDA outlined above, and in his challenge to the shift in a wider drug policy towards harm reduction, McKeganey (2007: 570) suggests that this shift is a concern because of the 'slim' evidential base, and cautions against a major change in the direction of drug policy. The question is what counts as an acceptable threshold of evidence to support 'evidence-based policy'?

Evidence-based policy?

There have been gathering calls for evidence-based policy both from the academic community across the board from Nutt to McKeganey, and also from the previous Labour government (e.g., Cabinet Office, 1999). This has to be set alongside the increased auditing of academic and policy activities or 'impact'; pressures to generate income; and restrictions on resources which have led to a shift in political and social science circles towards evidence-based policy. However, this prioritization of evidence-based policy, abstracted from a critical understanding of the relationship between academic research and practice, has led Smith (2010) to raise concerns about the resulting 'squeeze on intellectual creativity'. The different aims as well as communication gap between researchers and policy makers, combined with the tensions and differences within as well as between each group, may make a unilinear model of evidence-based policy unachievable.

A study by Jewell and Bero (2008) explored how evidence might be incorporated into decision making and identified key challenges to evidence-based policy through a qualitative study of US state legislators. These included variations in the quality of 'evidence', a lack of consensus among scientific advisers and competing interest groups, budgetary restrictions, lack of training for policy makers and a range of institutional hindrances. A prevalent form of political discourse, drawing on personal anecdotes and emotional or 'common-sense' appeals, could be considered at odds with research communication models. While in general the findings of well-conducted randomized controlled trials and well-conducted observational studies concur (Benson and Hartz, 2000; Concato *et al.*, 2000), there are also notable disputes within the scientific community regarding the hierarchy of research funding and research 'evidence' to policy makers.

Such issues have played out in recent years in the UK in the politically charged debate over what role cannabis plays in the development of psychosis. As Macleod and Hickman (2010: 1338) recently noted, the relationship between cannabis and psychosis may be due to 'residual confounding and measurement error . . . That is not to say they are not causal – they might be, but it is simply impossible to know'.

Treatment policy

It has been estimated that the social and economic costs of Class A drug use in England and Wales amount to over £15 billion in England and Wales (Godfrey *et al.*, 2002), with 90 per cent of these costs resulting from drug-related crime committed largely by 'problem drug users', with heroin and crack referred to as 'high harm drugs' (PMSU, 2007). The UK policy has increasingly focused on addressing this drugs–crime relationship through a programme of testing offenders, assessing their drug problems and referring them for treatment. This treatment regime was established through a series of legislation: starting with the Crime and Disorder Act 1998 which created Drug Treatment and Testing Orders (DTTOs). The Criminal Justice and Court Services Act of 2000 then enabled the police to drug test people charged with 'trigger' offences such as theft and burglary. The Criminal Justice Act 2003 created generic Community Orders and replaced DTTOs with the Drug Rehabilitation Requirement (DRR). The Drugs Act 2005 made it illegal to refuse a required treatment assessment along with introducing drug testing on arrest rather than charge.

This expansion of the treatment sector over the last decade, with a focus on substitute prescribing services, the local commission and provision of treatment services, and the introduction of the Integrated Drug Treatment System within prisons, have all been immensely beneficial. It is estimated that this has led to up to 58 per cent of Class A problem drug users (PDUs) being assessed for treatment (Reuter and Stevens, 2008) and a resulting reduction in both the quantity of drugs consumed and the quantity of crime committed, even if total abstinence from drugs is not achieved (McSweeney et al., 2007). However, as noted by Duke (2006), this has led to the 'drug problem' increasingly being framed as a 'crime problem' rather than a health, social, welfare or environmental policy, leading to the situation where nearly two-thirds of drug policy expenditure is used for enforcement. Public health and information campaigns, although (sometimes) well resourced, are difficult to evaluate and generally do not have a strong evidence base (ACMD, 2006). Furthermore, the focus on substitute prescribing and particularly methadone maintenance programmes, while desirable in terms of public health and crime reduction, have led to residential rehabilitation and abstinence-oriented treatment programmes becoming increasingly peripheral to the treatment system. The new government heralds a greater focus on recovery, rehabilitation and abstinence-oriented services in the coming years. However, some within the drug treatment field view this polarization of abstinence versus harm reduction as unhelpful to understanding treatment needs and suggest instead that treatment should be seen as a continuum with a range of different goals rather than a pendulum swinging between the prioritization of abstinence or maintenance.

Implications for social work practice

The challenge then is for social work practitioners (and indeed, researchers and policy makers) to forge a better understanding borne of respect rather than obligation, recognizing the complex and non-linear nature of the relationship between academic findings, political decision making and community-based practice. The challenge for social workers is to carry forward a more sophisticated understanding of drug users, the positive and negative effects of drugs, as well as the intended and unintended consequences of not just drug use but also drug policy, enforcement and treatment.

2   Defining drug users

Introduction

'Drug user' is potentially so broad a category that it can encompass almost all human beings who take any legal or illegal, prescription or over the counter (OTC), herbal or chemical substance that can alter the human body in some way. Politically, it has been seen by some drugs organizations, professionals and researchers as important to assert that there is an essential nature to substance taking across cultures, societies and time periods. Indeed anthropologists have suggested that all but the Innuit tribe are thought to have taken mind-altering psychoactive substances of some sort at some time in human history (Klein, 2008; Steinberg *et al.*, 2004; Weil and Rosen, 1993). Yet in contrast to these all-encompassing approaches to drugs and humanity, attempts to define and refine the landscape of drug consumption can result in a greater insight into the distinctions and differences between drug users, and for the purposes of regulation, intervention and service provision, between those activities which result in greater or lesser harm to drug users, their families and wider society. This chapter considers different ways of defining and differentiating between drug users and the implications of these different typologies of drug use for service provision.

How we might understand and attempt to develop some sort of typology of illicit drug use or indeed drug users depends to some extent on the criteria we focus upon. This chapter considers the various perspectives on ordering or categorizing patterns of drug use, through a consideration of the behavioural patterns, motivations and outcomes of illicit drug use and how these have impacted, both explicitly and implicitly, on social work with drug users and their families. Such typologies of drug users and the recent debate surrounding these challenge the notion of drug users as a single homogeneous group in need of a single policy response.

Behavioural typologies of drug use

In the 1980s the image of the 'typical' drug user exemplified in public information and drug prevention campaigns was most graphically illustrated in the
'Heroin Screws You Up' prevention initiative: drug users were portrayed in poor
clothes with bad skin, symptomatic of daily, dependent, injecting opiate users
deprived of food, shelter, money and sleep. In these images, drug use was clearly
and simply represented as a problem, specifically linked to a package of social
problems in the 1980s which included acquisitive crime, homelessness and life-
threatening infectious diseases. By the early 1990s, however, patterns of drug
use and the range of illegal drugs being consumed were diversifying which
resulted in a reconsideration of who a 'typical' drug user might be and a move
away from the overly simplistic 'junkie' stereotypes of the 1980s. It was in this
period that two distinct groups of drug users were identified: a small group of
'problem' drug users and a much larger group of 'recreational' drug users.

Problem drug use

Problematic-recreational models of drug use have developed since the 1990s:
Newcombe (1990, 1995) developed a 'group model' approach which contrasted
problem drug users with recreational drug users (see also Gilman, 1991).
Within a Venn diagram format, problem drug users (Group As) in the model
were estimated to make up about 5 per cent of the total number of drug users
in the UK and were characterized by their use of heroin, crack or benzodiazepines, in patterns of daily or dependent use, often by the route of intravenous injection. Recreational drug users (Group Bs) by contrast – accounting for
about 95 per cent of illegal drug users in the model – included occasional and
regular users of cannabis, and psychostimulant drugs such as amphetamines
and ecstasy, often associated with weekend partying and the 'rave' scene at
that time, and which were more likely to be swallowed, smoked or insufflated
rather than injected. Within or attached to this larger recreational drug-using
group, there were also groups of cannabis and solvent users (Group Cs and Ds).
Implicit in this 'problematic-recreational' group model of users was the recognition that high-visibility problem drug users, associated with mainstream
junkie stereotypes, despite being a very small minority of the total number of
drug users, were the focus for the majority of criminal justice, medical and
treatment interventions as well as press and public concerns.

    This identification of problem drug use (PDU) with the consumption of
specific drugs and specific drug-related problems has remained a cornerstone of
drug policy for the last two decades, used in government drug policy to identify those most in need of treatment. The UK drug strategy refers to 'problem
drug users' rather than 'problem drug use', who are defined as those people

using opiates and/or crack cocaine (Home Office, 2008: 50), whose use is more likely to be daily or dependent, and who may have a range of associated problems linked with their drug use. It is interesting to note that in a Home Office-commissioned study, problem drug use is defined in opposition to recreational drug use and the use of recreational drugs is assumed to be unproblematic:

> Problem drug users are generally understood to be those whose drug use is no longer controlled or undertaken for recreational purposes . . . It was assumed . . . that all opiate use and crack use . . . is problematic . . . All ecstasy, LSD and magic mushroom use is assumed not to be problematic.
>
> (Godfrey *et al.*, 2002: 9)

While there is a growing consensus in the UK that definitions of PDU focus on the types of drugs consumed, a review of definitions in the international literature by contrast suggests that there is less agreement on the types of drugs, patterns of drug use or consequences of use which might be considered 'problematic' (Cave *et al.*, 2009), with international studies tending to focus more on harmful outcomes than specific types of drugs. Nevertheless, successive UK drug strategies have prioritized treating opiate and/or crack users and tackling the problems for communities associated with PDUs, including open drug markets, acquisitive crime, health needs, supporting children at risk and harm reduction (HR) services. This focus on problem drug use was consolidated in the late 1980s with the identification of the link between injecting drug users (IDUs), shared needles and blood-borne viruses (BBV). In the UK this led to an innovative programme of HR for problem drug users, both at a local level spreading out since its inception in Merseyside (Eaton *et al.*, 1998) and also at the national level the Advisory Council on the Misuse of Drugs (ACMD) recommendations were 'a major catalyst for change' (Stimson, 1995: 700), accepted by a Conservative government which prioritized public health initiatives such as syringe distribution and methadone treatment over the criminal justice issues relating to Class A drug use and associated acquisitive and trafficking crimes (ACMD, 1988). It has been estimated that this period where harm reduction was prioritized directly saved the lives of many thousands of IDUs in the UK and stemmed the spread of HIV/AIDS in the early stages of a global pandemic (Stimson, 1995; Yates, 2002).

Harm reduction

Harm reduction (HR) – also called damage limitation, risk reduction and harm minimization – is a policy which prioritizes the aim of decreasing the negative effects of drug use over eliminating drug use or helping people stop their drug use (Newcombe, 1992: 1). It contrasts with the traditional approach to illegal drug use – defined as 'abstentionism' by Newcombe – which prioritizes the reduction of the incidence of drug use, with total abstinence as its target. More broadly, Newcombe sees HR as a term that defines policies, programmes, services and actions that work to reduce the health, social and economic harms to individuals, communities and society, a definition endorsed by the UK Harm Reduction Alliance (UKHRA, 2011). Harm reductionists argue their approach is pragmatic, in that they acknowledge that drug use 'is a common and enduring feature of human experience' and that 'harm reduction recognises that containment and reduction of drug-related harm is a more feasible option than efforts to minimise drug use entirely' (UKHRA, 2011). They argue their approach is a humanist approach, which chooses not to take a moral judgement concerning the drug user's behaviour; rather they focus on the associated risks and harms of drug use, on the basis that by 'providing responses that reduce risk, harm can be reduced or eliminated' (UKHRA, 2011). Harm reduction (HR) differs significantly from strategies aimed at complete abstinence, which undoubtedly have a place, but often only for those people who are already strongly motivated to give up drugs.

Characteristics of harm reduction strategy

Realism – acceptance that use of mind altering chemicals by some people is inevitable. An understanding that drug use offers benefits as well as costs to drug users and that limiting the damaging effects of drug use to individuals and communities is more effective than only trying to stop drug use.

Respect – the recognition that is unhelpful to allow moral judgements about drug use to interfere with work with drug users. Despite the frequent demonisation of drug users in the media, harm reduction strategies recognise that drug users have the right to be treated with as much respect and accorded the same human rights as everyone else.

A focus on reducing harm rather than drug use – although harm reduction approaches retain the ultimate goal of helping people become drug free, (because no drug use usually means no drug-related harm) responses are based on the idea that where this is not practicable, the priority is to reduce risks to the individual and society.

A hierarchy of goals – priorities have to be established for effective targeting of resources. Because the risks of an HIV epidemic to individuals and society, the hierarchy of goals for the UK has, since 1988, been to 1. Reduce the sharing of injecting equipment, 2. Reduce the incidence of injecting, 3. Reduce the use of street drugs, 4. Reduce the use of prescribed drugs and finally, 5. Increase abstinence.

Source: Preston, A., Derricott, J. and Hunt, N. (undated) *Harm Reduction* No 7 What and Why? Guide Produced by DrugScope Published by Exchange Publications/Department of Health

Rooted in a public health approach to illegal drugs, HR contrasts with traditional abstentionism, which maintains a strong emphasis on the need for punitive law enforcement when dealing with drug users. Though HR should also be understood as distinct from 'drug treatment'.

> Harm minimization is concerned with helping drug misusers limit the physical and social damage caused by their drug use. The aims of treatment are, in contrast, concerned with helping them to stop misusing drugs or deal with the drug dependence itself.
>
> (Keene, 1997: 124)

The term was adopted in the 1980s to describe the activities of services that were developed to limit the spread of HIV among IDUs and was a key factor increasing political willingness to provide more money to support drug services (Neale, 2002: 30; Keene, 1997: 135). Harm reduction (HR) goals have since been expanded to include hepatitis B and C prevention, reducing overdose deaths and improving the general health of drug users.

During the mid-1980s, increased resources designed to extend and improve drug services in England were provided by a new Central Funding Initiative (CFI). It was hoped that the CFI would begin to remedy persistent problems in existing drug service provision, such as lack of coordination and inadequate treatment (Neale, 2002: 30). One particular objective of the CFI was to draw large numbers of illegal drug users into services by making provision more accessible to a wider range of service users and, to achieve this goal, it is argued that professionals began to take a more tolerant approach to drug-taking (Neale, 2002: 30). The new emphasis of a more tolerant approach to illegal drug users in the mid-1980s coincided with the emergence of HIV/AIDS. Concern over HIV/AIDS underpinned the emergence of HR as an established approach. The governmental ACMD declared that 'the spread of HIV is a greater danger to individual and public health than drug misuse' (ACMD, 1988: 1) and policy-makers and practitioners came to identify IDUs as a high-risk group for disseminating the HIV virus into the general population (Neale, 2002: 31).

The ACMD stipulated a 'hierarchy of goals', namely, the cessation of sharing injection equipment; a move from injectable to oral drug use; a reduction in the quantity of drugs consumed; and finally, abstinence (Newcombe, 1992: 2). In this way, HR goals overtly took the priority over treatment goals. The changing priorities necessitated the provision of injecting equipment and condoms, health care facilities and prescription drugs. Drug agencies became more 'user-friendly' and therefore more accessible to a wider range of drug users (Keene, 1997: 137). Stimson (1992: 42) noting the relatively low number of IDUs testing positive for HIV observed that:

among long-standing regular drug injectors the message has got
through that sharing syringes is an effective mean of transmitting
HIV . . . people we have interviewed adopted a wide range of protective strategies against the risk of HIV infection and transmission . . .
sharing events [syringes] were usually described as exceptional.

Thus, there appears to be significant evidence that HR strategies in the late
1980s and early 1990s have been largely successful in curbing the spread of
HIV/AIDS. More recently, the Health Protection Agency (HPA) released their
study *Shooting Up: Infections Amongst Injecting Drug Users in the UK 2004* (2005).
The report noted a slight overall increase in infection rates among IDUs though
also found that 'while infection remains comparatively rare among this group
[IDUs] overall, with 1 in 65 infected, it is elevated among IDUs in London with
1 in 25 in infected' (HPA, 2005: 19).

Of more concern were infection rates for hepatitis C (HCV): 'the prevalence of Hepatitis C infection has also increased with more than 2 in 5 current
IDUs now having been infected' (HPA, 2005: 19). Its authors were also
concerned about syringe sharing, reporting that sharing increased in the late
1990s to a figure of 28 per cent of IDUs reporting sharing in the last 28 days.
This figure rises to 50 per cent when concerned with the sharing of other equipment such as filters, and spoons (HPA, 2005: 19). (See Chapter 3 for a more
detailed discussion about HCV.)

These concerns illustrate why HR remains an important part of
current drugs policy. The National Treatment Agency (NTA) emphasizes the
need for a reinvigoration of HR in all tiers of drug treatment recommending a
number of specific HR interventions including needle exchange services,
advice and support on safer injection, advice and information to prevent
BBVs, testing for BBVs (including before and after counselling) and vaccina-
tions (NTA, 2006a: 41).

Harm reduction (HR) approaches are clearly a vitally important part of
drug services and there is a significant amount of evidence they have been
successful in curbing the spread of infectious diseases and some evidence that
they can help reduce the numbers of deaths in relation to other drug use.

While accepting that there has been success in these areas, Newcombe
(2005) questions whether the potential of the HR has been fully explored.
For him the HR movement has been emasculated, its radical edge blunted
and reconfigured to fit with the new criminal justice agenda. Two decades
of research into HR, Newcombe (2005) argues, leads to the following
conclusions:

- Services for IDUs must be much more flexible with needle exchanges
  operating outreach and mobile services for evenings and weekends;
  specialist services including consumption rooms.

- The revival of the old 'British' system of drug treatment incorporating a flexible range of prescribed opiate substitutes in oral, smokable, sniffable and injectable forms. Allied to this would be a far greater range of treatment options.
- The need for screening for genes or other physiological indicators of potential 'addiction' properties in people.
- Prioritization of research into safer drug products.
- Tackling adulteration of drugs by among other things extending drug-testing methods.
- Legal reforms – reclassification, decriminalization, legalization and other reforms to distinguish social supply from commercial supply.

He wittingly offers a restaurant metaphor to emphasize what he sees are the problems with the current strategy.

> HR is presently like a restaurant where they provide you with a really detailed menu telling you what's in each meal, pretty good table service from attentive waiters and clean crockery to eat with. But where the food is poisonous, adulterated muck. I doubt anyone would want to eat there. Yet we expect drug users to attend services which do much the same – providing them with key workers, information on safer drug use and clean needles – while letting them use dirty, adulterated drugs.
>
> (Newcombe, 2005: 11)

Measham *et al.* (2001: 181) while not as strident asks what exactly is meant by the term 'harm', an ambiguous concept in itself. Harm reduction (HR) approaches in respect of IDU, they argue, have been less controversial for the government because they can be seen as 'problem drug users' who can be medicalized or seen as a wider health threat (p. 187).

In relation to widespread recreational drug use by young people, Measham *et al.* (2001: 181) has criticized the lack of a 'coherent management strategy', noting that the government drug strategy prioritizes 'problem drug users' of illegal drugs such as heroin. Measham *et al.* argue that while there were local initiatives, such as 'Safer Dancing' guidelines adopted by Manchester City Council, throughout the 1990s the government's response was primarily a 'law and order' response, including legislation such as the 1994 Criminal Justice and Public Order Act, which effectively criminalized open-air parties and raves. Concerned by the political costs of being seen to be 'soft on drugs', the government publicly maintained a 'no compromise' position, while quietly sanctioning local initiatives. Due to a lack of national guidance, such initiatives were patchy and inadequate (p. 187).

In January 2002, the Home Office published Webster's (2002) *Safer Clubbing: Guidance to Licensing Authorities, Club Managers and Promoters* signalling a shift in approach to a more comprehensive national HR strategy. The author notes that the purpose of the revised guidance is to 'improve the safety of club goers and in particular to reduce the range of harms associated with drug use and clubbing' (Webster, 2002: 4). The guidance is explicitly in favour of drug information and education both in and out of the club setting. The report makes clear that many club goers are in need of 'support to encourage them to reduce the amount of drugs they use or at least to use drugs as safely as possible' and they recommend outreach services and drug action teams work with club promoters and managers to find ways to improving awareness of drug-associated risks (p. 43). The report encourages that outreach workers operate within the club where possible, provide appropriate drug information literature, and advises that Drug Action Teams (DATs)[11] should consider commissioning local drug agencies to provide education and drug outreach services in their area (p. 43).

On a more practical level, the guidance recommends that clubs should have first-aiders available to club goers with an understanding of drug issues. Clubs should provide free drinking water, take measures to prevent over-crowding, and ensure proper ventilation. The report also makes various recommendations to improve security at clubs to prevent drugs being brought in as far as possible (p. 39).

Practitioners of HR will no doubt continue to be criticized by those who see the use of illegal drugs as a moral issue (McKeganey, 2005) or argue (e.g., Phillips, 2007) that HR policies tacitly encourage the use of illegal drugs and 'send the wrong message' to young people considering using them.

However, the contention that HR approaches encourage illegal drug use appears unfounded and while authors such as Hathaway (2000) have argued that the HR movement should adopt a more explicitly value-based approach its proponents argue that:

> rather than a paradigm which is failing to live up to underlying ideals of freedom and human rights, harm reduction is better viewed as an assemblage of pragmatic practices and practical goals with varied outcomes. Its pragmatism, avowed value-neutrality and constitution of drug use problems as technical rather than moral are themselves significant interventions in the moralised realm of drug debate.
>
> (Keane, 2002)

By continuing to work pragmatically and value-neutrally to develop a range of health-based responses to substance-associated harms and risks, social work practitioners will demonstrate their important part in responses to drug use.

Problematic-recreational dichotomy

The problematic-recreational dichotomy has served to highlight both the prioritization of the drugs–crime relationship and the predominance of the classic disease model of addiction as a way of understanding the underlying cause of such patterns of drug use. It also poses questions regarding what are the appropriate policy responses and resource allocations proportionate to different types of drug users, the problems they create and how society should respond. The application of this dichotomous distinction to policy can be illustrated by the Dutch model of drug policy which has distinguished between 'hard' and 'soft' drug use since the 1970s, linked to a market-driven view of gateway theory. Underlying the Dutch model is the aim of separating the markets for 'hard' drugs such as heroin and 'soft' drugs, particularly cannabis, so that 'soft' drug users are less likely to come into contact with the suppliers of 'hard' drugs, resulting in a reduction in opportunistic experimentation, supplier-driven initiation and escalation of drug careers. To this end, the Netherlands effectively decriminalized the personal possession of cannabis in the Opium Act 1976 initially for amounts under 30 grammes (reduced to 5 grammes in 1995), with the sale of cannabis tolerated in licensed coffee shops from 1980. This policy distinction between 'hard' and 'soft' drugs achieved its aim with the Runciman Report (Police Foundation, 2000) noting that 'Holland can justly claim to have separated the heroin and cannabis markets'. In recent years, however, there has been a shift away from this separation of the markets for 'hard' and 'soft' drugs in part due to restrictions on the smoking of tobacco in public places meaning that the smoking of tobacco/cannabis mixtures is no longer tolerated and in part due to a programme of coffee shop and cannabis sales restrictions aimed at reducing the 'honeypot effect' of drug tourism to the capital and associated pressures from neighbouring European countries. We turn now to the recreational drug users in this typology.

Recreational drug use

Research throughout the 1990s increasingly focused upon a large and growing group of 'recreational' drug users, their patterns of use and the wider implications. For example, use of the most popular illegal drug, cannabis, increased throughout the 1990s to a high point of 1998 (Roe and Mann, 2006). Other illegal drugs that are reported among the UK population include cocaine, ecstasy and amphetamines (Hoare and Moon, 2010). The characterization of this larger group of drug users as 'recreational' was in part in opposition to problem drug users, with the term providing a general overview of the types of drugs consumed, patterns of drug use, the social circumstances and consequences; that is the occasional or more regular use of drugs other than heroin and crack, most usually at weekends at social gatherings and in party situations where while intoxication may be both an aim and a desirable effect, drug use is not the sole or primary function of the gathering and is to a considerable extent controlled rather than compulsive.

This model of drug use should not imply that recreational drug use is a homogenous category. A longitudinal study in the north west of England of young people aged 14–28 tracked the uptake and patterns of legal and illegal drug use, characterizing them as the 'post-heroin generation' because of their very low levels of experimentation with opiates (Measham *et al.*, 1993). Among this sample of young people, none were daily or monthly heroin or crack users. However, within the group that could be considered 'recreational' users, there were differences in drugs careers, frequency of use, types of drugs consumed and attitudes to illegal drugs. Parker *et al.* (1998) created a 'drug pathways' analysis which divided young people into: *abstainers, current users, former triers* and those *in transition*. Abstainers had never tried illicit drugs, never intended to and held the most negative attitudes towards drugs. Within the recreational drug user category there were three clear subdivisions: current users had used drugs in the past, thought they would probably use them again, identified as current users and held the most positive attitudes towards drugs. Former users had experimented with drugs but did not intend to do so again and held neutral attitudes to drugs. The in-transition group was the most disparate: they may or may not have tried drugs in the past but none ruled out the possibility of future experimentation and they were mostly neutral in their attitudes to drugs. What is interesting is that at the age of 18 not only were young people divided between the four groups (31 per cent current users, 28 per cent in-transition, 11 per cent ex-triers and 30 per cent abstainers) but also throughout their twenties they continued to oscillate between the groups including a sizeable minority of the abstainers moving towards experimentation: from nearly a third of the sample at 18 down to a quarter of the sample at 22 and this had fallen to just under a fifth by the age of 27 (Aldridge *et al.*, 2011).

The policy implications of the large and growing numbers of recreational drug users in the last two decades regards the potential criminalization of otherwise law-abiding young people whose drug use may not have significant negative consequences on their health or social circumstances, nor for their communities or wider society beyond the law breaking itself. This was summed up by Parker *et al.* (2002: 960) in their development of the normalization thesis:[12]

> What the Class A stimulant drug users have done . . . is pose a very knotty political dilemma. As primarily educated, employed young citizens with otherwise conforming profiles, they challenge the war on drugs discourse which prefers to link drug use with crime & personal tragedy & utilizes this discourse as a reason for not calling a truce.

This dilemma is further illustrated by Mike Trace, Chairman of the Management Board of the European Monitoring Centre for Drugs and Drug Addiction, in an EMCDDA briefing in 2002:

> Recreational drug use, especially of synthetic drugs, is increasingly common. Notably, those using them are not found predominantly among the marginalised or socially deprived but among the young, studious, employed & relatively affluent. Such trends appear to have been established rapidly across the EU.

Between problematic and recreational drug use

The problematic-recreational dichotomous characterization of drug use has been further developed and challenged since its inception. First, to categorize people as problem drug users simply on the basis of whether or not they regularly consume specific illegal drugs is problematic. Not all opioid consumption is problematic and not all drug problems are directly related to opioid consumption. For example, in relation to the former point, McSweeney and Turnbull (2007) have challenged the inevitability of daily and dependent heroin use in an important longitudinal study which challenges some of the myths surrounding patterns of heroin use. McSweeney and Turnbull explored the characteristics of a sample of occasional and non-problematic heroin users, many of whom were not in touch with criminal justice or health services and for whom, for at least part of their drug-taking careers, heroin use could be considered controlled and unproblematic aside from the illegality of their actions.

In relation to the latter point, Hammersley *et al.* (2006) have suggested that there is a complex relationship between potentially any drug and crime, rather than a simple causal relationship whereby the need for opioids causes crime. This supports the estimate above by McSweeney *et al.* (2007) that only one-third of PDUs fund their use of opiates and/or crack through crime. Through interviews with 151 Scottish offenders, Hammersley *et al.* (2006) found that alcohol was associated with fraud, and that there was a stronger association between non-opioid polydrug use and theft than opioid use and theft. In a similar vein, de Dios *et al.* (2010) looked at problem marijuana use. They assessed the levels of abuse and dependence among a volunteer community sample of over 300 female US marijuana users aged 18–24 using the DSM[13] criteria. They divided marijuana users into three groups along a continuum from mild through moderate to severe problems. They found that over one-third of the sample were either unaffected by their marijuana use or had very low rates of abuse and dependence; over four in ten had moderate problems associated with use; and over one in five were categorized as severe problem marijuana users. Among this group of severe problem users, 90 per cent met the DSM criteria for abuse and 100 per cent met the diagnostic criteria for dependence. This group was also most likely to report using larger amounts than intended, spending a great deal of time smoking, being unsuccessful in attempts to cut down their use, and continuing to use despite associated problems. Severe problem marijuana use was associated with early initiation, problems with alcohol and other substances, and also lower socio-economic status. This final point of socio-economic position is a significant one.

MacDonald and Marsh (2002) have noted that, particularly in areas of entrenched social exclusion, the distinction between 'recreational' and 'problematic' drug use may break down, resulting in drug use patterns and repertories not typically associated with recreational use. Simpson (2003) has challenged the idea of so-called recreational drug use being unproblematic in his ethnographic study in the north east of England. Simpson (2003) suggests that 'persistent drug use' may exist alongside recreational and dependent use, and that drug use careers may slip from one to another of these characterizations and have complex relationships with crime. Simpson identified five key criteria in categorizing a user as recreational, persistent or dependent: frequency, quantity, drug types, route of administration and drug-related attitudes.

The problematic-recreational dichotomy has also been refined by Hammersley *et al.* (2003) in their longitudinal study of persistent young offenders which explored the relationship between offending and drug use. They found little use of heroin or crack and little evidence of progression on to these drugs in later years. Instead their study highlighted frequent, low-level offending alongside heavy and frequent use of alcohol, cannabis and tobacco, and less frequent use of other drugs. This led them to conclude that there were signs of 'normalization' of use of some drugs among young offenders in terms of easy access and acceptance of drug use. Forty per cent of the sample thought that there was a relationship between their drug use and their offending and 15 per cent were assessed by the researchers as having substance abuse problems. As Hammersley *et al.* conclude (p. 70), their cohort 'could not be neatly divided into normal substance users without problems and "addicts" with problems'.

When interrogating the research more closely, then, what we find is that while there are small numbers who commit petty and persistent crimes to fund a lifestyle which includes recreational drugs such as those in Hammersley *et al.*'s study, the majority of recreational and problem drug users appear to fund their drug use out of legitimate earnings. This then raises serious problems for the government because for many users the only drug-related crime involved is the criminal offence of drug possession which the government creates and enforces. The secondary concern is the mismatch between resource and service demands. For example, there is a growing population of younger entrants to treatment from predominantly deprived backgrounds who have problem family backgrounds, minor health and mental health concerns, low-educational and employment aspirations and achievements (Aldridge *et al.*, 2011). For many of these primarily 16–24-year-olds their drug problems relate to frequent and heavy use of alcohol, cannabis and more recently cocaine for which an increasing number are testing positive if arrested. While the casualty rate for adult non-PDUs may be growing, service provision is not in step. As Aldridge *et al.* argue, separate alcohol and drug strategies and funding streams have prevented integrated services developing, the National Treatment Agency continues to marginalize treatment for non-opiate users, and services remain dominated as much by a crime prevention as an HR or public health agenda. For this growing group there are few appropriate services and most reject attempts to be coerced into traditional treatment (Duffy and Cuddy, 2008). This group is distinct from the majority of recreational drug users and clubbers who are employed, less often caught up in drug testing and less likely to present to services in significant numbers.

Nevertheless, despite the drawbacks identified above, the problematic-recreational distinction has retained some salience to our understanding of twenty-first-century patterns of drug use in the UK. Parker (2005: 213) identified a 'welcome, fundamental shift in the official thinking about the need to recognise recreational drug use being widespread but distinctive from problem drug use'. This can also be illustrated in surveys of drug use in dance clubs (e.g., Deehan and Saville, 2003; Measham *et al.*, 2001). First, in terms of sheer numbers, surveys of clubbers have noted very high levels of use of a wide range of illegal drugs including ecstasy, cocaine, amphetamines and cannabis, but very low levels of use of heroin, crack and benzodiazepines, suggesting that in general terms there is some empirical grounding to making a distinction between these two types of drug use (Measham and Moore, 2009). Second, such surveys locate drug consumption away from the sphere of social problems and within the sphere of leisure time and consumption; for example, as part of the night-time economy of bars, clubs and parties, with different challenges in terms of public health and public order, education, treatment and service provision (Hunt *et al.*, 2010).

Motivational and career typologies of drug use

Other studies have distinguished between drug users according to their motivations for use. For example, motivations for use have been categorized as experimental, recreational, spiritual or dependent (Gossop, 2006a). A similar typology, which relates to both the reason for taking drugs and to their effect, is a Danish study which characterizes drug use as either pleasurable or addictive. As with the problematic-recreational model discussed above, it faces similar strengths and weaknesses in terms of being a simplistic dichotomy and is easily criticized for using two concepts – pleasure and addiction – which are both complex and disputed terms (Davies, 1992/1997; Farrell Brodie and Redfield, 2002), yet neither is mutually exclusive nor independently essential to psychoactive drug use. Nevertheless, such distinctions may carry weight in policy and practice terms regarding making necessary distinctions between the small cluster of daily, often dependent drug users, and the much larger cluster of occasional and weekend users.

Studies have also distinguished by the level of drug experience and length of drug careers. Most notable is the work of Becker (1963) and his application of social learning theory to the development of cannabis careers (and further developed by other researchers; e.g., Østergaard, 2009 in relation to Danish adolescents learning to become alcohol users) with drug users divided into the categories of novice, occasional, regular user and connoisseur. Finally, drug users have been categorized by the number of drugs consumed per session as well as the quantities of different drugs (ACMD, forthcoming). In O'Hagan's work it was suggested that the repertoire of simultaneous polydrug use was a key indicator for drug-related problems and is a particularly useful typology for policy-makers. Polydrug use has been used as a key marker for acute problems, as well as being associated with risk-taking behaviours, overdose and a range of health and social problems (Thiede *et al.*, 2003).

A critique of dichotomies

At a more abstract level, Fraser and Moore (2008) have provided a critique of dichotomous distinctions of drug use, specifically looking at chaotic versus ordered drug use, exploring the use of this dichotomy in discourses of drug users in the UK, the USA and Australia. They challenge such dichotomies on political grounds, suggesting that the chaos/stability pairing is used to affirm the illegitimacy of injecting drug users (IDU) by associating it with unproductive and disorderly lives and therefore justifying a high degree of regulation and intervention. This is contrasted with the normal, orderly and productive lives of non-injecting drug users and particularly non-drug users. In their critique of this chaos/stability pairing and their reconceptualization of chaos, they argue that academic and policy debates import 'largely unexamined normative assumptions about appropriate ways of living' (Fraser and Moore, 2008: 741), apply mainstream notions of order to drug users' lives, and emphasize neo-liberal individualized values such as reasoned decision making, healthy choices and lifestyles. Such a criticism can be levelled at much of the research on recreational drug use and the normalization thesis of recreational drug use (e.g., Parker *et al.*, 1998); with its overemphasis on rational choice, 'sensible' drug use and cost-benefit decision-making pathways through adolescent experimentation (see also Measham, 2004 for critique). Such discourses, Fraser and Moore (2008: 744) argue, create 'a mythical divide between those who are chaotic . . . and those who are orderly' with chaos itself portrayed as inherently and self-evidently problematic and non-pleasurable. Indeed for some drug users, a little bit of chaos, disorder, a 'controlled loss of control' or 'calculated hedonism' might be exactly what they are seeking from a drugs experience (Measham, 2002; Szmigin *et al.*, 2008). The problem for policy is that the 'blanket (perhaps complacent) charge of chaos' may serve to confuse rather than clarify appropriate interventions when there is a vital need to iden- tify exactly what the problems are for problem drug users (Fraser and Moore, 2008: 748).

At the heart of the problematic-recreational dichotomy, then, is this contrast between drug users as rational neo-liberal consumers who take respon- sibility for their lives and those who relinquish responsibility (and blame) for their actions, resulting in stigmatization, instability and intervention. Historically, such dichotomies could be seen to have their origin in the 'respect- able versus non-respectable' discourses surrounding the masses in Victorian England and judgements made about the 'deserving versus undeserving' poor in charity interventions and poor relief in particular (Steadman Jones [1971] 1984).

Implications for social work practice

The ways that we understand and differentiate between drug users has signifi- cance not only in terms of service provision but also for political reasons. The wide variety of patterns of drug use, motivations to take drugs and conse- quences of use means that there is no simple understanding of what a 'drug user' is and therefore what problems are faced by or caused by drug use in our society. It is necessary to understand each individual drug-using career before considering the ways in which drug use may impact upon or cause possible harms to that user, their family or community and wider society. Furthermore, the political reasons for such differentiation are also salient in terms of service provision and resource allocation, subjects we turn to in later chapters. The key point here is that drug problems are not confined to problem drug users.

3   Stigma, HCV and HIV

Introduction

In this chapter we consider the social context to drug use, how drug users are viewed by wider society and the implications of these perspectives to the experiences and consequences of illicit drug use. While historically studies of drugs have emphasized drug users as 'outsiders', the shift towards higher levels of availability and use of illegal drugs, and more recently the online marketing of novel psychoactive substances or so-called 'legal highs', have led to increasingly varied perceptions of drug users as spread across all social strata, with some drug users socially excluded whereas others are undifferentiated from the general population. In this chapter we consider such social perceptions of drug users, the enduring stigma that some face and the damage done to drug users, their families and wider society from the resulting marginalization and discrimination.

Stigmatization

Stigmatization is the process of marking individuals and groups judged to be unworthy of social investment (Reidpath and Chan, 2005). Such stigmatization may lead to an erosion of drug users' support networks as family, friends, colleagues and the wider community seek to disassociate themselves from the user and their deviant behaviour. Furthermore, users may come to recognize themselves as deviant and accept their ascribed role. This may lead to users' withdrawal from society as they exclude themselves from the places that *normal people* go, and the things that *normal people* do, often becoming part of deviant subcultures (Schur, 1965). As Buchanan and Young (1998: 222) state, 'they are forced into an underworld of criminal networks and secrecy, which then exposes them to other drugs and other criminal activity'.

The stigma and criminality associated with illicit drug use also has implications for drug users' help-seeking behaviour. Users will inevitably be discouraged from accessing services if they believe that their problems will be met by disapproval, judgement or punitive action. The implication for practice is that social workers should seek to facilitate inclusion. This may involve supporting users to re-establish existing support networks or introducing users to alternative support networks such as user organizations where they may benefit from peer support. Workers may also engage in outreach work with users in order to facilitate reintegration into society. This may involve supporting users to access local facilities and services or to find employment for example. Because the stigma associated with illicit drug use makes users hard to reach, drug services must be proactive in devising ways to engage with users and must capitalize on every opportunity for contact. This suggests an increasing role for peripatetic drugs work which seeks to make contact with users at the point of drug use or at users' points of access to other services such as needle exchanges or via GP and pharmacy liaison work for example. The overarching message to social workers is that they must seek to work with users in a non-judgemental and anti-oppressive manner in order to challenge stigma and build capacity for change.

HIV and AIDS[14]

The word 'stigma' has become virtually synonymous with HIV/AIDS (Parker and Aggleton, 2003). In relation to HIV/AIDS it could be suggested that stigma also reinforces and promotes the blame culture that exists. The issue of stigma, disclosure and confidentiality are all significantly linked in relation to HIV and AIDS. For example, parents may choose not to tell their children they are HIV positive or have AIDS because they may be afraid that their child cannot keep the secret (Miah *et al.*, 2004); that is, they may be afraid of the adverse reaction of 'others' (whether this is family members, friends or people within the community), finding out about their illness because of the effect this may have on their lives and the lives of their children in relation to rejection and discrimination (Miah *et al.*, 2004). As Antle *et al.* (2001: 162) highlight, for most families, secrecy 'appeared to be based on a desire to protect their children from perceived hardships that this knowledge brings and on their own concerns about death or how they became infected'. It is additionally important to understand that individuals may not want to talk to professionals because they are worried about being judged, treated differently and concerned about the issue of confidentiality.

An individual's concerns are often justified in relation to HIV/AIDS. HIV and AIDS are connected to discrimination and prejudice and are stigmatized in a way that other illnesses are not (Waugh, 2003). Research (Bor and Elford, 1998; Berger *et al.*, 2001) shows that it is the very particular nature of HIV stigma which sets HIV apart from other chronic and life-threatening conditions. HIV/AIDS-related stigma compounds the social exclusion experienced by injecting drug users (IDU), gay men and African communities and 'promotes discrimination' in the workplace and intensifies poverty and isolation (Dodds *et al.*, 2004). As Reidpath and Chan (2005: 425) argue, 'HIV related stigma is regarded as one of the major barriers in the development of effective prevention and care programmes'.

Goffman (1963) describes and allows us to see clearly the process of stigmatization and mortification of the self irrespective of the nature of the stigma or deviance and irrespective of any harm or injury (to the deviant or to a victim) that may result from the stigma itself or from the stigmatization. Stigma is therefore a negative consequence of not matching social expectations of normality with discrimination as a consequence of a person acting in relation to their stigmatized views of 'others' (Dodds *et al.*, 2004). An individual's character is also questioned because HIV/AIDS is often associated with drug use and promiscuity, particularly associated with gay men. People are blamed by 'others' as being responsible for putting themselves at risk and failing to protect themselves (Cree *et al.*, 2004).

HIV stigma is therefore not straightforward because it is not only attached to an individual's diagnosis, but also to 'risk factors associated with the routes of transmission and also other personal characteristics such as ethnicity' (Reidpath and Chan, 2005: 425). Thus, when an individual is diagnosed as HIV positive they not only have to deal with the stigma that is attached to the disease, but they additionally face different levels of stigma depending on how they contracted the disease and who they are (Reidpath and Chan, 2005). Haemophiliacs, in particular, have been portrayed as innocent and blameless. When concerns began about HIV/AIDS transmission through blood products in 1983, they were advised to continue with their treatment as there was no conclusive proof that HIV/AIDS was transmitted through blood products (Berridge, 1996: 40). The dichotomous labels of blame and innocence continue in the twenty-first century and continue to feed stigmatization.

Hepatitis C (HCV)[15]

Stigma and discrimination is also recognized as being one of the main issues faced by people who live with HCV (Paterson *et al.*, 2007). The relationship between HCV and stigma are particularly pertinent in that HCV can be experienced as both what Goffman (1963) describes as discredited (i.e., visible) perhaps in an exchange with a social worker who has access to service user notes (Hopwood and Treloar, 2003) or discreditable (not visible but the possibility of being exposed is ever present) in interactions with friends, work colleagues and partners (Fraser and Treloar, 2006).

The World Health Organization (WHO) estimates that HCV infects 170 million people worldwide and thus represents a viral pandemic, one that is five times as widespread as infection with the HIV. Blood-screening measures in developed countries has decreased the risk of transfusion-associated hepatitis to a negligible level, but new cases continue to occur mainly as a result of IDU. Progression to chronic disease occurs in the majority of HCV-infected persons, and infection with the virus has become the main indication for liver transplantation. HCV infection also increases the number of complications in persons who are co-infected with HIV.

Current estimates of infection prevalence in the UK vary from 250 000 (Department of Health (DoH), 2002) to 600 000 (Royal College of General Practitioners (RCGP), 2007) and the percentage of the population living with HCV is 0.5 per cent in England, rising to 0.8 per cent in Scotland and 0.4 per cent in Wales (Health Protection Agency (HPA), 2008). It is estimated that only 17 per cent of the people living with the virus are currently diagnosed and only 2 per cent of those are receiving treatment (RCGP, 2007). This will cost the NHS an expected £8 billion over the next 30 years as more and more people require liver transplants, treatment for end-stage liver disease and liver cancer. The Advisory Council on the Misuse of Drugs (ACMD) (2009) estimates that 80 per cent of current infection can be attributed to past or present IDU and 50 per cent are people who are currently injecting drugs have HCV, with approximately half of these being unaware of their infection.

The reason for this lack of awareness around infection is because HCV is slow to proliferate in the body (Dolan, 1998) and can therefore take between 10–40 years to develop serious liver disease (Foster, 2008). This means symptoms can be 'chronic and debilitating rather than fatal' (Dolan, 1998). RCGP (2007) maintain that symptoms are difficult to recognize, given they may be general or asymptomatic until the liver disease has significantly advanced and even then may only present mild symptoms.

However, Temple-Smith *et al.* (2006) explain that for many people, symptoms of HCV can severely affect their ability to carry out day to day tasks, and Foster (2007) maintains that the symptoms of HCV which, although variable, can include poor concentration, poor memory, difficulty in completing mental tasks, feelings of chronic fatigue and experiences of non-restful sleep, pain in the liver, joint pains, irritable bowel syndrome and bladder symptoms. Crofts *et al.* (1997) discusses HCV in the context of disability legislation and as such may constitute impairment under the Disability Discrimination Act 1995.

Despite the diverse symptoms and implications of living with the disease, respondents experienced their health and their identity in extreme terms; notably feelings of 'absolute contamination' – shifting their self-perceptions and identify 'from good to bad, healthy to sick and clean to dirty' in the context of the highly stigmatized nature of living with HCV because of its association with IDU (Fraser and Treloar, 2006: 108). Social workers have a difficult but vital role in conveying the seriousness of the infection, while balancing this with the need to disrupt the extreme responses where people perceive themselves as being worthless; this would include explaining the variable nature of living with HCV and as such the continuum of health and illness involved.

Clearly, the possibility of this occurring depends to a significant degree on social workers being equipped with appropriate and accurate knowledge concerning HCV, as well as the appropriate non-stigmatizing professional response encouraging interaction with the person. This interaction between professional and individual is the key in responding to HCV which has been termed 'the silent epidemic' (DoH, 2002).

The major route of transmission for HCV in the UK is via sharing injecting equipment (Coffey *et al.*, 2005; Judd *et al.*, 2005) and this has resulted in IDU accounting for the majority of new infections (DoH, 2002). HCV has two stages of infection: the asymptomatic acute stage generally lasts about six months and is followed by the chronic stage, which affects 80 per cent of those initially infected. Chronic HCV varies wildly. Many people will experience few symptoms for a long period of time whereas others can be symptomatic from the onset. Twenty per cent of people who are infected will develop cirrhosis. Lack of awareness and the asymptomatic nature of the disease mean many of the infected have not been diagnosed and are therefore not able to access treatment. Awareness of HCV and its transmission must be raised among professionals, the public and IDUs in order to get more people into treatment and prevent further infections. The scale of new diagnoses have reached '. . . epidemic levels' (McKeown and Gibson, 2007: 1211).

It appears that the strength of the harm reduction (HR) message for HIV has provided false reassurance and overshadowed concerns about HCV among IDUs and thus contributed towards risky injecting behaviour. HIV is still perceived to be the primary risk and reason behind safer injecting practices for older injectors and this belief may have been passed on to younger injectors (Paylor and Orgel, 2004). It would seem that the knowledge IDUs have in regard to BBV is an important factor in preventing HCV. In many ways, empowering IDUs to gain and pass on a knowledge concerning BBV can be influential in reducing risk-associated behaviours. Research has indicated that instances in which IDUs displayed knowledge regarding the possible transmission of HCV through injecting paraphernalia resulted in more care being taken in reducing sharing (Wright *et al.*, 2005). However, HCV is not the only BBV that is often associated with IDUs and this presents a problem in developing interventions that are specific to HCV. HIV serves as a 'master status' (ACMD, cited in Rhodes *et al.*, 2004) for how HCV and the associated risk environments are understood. HCV is '. . . blinkered' (Paylor and Orgel, 2004: 903) by HIV as the greater emphasis by drug services in preventing the spread of the disease has undermined the seriousness of HCV (Rhodes and Treloar, 2008). This has resulted in IDUs perceiving HCV as a lesser danger in comparison to HIV

(Rhodes *et al.*, 2004) which in turn makes preventing the disease much more difficult.

The influences of HIV have also led to IDUs being either confused (Rhodes *et al.*, 2004) or having a lack (Paylor and Orgel, 2004; Wright *et al.*, 2005) of knowledge that is specific to HCV. A lack in knowledge has heavily contributed to the HCV epidemic in the USA (Grow and Christopher, 2008) and there is a strong possibility that the UK is heading in the same direction. Educational interventions are needed which enable the majority of IDUs, and not just those in either treatment or caught up in systems of law enforcement, to become aware of HCV. IDUs need to be targeted through other HR interventions like needle exchange schemes in which clean injecting paraphernalia (Wright *et al.*, 2005) is given to IDUs in the community in order to reduce the possibility of acquiring HCV and other BBV (Van Den Berg *et al.*, 2007). Establishing contact with IDUs in the community and empowering key members from injecting networks will allow them to obtain a knowledge concerning HCV which can both help to protect themselves and be passed on throughout other 'overlapping' injecting networks in order to protect others (De *et al.*, 2007).

People who inject drugs and who experience marginalization and stigma, often substitute trust and social relationships for professional knowledge which act symbolically to interpret and rationalize risk practices as constituting reduced risk of contracting HCV. However, the fragility of these social relationships given the cultures of silence, shame and secrecy that often surround antibody status means that having a knowledgeable supportive professional who can maintain confidence and provide support is even more vital (Rhodes and Treloar, 2008). A significant amount of confusion reigns among those who are not in touch with services reinforcing the importance of accessible services (DrugScope, 2009).

National campaigns, such as 'FaCe It', have a limited effect and more successful awareness-raising strategies to encourage safer injecting and increase testing must be implemented. Short one-off counselling sessions, or brief behavioural interventions, are a means of directly engaging a service user, getting them to consider their own risky behaviour and providing them with information on safer injecting and sexual practices in order to decrease their risk of contracting or transmitting HCV. These are even more effective if they are led by service users. Drug users are more likely to approach and respond to peer-ran services as peers may be seen to be more understanding of their situation and less judgemental. There is evidence that peer-led services lead to a higher awareness of HCV and reduced risky behaviour (Aitken *et al.*, 2002, cited in Mack, 2007) and, on a positive note, the National Treatment Agency (NTA) (2008) reports a significant increase in service-user-led programmes in drugs partnerships.

Social work has a crucial role in preventing HCV infection through its core practice of focusing on the environment and the relationship that individuals have with it (McCarthy and Galvani, 2004). The transmission of HCV is a product of aspects from society that have resulted from a complex interplay of social and environmental factors (Rhodes and Treloar, 2008). The social context in which IDUs inject is associated with HCV status. Smyth *et al.* (2005: 171) found that IDUs who reported closer social relationships with other IDUs were at an increased risk of infection as drug injecting was a '. . . socialized behaviour'.

The concept of socialized behaviours in IDUs allows conclusions to be formulated that suggest that acquiring a knowledge which relates directly to both the social and environmental factors of injecting drug cultures may be beneficial in preventing HCV. Support for such a statement can be found by examining research which argues that the most common mode of HCV transmission for IDUs is through the direct or indirect sharing of injection paraphernalia. Such paraphernalia does not just include needles and syringes. Spoons and other forms of containers used for 'cooking' and mixing drugs, water in order to dissolve the drugs or rinse syringes, swabs to wipe the site of injection and filters, which prevent particles from being drawn up into the needle, have all been associated with HCV transmission (De *et al.*, 2008; Mathei *et al.*, 2006; Rhodes and Trelaor, 2008; Wright *et al.*, 2005).

Drug paraphernalia sharing is viewed as normative behaviour within many injecting cultures (Rhodes *et al.*, 2004; Rhodes and Treloar, 2008). Koester *et al.* (2005: 35) argue that IDUs might acquire, prepare and inject together because drug use is a '. . . social activity'. Paraphernalia sharing can often be as a consequence of how the drugs are obtained as the pooling of resources can allow users to get a better deal or enable them to afford to buy the drug (Koester *et al.*, 2005).

There is a clear need for services, whose goal is to decrease the prevalence of HCV among IDUs, to either adopt or support a practice which has the ability to reduce drug-related harm through targeting risk behaviours that are associated with HCV. This allows the limitations of individual approaches in reducing drug-related harm, which are a consequence of both medicine and law enforcement (Koester *et al.*, 2005), to be swept aside in order for interventions to be developed that specifically reduce the risk of both transmitting and contracting HCV. It is therefore imperative that social workers, whose interventions are aimed at the social circumstances of individuals (McCarthy and Galvani, 2004), to become involved in using their experience in attempting to improve both the social and individual circumstances of IDUs.

Factors such as homelessness, a subject which social workers have knowledge in (Paylor and Orgel, 2004), highlight how non-health-oriented interventions can help create the '. . . climate' (DoH, 2002: 16) of HCV prevention. Research identifies that homeless individuals in the UK take risks in their injecting practices (Wright *et al.*, 2005) and that the concept of 'not sharing' drug paraphernalia is '. . . probably beyond what can be expected' (Mathei *et al.*, 2006: 567). This is further compounded by research which suggests that users inject more when homeless and that for some individuals being home-less was a factor in initiation into intravenous drug use (Wright *et al.*, 2005). Wright *et al.* emphasize the role poverty has in influencing homeless IDUs to share paraphernalia. They found that equipment such as spoons and filters can often be reused by groups of individuals who have pooled their resources together in order that any drug residue is not discarded.

Identifying the risk of homelessness gives a good example of how inter-ventions, other than those influenced by health and law enforcement, are needed in combating HCV. A focus on risk environments enables social workers to think about social situations and helps in developing interventions that aim to change environmental conditions (Koester *et al.*, 2005; De *et al.*, 2007). An understanding of the environmental determinants which influence the risk behaviours associated with HCV will allow 'enabling environments' to be developed that can reduce risk (Rhodes, 2002; De *et al.*, 2007).

There is a clear need for social workers to use their experience, skills and knowledge in combating HCV transmission as: '. . . if the primary determi-nants of harm are economical and social then remedies must also be econom-ical and social' (Rhodes, 2002: 91).

Social workers have the ability to support service users in reducing the risk of drug-related harm (Keene, 2001). Drug-related harms like HCV can be prevented through social workers role as '. . .change agents' (McCarthy and Galvani, 2004: 92) in working with service users in order to change behaviours. Maximizing contact and empowering IDUs to become an integral partner has been found to be an important aspect in preventing BBV (Grund *et al.*, 1992). In terms of risk environments, in which peripheral network members pass from group to group (De *et al.*, 2007), harm-reducing interventions, which empower IDUs, may be critical in controlling the spread of HCV. Social workers can work alongside IDUs in enabling them to take up a peer educator-style role in which IDUs themselves take responsibility for providing informa-tion and aid to others (Fraser, 2004). Interventions like these, in which peer leaders of injecting networks are identified through being nominated by other IDUs and taught to discuss safer 'risk' behaviours, have been found to signifi-cantly reduce the sharing of needles (De *et al.*, 2007).

It is clear, however, that social work is not responding effectively enough to HCV. There are a lot of improvements; HR services are more effective and there is evidence that local authorities can adopt successful HCV strategies. However, there is still a lack of consistent information and services for at-risk groups and a high degree of stigmatization surrounding the virus. Social work as a whole must take a substantial role in preventing HCV, yet there has been little expansion of integrated services (Paylor and Orgel, 2004). HCV has the ability to infect a wide variety of individuals from mostly socio-economic deprived areas because they have chosen to inject drugs. Notions of individual responsibility and 'it serves you right' do little to prevent the disease, as does the influence of health in focusing on beating the addiction and law enforcement in punishing criminality. There is a clear need for a different ideology, a need for social workers, who neither punish nor treat, to go out into communities and establish contact with as many IDUs as they can. They need to reach out to those who do not want to give up and develop interventions that are both relevant to specific environments and relevant to HCV. Most of all, social work needs to realize the important role it can play in preventing HCV and make the appropriate adjustments that will enable it to take a leading role in combating this epidemic (Paylor and Mack, 2010).

'Clean/dirty' dualism

The dichotomy between clean/dirty sets the body in a context of utopian ideals and the sense of being 'dirty' ignores the fact that bodily boundaries are fluid and things enter and leave the body daily. The idea of the body as closed and pure or open and contaminated is part of Western medical discourse which conceptualizes the body as rigid (Fraser and Treloar, 2006). HCV poses a particular threat to the science and the authority of Western medicine (Jenner and Scott, 2007). HCV has always been characterized by confusion (knowledge and responses are still developing now) and as a result, anxiety. Jenner and Scott maintain that science has been unable to fully understand the phenomenon and given that HCV does not move in a predictable fashion (RCGP, 2007) have a lack of control over the body. Therefore prejudice and discrimination emerges from the threatening of authority.

Rhodes and Treloar (2008) also draw attention to the risk environment as a key theme in HCV literature (their review focuses specifically on people who use drugs) and the way in which hostile or unpredictable environments can not only disrupt risk reduction measures but also reinforce barriers between people who may be living with HCV, and the services they need, potentially compounding the 'trivial' nature of HCV and pushing it further down the list of competing priorities 'when you're taking drugs all the time, you don't think you will live long enough to die from HCV'.

Additionally Link and Phelan (2001) discuss the fact that although an individual can exert effort to reduce the impact of stigma, this can have a significant impact on other areas of life; this is evident in phase 2 of the Scottish Action Plan (The Scottish Government, 2008), which provides evidence that people are not approaching services because they fear that their injecting behaviour will be met with disapproval. In the immediate term this means that the individual may not have to face disapproval (Scambler's, 1998 enacted stigma) but in the long term could potentially experience poorer health as a result of unsafe injecting, would not be signposted to services and may contract and live with unmanaged or untreated HCV for a longer period.

Importantly feelings of stigma are shifting and likely to change as a person comes into contact with other different individuals such as family members or social workers (Hopwood and Treloar, 2003). Fraser and Treloar (2006) similarly discuss 'social identity theory' and how discrimination by professionals may serve a socially adaptive function, reinforcing norms which are perceived as being at odds with those of 'out groups'. Professionals who employ discriminatory practices are making judgements concerning a person's moral adequacy and positioning those with the virus as deviant (Fraser and Treloar, 2006). This serves to marginalize those who are already ill. Following a bad experience, people with HCV (and their friends) are less likely to engage which can adversely affect HR and engagement with services and professionals (Simmonds and Coomber, 2009), which in turn reduces access to information and support which has consequences for wider society and transmission (Temple-Smith *et al.*, 2006).

Stigma can become so internalized that people can become accustomed to discriminatory attitudes even failing to notice them or merely accepting them (Harris, 2005). This may serve to perpetuate the socialized nature of discrimination observed (Butt *et al.*, 2008) and reinforce stigmatizing behaviour from professionals by allowing it to go unexamined. Alternatively the perception held by professionals that people with HCV will be less grateful and more aggressive acts as something of a self-fulfilling prophecy (Paterson *et al.*, 2007) given that people with HCV experienced frustration with their treatment (Hopwood and Treloar, 2003). Stigma can also cause the individual with HCV to expect the discrimination which then reinforces the perception of people with HCV as undesirable.

Day *et al.* (2003) recognize there is a dearth of literature available on the impact of the method of HCV transmission but recognizes that the stigma associated with HCV is strongly related to assumptions concerning injecting drug use. Participants in Golden *et al.*'s (2006) study reported experiencing this directly from the nursing staff (having their arms checked for track marks, even though not all IDUs inject in their arms (for discretion) and combated this by introducing themselves as an 'innocent victim' and emphasizing the distance between themselves, who contracted HCV from blood products after giving birth between 1977 and 1994, and those who knowingly put themselves at risk of contracting HCV (see Simmonds and Coomber, 2009).

Golden *et al.* (2006) found that those who did not know how they had contracted the virus had the lowest stigma score and those who injected drugs felt it most keenly. They discuss the difficulties the women felt in needing to speak out publicly about the fact they had contracted HCV but at the same time experiencing this as profoundly distressing, being seen to have ties to groups such as IDUs. This was remedied by professionals by holding treatment and clinics for the two different groups on different days which may perpetuate the perception of difference not only for those people living with HCV but chiefly for the workers. In this way, stigma becomes socialized and institu-tionalized (Butt *et al.*, 2008).

Until stigma is effectively addressed people are likely to be deterred from accessing testing and therefore treatment. Subsequently, they are then less likely to protect themselves and others (Dodds *et al.*, 2004).

Disclosure

Disclosure is closely associated with HIV- and HCV-related stigma. Non-disclosure may be a way, for example, of parents who are HIV positive trying to protect their children from discrimination. However it can also have a detri-mental affect on the child in the long term because it not only prevents access to services, but also impedes permanency plans being developed (Knight *et al.*, 1999). There is also the conflict between a child's right to know and a parent's right to confidentiality (Lewis, 2001). Kay *et al.* (2002) through their research with 28 affected children who had been told about their parents' HIV status, found that most children and young people acknowledged that it was a difficult decision for parents to decide when the best time was to inform them of their HIV status. The study showed that the majority of children were told about their parent's illness at the age of 8 or between the ages of 11 and 12. Their research also highlighted that while some children were shocked and believed that their parents were about to die very soon, other children had to additionally come to terms with their own negative beliefs in relation to HIV and change their own moral outlook. For example, because a number of the children had simply learnt about HIV from their friends or through school, they were under the impres-sion, as many people are, that HIV is bad and some kind of punishment for risky behaviour (Kay *et al.*, 2002). While stigma may not excuse a parent's decision to hold back on disclosing their HIV status to their children, it does however explain it. While some people may view this as selfish, a comprehension of stig-matization and discrimination makes the decision understandable. No other illness carries a stigma that induces people to feel ashamed and reluctant to confide in or ask for support from their family in the same way HIV/AIDS does.

Gender and stigma

For women, drug use and poverty can be compounded by a further layer of disad-vantage due to gender discrimination. With increased interest in how gender impacts on drug use, harms and risks, research has explored how to improve women's access to drug services and the barriers which may be faced by female drug users, especially drug-using mothers, when trying to access services due to the stereotypes which surround what constitutes cultural ideals of femininity, female sexuality and motherhood. Studies have highlighted how the layers of disadvantage and also the multiple identities held by problem drug-using women result in the magnification of discrimination (Ettore, 2007; Lloyd, 2010). A qualitative study by Mulia (2002), for example, found that not only did formal institutional rules and informal practices restrict female drug users' access to drug services, but that women themselves employed 'forms of resistance' to intervention, some of which were protective but some of which were potentially harmful. Utilizing the concept of 'everyday resistance', Mulia (2002) suggests that women's strategies of resistance can be understood as acts of defiance or self-defence against a perceived threat to their physical or emotional well-being or to their basic dignity and human rights. Because of the power imbalance between most users and service providers, this resistance tended to take non-confrontational forms such as non-disclosure of HIV status or other medical information, or telling service providers what they thought they wanted to hear, in order either to access or to avoid health and social services interventions. Such resistance can be interpreted by the authorities as manipulative, non-compliant or self-destructive, however, and overall can lead to a negative impact upon the level and quality of service provision and treatment that female drug users receive.

Because of this greater stigma associated with female drug users, gender can also influence willingness to disclose drug use and drug-related problems to officials, to academics and to practitioners (Hoare and Moon, 2010; Measham *et al.*, 2011). The gender of the interviewer has also been demonstrated to affect women's responses to questions. For example, respondents have been shown to be more willing to reveal 'non-traditional' responses to female interviewers than to male interviewers (Flores-Macias and Lawson, 2008). Thus practitioners cannot discount the possibility that gender may influence the willingness of women to disclose drug-taking, particularly when that drug-taking is associated with stigma, or where respondents perceive that interviewers judge the circumstances of their lives as inappropriate to drug-taking; for example, where respondents are mothers being interviewed at home and in the vicinity of their children.

Because of issues relating mainly to stigma, parents and children are unable to freely access HIV/AIDS services and therefore inadequacies in provision remain hidden. Those specialist services that are available are few and far between, which means that there is a need for practitioners in social work to have up-to-date information about HIV, its treatment and the stigma which HIV brings (Cree *et al.*, 2004).

Implications for social work practice

Social workers must consider the interplay of wider social and cultural factors that may affect drug use and plan interventions which seek to address these issues rather than attempting to tackle 'drug use' *per se*. From US studies of juvenile delinquents and jazz musicians through to contemporary UK drug users, we can identify certain groups of drug users who have been marginalized from 'respectable' society. There is evidence that for some recreational users, access to material resources can mean that their drug use remains hidden from the authorities and does not become a criminal justice issue, meaning that they are able to progress through their drug-using careers with minimal harm to themselves and their future life outlook. For other drug users, however, the stigma, blame and discrimination associated with 'addiction' and injecting can lead to an outsider status which results in added problems such as reduced access to employment, housing, health services and sometimes even basic human rights.

Social workers (particularly those working with physically disabled adults or older people) will find themselves with increasing caseloads as HIV and HCV increase. This will necessitate them being able to adequately support families in an open and non-judgemental way and if and when disclosure happens, any additional support that is needed should then, through discussion, be put in place. In areas where there are no specialist agencies, generic teams should spend time with specialist teams outside their area, where possible, to develop the types of support that are available from the specialist agencies.

4 The service user's perspective

Introduction

As discussed in the previous chapters, drug users are one of the most demonized groups in society, the basis of many 'moral panics' within the media (Goldsmith, 2008) which portrays them as the source of many of society's ills, and as such they are the focus of a great deal of prejudice and stigma. The popular conception of substance users among health and social care professionals is often that they are: undeserving (Shapiro, 2005; Griffiths and Pearson, 1988); unmotivated (Bien *et al.*, 1993); hostile towards treatment, help, support and interventions; dishonest and manipulative (Fischer and Neale, 2008; Griffiths and Pearson, 1988); morally bankrupt; unable or unwilling to help themselves and unlikely to change (Rassool, 1998) and have only themselves to blame (Lloyd, 2010). This chapter will explore the perceptions and experiences of service users themselves, especially in terms of prejudice and stigma; provide a discussion of how these can be potential barriers to treatment for service users; and look at how these influences can be minimized. It will discuss ways in which substance users can be engaged and retained in treatment; how therapeutic relationships can be established and fostered; and is designed to enable a more empathic and holistic approach to drug support.

Factors, effects and attitudes

Social attitudes to drug use and drug users can be influenced by a range of factors including: the source from which the substances are obtained; the drug's legal status; familiarity with the substance and its effects; familiarity with users of a substance; the reasons behind use; and wider cultural factors (Griffiths and Pearson, 1988). Drugs prescribed by a doctor are usually seen as more socially acceptable, and use of the same substance, such as methadone, is viewed differently if it is prescribed by a doctor than if it is used illicitly for perceived 'hedonistic' purposes. This also highlights the different perceptions between legal and illegal or illicit use, where the 'control' of a substance is seen as evidence of its greater potential for harm, even where we are looking at the legal or illicit use of the same substance, as in the case of methadone. As Lloyd (2010) suggests, the illegal status of drugs plays a significant role in the stigmatization of drug users, especially when combined with the current politic rhetoric of the 'War on drugs' and 'Tough Choices', and this commonly elicits responses that support punitive measures being taken against those identified as being responsible for their own condition.

Additionally, attitudes to substances with widely known effects, such as alcohol, may differ to those about which less is known, such as heroin (Forrester, 2000). Society has 'a detailed body of folk knowledge about alcohol, and elaborate sets of social rules for regulating its consumption' (Griffiths and Pearson, 1988: 11) and establishes consensus about 'controlled drinking' and 'problem drinking'. Conversely, few people have personal experience of heroin, and its use is generally viewed as being inherently problematic, a view challenged later in this chapter. The use of 'problematic' drugs such as heroin and crack cocaine are more commonly associated with the socially marginalized and 'drug-using subcultures' than the social circles in which mainstream society, particularly professionals such as social or healthcare workers are likely to move in, and as Griffiths and Pearson suggest: we fear what we do not know; the less contact we have with users of such substances the easier we can project our fantasies on to them; and that perceptions of some drugs are damned by the association that they have with already stigmatized groups of users. Such groups are further stigmatized by the perception of them as hedonistic, obtaining 'unearned pleasures' and as a consequence the media relish in recounting the problems associated with use and the horrors of withdrawal (Griffiths and Pearson, 1988).

Professionals' attitudes can be influential in the way they assess and respond to substance use, the quality of the relationships that they develop with substance-using service users, and can deter professionals from supporting their service users adequately either through prejudice or lack of knowledge and understanding. The shame and stigma associated with problematic drug and alcohol use can also dissuade service users from disclosing, and, where social work interventions are statutory rather than voluntary, to the fear of increased involvement of social services. For some drug users, the act of seeking treatment may reinforce the 'addict' or 'junkie' identity, which in itself may dissuade drug users from seeking treatment (Lloyd, 2010). A common intervention used with drug and alcohol users is the decisional balance which compares the positives and negatives of continuing substance use against those of changing use, but the same type of decisional balance will be evident, albeit perhaps subconsciously, with those considering disclosing drug or alcohol use, where they have to balance the positives of disclosure, such as increased support, against the perceived negatives, such as increased social service involvement (especially where children are involved), shame and stigma. For these reasons the level of perceived problems and the corresponding desire for support may need to be quite high before service users will self-disclose, and thus social workers may need the skills and competences to identify problematic substance use in service users who do not voluntarily disclose. Conversely, social workers also need the skills to assess the extent to which substance use may contribute to their service users' problems and not conclude that where drug use is evident or disclosed, that it is automatically problematic. Service users who are incorrectly labelled as problematic drug users can find themselves with additional problems related to such inappropriate and loaded labels (Griffiths and Pearson, 1988) and this can direct attention away from the real sources of problems.

Social work as a profession seeks to understand and respond to the social factors in service users' lives that cause or contribute to their problems (Barber, 2002) and this can often necessitate identifying and responding to environmental factors, in addition to addressing problems such as substance use itself. A study by the Institute for Criminal Policy Research (Warburton *et al.*, 2005b), published by The Joseph Rowntree Foundation, explored the concept of controlled heroin use and found that some long-term heroin users report quite controlled use that results in few social, physical, psychological or legal problems. As well as casting doubt on the dominant assumption that heroin use is inherently problematic (as discussed earlier), the report highlighted several important factors. A comparison of the heroin users studied, to heroin users in treatment and in the Criminal Justice system, revealed that those who experienced comparatively few problems on the whole had noticeably better social capital: most were working or studying; had better accommodation; and were more affluent. While it is impossible to determine conclusively the direction of causality, the study concluded that problematic drug use is caused more by inequality in access to social goods such as employment, education and housing than to the features of the drug itself (Warburton *et al.*, 2005b). This concept is also of relevance to the current focus on the links between drugs and crime, in that there is evidence that suggests problematic drug use and crime may share similar risk factors such as social exclusion and poverty. Thus the socially excluded may be more likely to be problematic drug users (and problem drug use may compound social exclusion) and they may be more likely to resort to crime to pay for the economic costs of this (Parker *et al.*, 1998; McIntosh and Saville, 2006).

If problematic drug use has less to do with lifestyle choices *per se* and more to do with socio-economic factors in the service user's history beyond their control, then rather than focusing solely on their substance use, a more positive outcome might be achieved by a holistic approach that addresses the underlying factors such as access to adequate housing, employment and education. This approach, together with drug treatment and support, is now commonly seen as an essential part of helping this service user group (Straussner, 2004; Goldsmith, 2008) and a framework to assist social workers in identifying, providing and coordinating this type of holistic support is described in Chapter 5.

A further point for consideration is the perception of the role of different substances in causing or contributing to such social problems and the direction of causality. The research conducted by Warburton *et al.* (2005b) would suggest that problematic drug use is caused by socio-economic deprivation instead of, or as well as, causing it, and Forrester (2000) comments that social workers in a study of parental substance misuse had a familiarity with alcohol which led them to view alcohol use as a contributory factor in wider social problems, whereas their lack of knowledge about heroin use led them to see heroin as *the* problem rather than just as a contributing factor. This raises specific issues relating to social workers' perceptions of the parenting skills of heroin users in comparison to alcohol users, and from the service user's perspective may be highly influential in their willingness to self-disclose substance use. Additionally, if socio-economic factors are implicated in greater use of drugs and an increased likelihood that such drug use will become problematic, it also challenges the degree to which an individual is solely to blame for their experiences of problematic drug use that underpins their stigmatization.

There is evidence of a blame culture underpinning drug treatment provision in the UK which manifests itself in terminology such as 'problematic drug users', 'difficult clients', 'chaotic lifestyles' and 'hard to reach groups.' Perhaps the focus should be shifted to the services themselves, which might be described as having 'problematic treatment regimes', 'chaotic bureaucracy', 'difficult providers' and 'hard to access services'; thus, drug users are often socially excluded while treatment providers fail to provide socially inclusive services (Garret and Foster, 2005). Thompson (cited in Sampson, 2008) suggests that it is more commonly the failings of mainstream services to provide appropriate and attractive services than that certain groups of drug users are 'hard to reach' and this highlights the need to provide services that meet a service user's, or a potential service user's needs. Montagne (2002) describes how research into compliance with methadone prescriptions has assumed that non-compliance was caused by a lack of 'something' on the part of the patient which could be improved by seeking ways to force patients to be more compliant, rather than by asking patients themselves why they failed to comply, and suggests that gathering information from the service user's perspective can be of great help in 'determining the reasons for using drugs, identifying those prevention and treatment programs that could be the most effective' (Montagne, 2002: 568).

While the dominant view of substance users is that they are unwilling to change and unreceptive to treatment, McIntosh and McKeganey (2001) highlight two critical factors. They suggest that an important distinction needs to be made between individuals feeling that they *should* stop, and their *wanting* to stop. They also note that there is a wealth of evidence that most drug users (including those dependent on drugs) will eventually stop using drugs and enter 'recovery,' and that a substantial number of these will do so 'naturally' without professional interventions. Therefore the role of professional involvement could be conceptualized in terms of bringing forward the point at which substance users *choose* to decide that they want to stop and facilitating this change and the service user's motivation plays a key role in this.

Motivation plays an important role in all therapeutic interventions, and perhaps more so in drug treatment, as the competing influences of desire to change and positive reinforcement of the drugs themselves may create greater ambivalence about the change process. The 'failure' of individuals to enter, continue in, comply with and succeed in treatment is often attributed to a lack of 'proper' motivation (Simpson and Joe, 1993).

> A client tends to be judged as motivated if he or she accepts the therapist's view of the problem (including the need for help and the diagnosis), is distressed, and complies with the treatment prescriptions. A client showing the opposite behaviours – disagreement, refusal to accept diagnosis, lack of distress and rejection of treatment principles – is likely to be perceived as unmotivated, denying and resistant.
>
> (Miller, 1985: 87–8)

The use of language such as 'resistant' and 'denial' suggests that the problem and the blame lies with the individual (López Viets *et al.*, 2002; Miller and Rollnick, 1991, 2002). However, this 'trait concept' can lead to confrontational approaches based on the idea that if you can make someone feel bad enough, they will change, or that readiness can be forced on someone (López Viets *et al.*, 2002). This type of confrontational style often drives away less motivated service users, and studies indicate that social workers with more introspective, accepting and nurturing styles usually have fewer service users who disengage from treatment than those with a more aggressive, controlling and critical style (Washton, 1991, cited in Straussner, 2004; Bien *et al.*, 1993).

Miller and Rollnick (1991) suggest that rather than perceiving motivation as a trait, it should be thought of as a state of readiness which can be influenced and is modifiable. Whereas historically motivation was seen as a prerequisite for treatment to begin, increasing service user motivation is now commonly seen as an essential part of clinical practice (Hanson and El-Bassel, 2004). As López Viets *et al.* (2002) propose, the question is not whether service users are motivated, but rather how best to enhance their motivation, and in this way social workers increasingly perceive service user engagement and motivation as a part of their job and recognize that it is not effective to wait passively for service users to 'get motivated'. It is most important at this stage in the process that social workers match the support and interventions they offer to the service users' level of motivation. If social workers do 'passively wait for service users to get motivated', or fail to use appropriate interventions to engage service users in treatment and to raise motivation and confidence in the change process, then valuable opportunities may be missed (Hanson and El-Bassel, 2004). Additionally, those involved in discussions with service users around changing behaviour, whether substance-use-related or not, should recognize that there is a difference between motivation to change and motivation to talk about problems and potential solutions. Counselling approaches and other approaches based on honest discussion about problems and articulation of feelings may be at odds with cultural norms and may present as an alien means of problem solving for some groups making it harder to discuss emotional pain and problems (Griffiths and Pearson, 1988). As such it is important to assess the degree to which service users have the motivation and also the emotional intelligence or maturity to discuss their problems as much as to assess their motivations to change.

Motivational interviewing

With increasing measures to coerce drug users into treatment, it is likely that more 'precontemplators' (see Chapter 5) will find themselves in treatment (Paylor, 2008). This suggests a greater motivational role for social workers. One point of the programme is to attract service users who would not normally attend and who do not come with ready-made motivations to change. Motivational interviewing gives you a constructive way to work with these service users, avoiding the confrontations or demands that would merely drive them out the door. Wahab (2005: 47) argues that simply telling people what to do, or how to do it, is rarely effective in supporting people to change their desired behaviour. Motivational interviewing instead expects motivation to change problem drug use to be 'elicited from the client, and not imposed from without'.

Practitioners may choose to employ motivational interviewing techniques to motivate users for behaviour change, the most widely utilized of these being Miller and Rollnick's (2002) motivational interviewing approach. This involves applying a series of interviewing techniques such as reflexive listening to encourage development of the service user's own intrinsic motivation and improve treatment outcomes (Miller and Rollnick, 2002). Motivational interviewing has been shown to be effective in a range of contexts (Gray *et al.*, 2005; Martino *et al.*, 2006; McCambridge and Strang, 2004; Stein *et al.*, 2006). Burke *et al.*'s (2002) review of the evidence on motivational interviewing found that few services actually applied the full technique, generally using instead adaptations of the technique. Nevertheless, they concluded that motivational techniques were efficient at improving outcomes for dependent service users. Studies on drug abuse that had only used adapted motivational interviewing techniques as a prelude to further treatment also indicated efficiency. There is no simple relationship, however, between motivational interviewing and improved outcomes. Project Match, a multisite clinical trial designed to test a series of a priori hypotheses on how service user–treatment interactions relate to outcome found that motivational interviewing had better results than twelve-step facilitation for service users with poor support networks but that for those with a high level of support the opposite was true (Project MATCH Research Group, 1993).

Motivational interviewing places responsibility for behaviour and decision making on the user themselves, with the worker in a facilitative or guiding role and as such is particularly congruent with an anti-oppressive approach to practice. The aim of motivational interviewing is 'to stimulate the client into starting an internal re-evaluation of his situation in such a way that leads to a "wise" (all pros and cons considered) decision', Van Bilsen and Van Ernst (1990: 29). According to Van Bilsen and Van Ernst (p. 30), the service user can only motivate him/herself for change if he becomes more aware of his behaviour and its potential consequences. He must also become aware of the motives for his behaviour and the possible contradictions therein. The motivational interviewer, in employing various reflective techniques, seeks to stimulate a re-evaluation of these factors.

Motivational interviewing may be considered preferable to the more traditional 'pro-social approach'. The pro-social approach involves the worker identifying pro-social behaviours or comments made by the service user and reinforcing these with praise while challenging those seen as undesirable. The worker may also undertake 'pro-social modelling' whereby they present in themselves behaviours or attitudes which they wish to foster in the service user. This approach has been strongly criticized (Trotter, 1999), in that it disregards the service user's own values and beliefs and seeks to impose those of the worker. The pro-social approach has also been criticized for its ethnocentrism in that it ignores the cultural context of socially acceptable behaviour, reinforcing only the values of the dominant culture (Trotter, 1999).

There is little point in employing motivational interviewing if one starts with the idea that drug use must stop before treatment can begin and that service users have no power over their addiction. Van Bilsen (1991) has described the key principles of the approach as:

- Accepting the service user in a complete and unconditional way.
- The service user is a responsible person.
- The service user must be ready for change and not forced into it by the counsellor.
- The goals and forms of treatment must be negotiated.

Non-adherence to principles such as those behind motivational interviewing often leads to a breakdown of relationships with service users who may not return to treatment centres for fear of disapproval from staff.

There are many pitfalls social workers need to guard against. Motivational interviewing demands that we do not reinforce labels, whether self-attributed or given to the drug users. Information on the service users' situation can be fed back to them in a neutral way, not to force change.

Another pitfall may be the perception of drug users as telling lies and untrustworthy in reporting their own drug use. Confrontational approaches can make this a self-fulfilling prophecy. Denial and lies are often a product of the treatment programme or drug service. For example, if the methadone programme requires abstinence from other drug use, will the service user be honest if the consequence is the loss of a prescription?

These counselling techniques are not new to the helping professions but in the context of the motivational approach they do provide you with a fresh approach to working with those experiencing difficulties with their drug use (see www.motivationalinterview.org/quick_links/bibliography.html for an extensive evidence-based bibliography).

Engagement, retention and the therapeutic working alliance

Engagement of service users in treatment services can also, of course, be conceptualized in terms of their active participation in the treatment process, recognition of problems, receptivity to suggestions and a desire to be involved in the treatment process (Cournoyer *et al.*, 2007). Engagement is sometimes viewed in terms of duration of treatment (Fiorentine *et al.*, 1999; Simpson *et al.*, 1995) though intensity and duration of treatment participation may be more accurately interpreted as consequences of positive engagement rather than engagement itself. Treatment duration may also not be the best indicator of treatment engagement as attendance at treatment may not be voluntary (Joe *et al.*, 2001; Joe *et al.*, 2002) and it should be recognized that treatment duration does not always equate to treatment benefit (Beutler *et al.*, 1997).

The National Treatment Agency Care Planning Practice Guide suggests that treatment engagement is the first, and one of the most important phases of the process of drug treatment. It lasts until service users are able to start looking at goals specifically directed at their treatment needs, rather than outcomes specifically concerned with keeping them in treatment (NTA, 2006b). Meier *et al.* (2005a: 309) report that 'a consistent finding in the drug treatment literature is that successful engagement of clients in the treatment process predicts positive treatment outcomes over and above client factors'.

It is noteworthy that discourse describing services engaging service users in treatment reflects a change from the philosophy that 'treatment receptive' service users themselves are the most active force in treatment engagement and recovery, to one where the perceived helpfulness of services and a favourable service user–counsellor relationship actively engages the service user in treatment (Fiorentine *et al.*, 1999). It is increasingly recognized that in terms of providing effective support and interventions with drug users, the quality of the relationship between the worker and their service user is highly influential on the outcomes of drug treatment, both in terms of the duration that the service user is retained in treatment (which in itself is associated with positive outcomes) and also in terms of their making and maintaining positive changes to their drug use (Barber *et al.*, 2001; Gossop, 2006b; Luborsky *et al.*, 1997; Meier *et al.*, 2005a; Wanigaratne *et al.*, 2005). As Hougaard (1994: 67) describes, 'the most common concept for the therapeutically important aspects of the relationship today is the therapeutic alliance, or related terms like the treatment alliance, the working alliance, or the helping alliance'.

The development of a strong therapeutic working alliance early in treatment is important for several reasons. First, evidence suggests that a strong early alliance is a key indicator of positive outcomes later in treatment (Meier *et al.*, 2005b; Meier *et al.*, 2006; Dundon *et al.*, 2008), but more obviously that a failure to engage with treatment in the early stages, an inability to agree on the nature of problems and the desired outcomes, and a lack of trust and rapport between providers and service users, are likely to result in early disengagement from treatment (Bordin, 1994). Meier *et al.* (2005a: 305) propose that the therapeutic alliance is also important because there is evidence that supportive therapeutic relationships not only enhance engagement and retention of substance users in treatment, but also may provide 'a model for improved relationships outside of therapy [an important consideration as] many drug-using clients report unsatisfactory relationships [which] have been implicated strongly in the aetiology of drug use', a view supported by Henry and Strupp (1994).

Hanson and El-Bassel (2004: 46) suggest that during the engagement phase of treatment, three essential objectives need to be reached in order to successfully engage service users and develop a Therapeutic Working Alliance:

1. They must create a 'safe space' so that service users *can* talk to them.
2. They must establish a collaborative partnership so that service users *will* talk to them.
3. They must reach a preliminary agreement that a problem exists so that the service user has *reason* to talk with them.

Bordin (1979) conceptualized the therapeutic working alliance as having three key features: an agreement on goals; an agreement on the assignment of tasks; and the development of a bond between the worker and service user. For substance-use treatment to be effective it needs to be delivered within a framework in which the service provider and the service user both agree upon what the goals of treatment are, how they are to be achieved, and who is responsible for the different components, rather than treatment being perceived by either party as something that service providers 'do' to service users. In this way, service-user involvement in treatment decisions is acknowledged as a key feature of successful treatment (for more details on involving service users in treatment see Chapter 7). There is, however, great potential for service providers and service users to have different views about what the desired outcomes of treatment are. Services may expect service users to seek abstinence or changes in their substance use, whereas service users may be seeking better relationships with close and significant personal others, getting a job, or achieving a more stable and 'normal' life (Fischer *et al.*, 2007). Thus it is important for services to identify what the service user sees as the most important problems to solve rather than, or as well as, those that the service provider believes are the most important. As Berg and Shafer (2004) note, there is often a difference between what the social worker feels is good for the service user and what the service user feels is good for the service user. Similarly, as Shapiro (2005) describes, there is an important difference between what is important *to* someone and what is important *for* them. From the professional's perspective, it may appear obvious that stopping detrimental behaviours and practices such as substance use would be beneficial and important *for* a service user, but from the service-user's perspective, it may not be as important *to* them. Substance use may provide an important function for the service user, such as a common bond within their social circle, a coping mechanism, or a source of pleasure.

There may also be a range of additional, non-substance-use specific factors which need addressing first or at the same time, before changes in substance use can be achieved or become relevant to the service user. For these reasons it is imperative that agreeing goals which can compensate for the functions that substance use serves, and address the wider needs of the service user are agreed as a part of the care planning process. Once such goals have been agreed then it is also necessary for the two parties to agree on what needs to be done for the goals to be reached, and who will do what (agreement on the assignment of task). This process may require compromise and negotiation but is an integral part of alliance building process (Bordin, 1994): involvement in the decision-making process and the provision of choice can be very empowering to service users.

The third component of the therapeutic alliance is that of 'bonding' between the service provider and the service user and Bordin (1994) suggests that this grows out of the experience of shared activity and is often felt in terms of mutual liking, trust and respect from each other. Bonding may be seen as similar to rapport, and as such dependent on what Rogers (1951) considered the core conditions for therapeutic change: empathy, congruence and unconditional positive regard. However, the perceptions of drug users as undeserving, untrustworthy, hostile and manipulative may influence service providers' ability to develop such therapeutic relationships. Research by Allman *et al.* (2007) into the characteristics of effective relationships between service providers and service users, from the service users' perspective, identified a range of factors that facilitated or damaged effective relationships. Non-judgemental service providers who focused on the service user rather than their substance use, who set explicit boundaries, but who could be trusted to maintain confidentiality within these boundaries and who were communicative, approachable, caring, honest and authentic, were seen as developing effective relationships. Those service providers who were suspicious and unable to see beyond the substance use, who believed that 'all needs are motivated by drug use', who attempted to 'force their answers or solution on you', or who broke trust, were seen as having a negative effect on the relationship.

Hanson and El-Bassel (2004) describe six core features for forming a therapeutic alliance based on the research of Bien *et al.* (1993). These core features are summarized by the acronym *FRAMES:* Feedback; Responsibility; Advice; Menu of options; Empathy and Self-efficacy (Bien *et al.*, 1993).

Feedback

Most interventions involve some element of assessment which allows feedback about the service users' current circumstances, including the social consequences of their substance use and other substance-use-related difficulties (Hanson and El-Bassel, 2004). Participation in this type of assessment, and the resulting feedback, can in itself have a therapeutic impact (Bien *et al.*, 1993) and because such feedback relates specifically to the service users' own experiences, it is personalized and specific to the service user (Hanson and El-Bassel, 2004).

Responsibility

Effective substance-use interventions are usually collaborative in nature, emphasizing that the service user has a shared responsibility in the process (Hanson and El-Bassel, 2004) but recognizing that they alone can decide whether or not to make changes to their substance use. Feelings of personal control are an important element of motivation for behaviour change (Bien *et al.*, 1993; Miller and Rollnick, 2002) and this notion of choice can be empowering, reducing resistance and increasing commitment to change (Hanson and El-Bassel, 2004).

Advice

Part of the role of social workers is to help the service user recognize problems and provide advice on possible solutions. Research has shown that participatory dialogue in which the advantages and disadvantages of different option are discussed (Hanson and El-Bassel, 2004), and where the service user is free to accept or reject the advice offered, is more likely to result in motivation towards positive behaviour change (Bien *et al.*, 1993).

Menu

Where a range of options has been generated by the service user in collaboration with the social worker, it is more likely that an approach will be found to solving problems that is appropriate to the service users' situation (Bien *et al.*, 1993) and more attractive and acceptable to them. As discussed previously, this notion of choice is empowering and often elicits greater commitment to change. Active involvement also lowers service-users' resistance towards service providers (Hanson and El-Bassel, 2004; Fischer *et al.*, 2007) and increases retention in treatment and treatment satisfaction (Neale, 2006; Simpson and Joe, 1993; Simpson *et al.*, 1997a, 1997b).

Empathy

Rogers (1951) describes empathy as the ability to develop an accurate understanding of the service users' meaning through reflective listening, and warm, reflective, empathic and understanding approaches to facilitating change are considered to be far more effective than directive, aggressive, authoritarian and coercive styles of intervention (Bien *et al.*, 1993; Miller, 1998; Miller and Rollnick, 2002).

Self-efficacy

Self-efficacy is the service users' belief that they are capable of the actions necessary to achieve desired outcomes and must be enhanced, and feelings of self-efficacy encouraged, in order to maximize the potential for change. In terms of making changes to patterns of substance use, several types of self-efficacy have been identified (Hanson and El-Bassel, 2004): treatment self-efficacy relating to service users' belief that they can complete the necessary tasks; resistance self-efficacy pertaining to service users' belief that they can avoid a return to previous patterns of substance use (relapse); recovery self-efficacy focusing on service users' beliefs that they can recover from lapses and relapses; and action self-efficacy addressing service users' beliefs in their ability to achieve therapeutic goals. Social workers need to encourage and communicate confidence in their service users' ability to achieve change in order to strengthen their commitment to change (Hanson and El-Bassel, 2004).

Implications for social work practice

At an agency or service level, a whole person focus is required, rather than seeing problem drug users solely as problem drug users, and at a practitioner level, in order to successfully engage substance users into beneficial forms of treatment and support, practitioners often need to 'put themselves in the service user's shoes' and try to understand the position that the service user finds themselves in, the function that substance use may play in their lives and try to see the situation from the service user's perspective. While practitioners may be more familiar with the positive and negative effects and consequences of alcohol use, because of a lack of familiarity with them, they may often struggle to perceive the use of illegal substance in the same way. This can result in approaches and ways of working that often see the use of alcohol as contributing to a service user's problems, but the use of other drugs as being 'the problem' and can alienate service users for whom drug use is part of a wider range of socio-economic and lifestyle factors. Failure to provide services and responses which are appropriate and attractive to the service user reduces the potential for active participation in the processes of change and may lead to service users being labelled as unmotivated. Increasingly, however, social work practitioners are recognizing that passively waiting for service users to become motivated is often ineffectual and that there is a role for them to play in motivating their service users to engage with treatment. This is especially true with practitioners such as social workers who work in non-substance-use specific services, but who have regular contact with substance users. This is because service users who do not self-refer into services may need motivating to engage with the services available and social workers are in a position to play an important role in bringing forward in time the point at which their service users decide to engage and actively participate in treatment. It is also important to recognize the potential for people working at this level to put service users off accessing services, at the present time or in the future, if they perceive the experience as a negative one in which they feel forced into treatment that they see as unsuitable, unnecessary or not meeting their needs. Thus for social work practitioners to successfully encourage their service users to engage with treatment and support services, they need to offer appropriate support and advice in an empathic and non-judgemental way and ensure that the process is a shared and negotiated activity.

5   Care and control

Introduction

While the previous chapter offered the client's perspective, this chapter will provide a sharper focus on the consideration of recurrent dilemmas for social workers involved with drug users, particularly around the need to find a balance between 'care' and 'control'. Additionally, an overview of models or approaches to substance-use problems is explored before offering a view on the pros and cons of each one. This is followed by a description of a 'process model' for working with substance users before a short examination of 'brief' interventions followed by a section on the 'cycle of change'.

Intervention

There are predominantly four different models, or approaches to substance-use problems; the disease model – which sees substance dependency as an incurable disease; the cognitive behavioural model – which uses psychological theory and methods to approach substance problems; the medical model which is the treatment of the physiological *effects* of problematic substance use; and the biopsychosocial or 'dependence syndrome' approach which contains elements of all three of the above approaches. Existing research into the effectiveness of the different methods is largely inconclusive as it has been shown that there is little evidence and even less consensus that any one approach is significantly more effective overall than any other (Collins and Keene, 2000; Lindstrom, 1992; Project MATCH Research group, 1997, 1998; United Kingdom Alcohol Treatment Trial (UKATT) Research Team, 2001, 2005).

The 'disease model' approach of treating 'substance misuse' could be argued to be the approach that is most familiar to the wider general public, as it is Alcoholics Anonymous (AA) or Narcotics Anonymous (NA) that is often depicted within popular media as the only method of addressing 'substance misuse' (Emmelkamp and Vedel, 2006). The disease model is also currently the most dominant treatment philosophy in the USA (Emmelkamp and Vedel, 2006). While the most commonly known method of treating 'substance misuse' within the disease model is AA (Denzin, 1987), there are other slightly different approaches within the model such as the Twelve Step Disease Model and the Minnesota Model (Collins and Keene, 2000).

The disease model is based on the premise that the individual has an addictive personality where they suffer from an illness or 'spiritual disease'. The expected 'goal' of the 'substance misuser' undertaking treatment within the disease model is reaching and maintaining total abstinence based on the view that 'substance misuse' is a disease that will progress as long as the individual continues to use (Emmelkamp and Vedel, 2006). Lifelong abstinence is supposed to be reached by following a set of 'steps', which differ slightly within each programme. These generally include surrendering to the disease and removing any 'false' sense of self-reliance (Collins and Keene, 2000). The disease model also stipulates that there is a crucial distinction between the 'misuser' and other types of substance user (Barber, 2002), and that the 'misuser' is not normal, that they suffer from an illness of the whole person (Collins and Keene, 2000). The misuser is seen to have a spiritual sickness, a physical allergy to the substance and an addictive personality of which they themselves are powerless to change (Collins and Keene, 2000).

For a number of reasons the disease model is not well equipped to suit the values of the social work profession. The notion of irreversibility and the 'emphasis on acceptance of personal powerlessness' (Collins and Keene, 2000: 31) (that as an addict they have no control over their drug-taking behaviour) goes directly against the idea of empowering individuals to change, which could be described as an essential part of social work practice. The 'labelling' (Becker, 1963) of problematic drug users as 'addicts' provides the individual with a stigma, and as such does not provide the user with an empathic, non-judgemental service nor will it enhance the problem users' well-being. Additionally, it could be argued that such an approach where there is a definite set of 'steps' to be followed until one can be seen to be a recovering addict lacks the opportunity for individuality and autonomy when working with problematic substance users.

However, it would appear that despite the apparent inappropriateness of the disease model, there is a possibility that the methods within it could contain elements that are already considered to be a part of a social worker's repertoire. Collins and Keene (2000: 34) do note that the disease model 'contains elements of significance to the field of drug and alcohol studies as a whole' and some of the techniques used, such as the encouragement of the support of families and social networks in the 'recovery' of the problem drug user and creation of support networks through group attendance and in teaching strategies for coping with dependence do have an amount of relevance to social work practice (Emmelkamp and Vedel, 2006). Similarly, the aftercare provided (or rather the overall length of such programmes) are seen to be productive in preventing relapse (Thevos *et al.*, 2001).

The medical model makes the distinction between individuals who are physically dependent and those who are dependent because of their beliefs and expectations about drug-taking (Collins and Keene, 2000). It addresses the physical dependency elements of problematic substance use and looks at how to treat them medically. Therefore the medical model does not look outside the individual, that is, at the environmental factors that could have caused an individual to engage in problematic drug use in the first place. Instead the medical approach focuses on treatments through pharmacotherapy which can either reduce the craving for or cause an adverse physical reaction when the substance is consumed. Similarly, it considers suggestions such as the idea that some people are genetically predisposed to be at a greater risk from substance dependency (Cloninger, 1999; Gorwood *et al.*, 2002).

The administration of drugs with therapeutic intention is problematic. Treating people medically, or suggesting that their genetic makeup is responsible for their drug-taking behaviour may reduce consumption but does not go any way to address the factors that may have caused the individual to engage in problematic drug-taking behaviour (Harris, 2007).

This highlights the point surrounding mistaking dependence for addiction. Addressing dependence without significant lifestyle changes does not necessarily help in dealing with problems in the person's life. Dealing with physical dependency and addiction are very different challenges (Harris, 2007).

Interestingly, a more holistic version of the medical model, using alternative or complementary therapies such as auricular acupuncture, homeopathic teas which are used in the detoxification process and can help problem users get back to regular sleep patterns (a notoriously very difficult thing to achieve), is being offered in some community-based services (Sukul, 2000). Arguably, this only differs in technique rather than theory from the medical model and only still in most cases only treating the physical effects of drug problems rather than the wider social context. However, the risks of adverse effects are low unlike prescribed drugs which may be hazardous (Raistrick *et al.*, 1999) not to mention the financial burden to the health service.

The 'biopsychosocial' or 'dependence syndrome' approach, developed by Edwards *et al.* (1976) suggests that dependence can be 'understood as a biopsychosocial continuum along which anyone can travel under certain circumstances' (Collins and Keene, 2000: 26), meaning that the biopsychosocial approach (much like the idea of genetics in the medical model) suggests that there are inescapable physiological, behavioural and social factors that cause an individual to develop drug problems (Edwards and Grant, 1977; Collins and Keene, 2000).

The biopsychosocial approach is seen to be closely related to the disease or medical model approaches to drug problems, despite containing aspects of the cognitive behavioural approach (see below) as well as aspects of the other two models. Because of this advocates of the cognitive behavioural approach see it as too closely related to the medical and disease models, whereas proponents of the disease model see it as too closely entwined with the medical model, which does not corroborate with the disease model view that 'addiction' is an incurable disease (Collins and Keene, 2000).

As with the medical model the dependency syndrome does contain elements that could be useful to social work practice, some of which are not overtly considered by other more popular approaches, such as recognizing different levels of problematic substance-taking, and others which are, such as the idea that in some circumstances substance-taking behaviour can be controlled rather than requiring complete abstinence from the individual.

The cognitive behavioural therapy (CBT) model, largely developed by Beck throughout the 1980s, initially focused on treating depression, but became increasingly applied to substance-use disorders (Beck, 1993; Heather, 2000). Cognitive behavioural therapy (CBT) draws on methods from psychological, behavioural, cognitive and humanistic approaches (Coulshed and Orme, 2006). Far from being a unified theoretical approach it is best understood as describing a range of interventions (McGuire, 1995) with numerous programmes and methods of working with individuals with drug problems that fall under the spectrum of the cognitive behavioural approach (Ronen, 2008).

Cognitive therapy helps service users reduce the frequency and severity of drug use by uncovering, examining and altering the thoughts and beliefs that accompany urges to use. In addition, cognitive therapists teach coping skills to service users so drug use is replaced with other strategies for managing moods, social situations and life problems (Padesky and Greenberger, 1995). Cognitive behavioural therapy (CBT) places 'emphasis on the direct modification of behaviour in the treatment progress' (Heather, 2000), working from the principle that problematic drug use is learnt by the individual and therefore through CBT can be 'unlearnt' (Coulshed and Orme, 2006).

Whereas the disease model requires total abstinence, CBT when used to treat drug problems, usually advocates a controlled approach (Collins and Keene, 2000). The concept that the individual is able to control their drug-taking is based on the individual choosing and maintaining an achievable level of substance use (or abstinence) at which they would feel that their life quality would be improved (Heather, 2000). This element of choice and control, while still under the observation of professionals is arguably why the cognitive behavioural approach is seen as a suitable method to use within social work practice.

Derived from evidence-based medicine (Gould, 2006; Tanenbaum, 2006) evidence-based practice (EBP) has become a dominant theme within social work (Cournoyer *et al.*, 2004) although there are competing claims about what is exactly meant by 'evidence'. Debate principally hinges upon two assumptions; the nature of evidence and 'what works' for *whom*? Evidence-based practice (EBP) promotes a hierarchical framework that privileges the randomized control trial (RCT)[16] or type I evidence (Department of Health (DoH), 1999a: 6) over other forms of evidence. Nevertheless (and even within DoH literature) there is evidence to suggest that in certain contexts such as longer-term conditions, the use of well-designed qualitative work may be more appropriate (DoH, 2005, 2007). Trinder (2000) describes the two emerging distinct approaches as falling into two opposing camps – the experimental and the pragmatic. Webb (2006: 158) sums up the differing views thus:

> For the adherents of experimental EBP randomised controlled trials are the gold standard. The main concern of experimental EBP is that social workers rarely use evidence or models that are falsifiable. That is, they make little effort to find refutations for their own practice and thus operate according to opinion-based beliefs rather than hypotheses or facts that allow for specific predictions. On the other hand, EBP pragmatists argue that the strict adoption of randomised controlled trials as the gold standard is reductionist and inappropriate for the kinds of social, emotional and value-laden problems faced by social work.

The current social and policy contexts that surround social work such as value for money, managerialism and performance indicators, 'best value' and effectiveness goals, outcomes and evidence for 'what works' have a degree of resonance when thinking about CBT.

The recent and actual political and social policy climate would seem favourable to the advancement of the principles of CBT (Cigno, 2002). Pragmatic concentration on presenting situations and problems, on planned focused work, on contracts, and attention to detail fits in with methods within the cognitive behavioural approach which do complement the expectancy that social work practice needs to be 'increasingly demanding that models of practice be subjected to systematic examination' (Cohen, 1985: 622).

There is a possibility that rather than it being the effectiveness of the treatment making the cognitive behavioural approach the most appropriate, it is deemed most appropriate as it has developed within the procedures that are already in place. Cigno (2002), drawing from Payne (1991: 186), goes as far as suggesting that at front-line level social workers 'do not find cognitive behavioural theory attractive'. Collins and Keene (2000) also note that the cognitive behavioural approach also often fails to take adequate account of the physiological/psychological effects of problem drug use on the individual.

Unlike the cognitive behavioural approach, the medical model predominantly concentrates on the 'short and long-term physiological effects' (Collins and Keene, 2000: 25) of problematic drug use. Whereas the cognitive behavioural approach primarily sees problematic drug-taking behaviour as learnt behaviour and the disease model primarily sees 'addiction' as incurable, the medical model looks at problem drug use as it would any other physical illness.

A review of the main approaches to drug problems suggests that treating problematic drug use through social work requires the social worker to have knowledge of a variety of approaches.[17] To define any of the approaches as wholly inappropriate to social work practice would be wrong, as all have aspects that can add to the service provided by the profession. The social work profession could certainly take note of the aftercare services provided by methods within the disease model, as it is suggested that it is the provision of aftercare that is seen to be the greatest prevention against relapse. Similarly, it is important that social work if using cognitive behavioural approaches takes adequate account of physiological factors and the different levels of dependency described within both the medical and biopsychosocial models.

What must be noted though is that the cognitive behavioural approach and social work practice have developed from similar perspectives and values and as such have found each other as ideal allies. Certainly from within a policy context, the cognitive behavioural approach appears to be most suited to social work practice as it works within the constraints of 'what works' and EBP. Perhaps it could be argued, however, that rather than finding the cognitive behavioural approach most appropriate to social work practice, social work practice (in line with its values such as promoting human rights and social justice) should find the approach that is appropriate for each individual, or perhaps even explore other areas of practice, rather than trying to work within the confines of a defined set of values. Unfortunately, this of course would not be cost effective and would be difficult to justify under the remit of EBP.

Therefore, it may well be that the cognitive behavioural approach to helping individuals with drug problems is the most suitable approach to use within social work, both in practice and as a theory. However, it is important that other approaches are also considered in regard to individual service users with drug problems.

Models of Care[18]

Services for drug and alcohol users have been arranged into four tiers following publication, by the NTA of Models of Care 2002 – updated in 2006. Tier 1 interventions include provision of drug-related information and advice, screening and referral to specialized drug treatment and are provided in the context of general healthcare settings (e.g., liver units, antenatal wards, Accident and Emergency and pharmacies), or social care, education or criminal justice settings (probation, courts, prison reception) where the main focus is not drug treatment. Tier 2 interventions include provision of drug-related information and advice, triage assessment, referral to structured drug treatment, brief psychosocial interventions, harm reduction (HR) interventions (including needle exchange) and aftercare. Tier 2 interventions may be delivered separately from Tier 3 but will often also be delivered in the same setting and by the same staff as Tier 3 interventions. Tier 3 interventions include provision of community-based specialized drug assessment and coordinated care-planned treatment and drug specialist liaison. Tier 3 interventions are normally delivered in specialized drug treatment services with their own premises in the community or on hospital sites. Other delivery may be by outreach (peripatetic work in generic services or other agencies or domiciliary or home visits). Tier 4 interventions include provision of residential specialized drug treatment, which is care-planned and care-coordinated to ensure continuity of care and aftercare.

Full details can be found on the NTA website at: www.nta.nhs.uk/publications/documents/nta_modelsofcare_update_2006_moc3.pdf

The guidelines set out in Models of Care are clear; social workers have a range of options available to them and should be aware of all the services available in their area. What is clearly important is that social workers take a holistic view of drug-related problems and provide a full and comprehensive assessment of needs. Social workers are required to treat 'each person as an individual' (General Social Care Council (GSCC), 2002: 1.1) and as such, approaches should be tailored to the individual.

Social workers have a duty to assist in dealing with drug-related harm. More social workers should have confidence in their skills and abilities and 'wake-up' to their responsibilities. Given the extent of harm drug misuse presents to society and individuals, it is not important for social workers to evaluate which interventions are most effective in dealing with drug-related problems, or whether or not interventions share the same underlying knowledge and ethical base as social work. What is important is that interventions work, intervention should take place and there should be a range of interventions available (Collins and Keene, 2000).

Interventions cannot be seen as a one-off treatment as they do not necessarily lead to individuals making significant changes to their lives (Keene, 2001). Instead there has to be an emphasis on support and maintenance and the social worker therefore plays a vital role in ensuring the individual has support networks and the necessary coping skills to maintain the benefits of treatment.

This does not eliminate the option of referring a service user to other treatment approaches such as AA or interventions discussed earlier. This will depend on the service users' needs as different approaches will suit individuals at different times and therefore requires appropriate matching. Keene (2001: 194) argues that 'although treatment is useful . . . inappropriate . . . treatment may cause more harm than good for some service users and social work models of intervention may be more effective for a wider range of clients'. Social workers therefore have a range of options and interventions, which may mean working with service users themselves and/or referring them to other agencies. Indeed, it may be that the social worker co-works with other agencies from specialists to other generic professionals (Collins and Keene, 2000).

Brief interventions

Most of the useful recent research in this field has been carried out by psychologists in the areas of 'early intervention' and 'brief interventions'. Relatively brief interventions have consistently been found to be effective in reducing drug consumption or achieving treatment referral of problem users (Bien *et al.*, 2008).

Brief interventions using the cognitive behavioural approach are currently very popular throughout social work practice. By providing a more liberating approach in tackling individual drug problems over what could be seen to be the oppressive methods of the disease model as they encourage the individual to explore their negative automatic thoughts, rather than having to 'surrender' to the idea that they are an addict. Simultaneously, they also have the benefit of being relatively short (hence 'brief') and low cost, which is advantageous to a social work agency with a limited budget and workforce.

Brief

Benefits – informing service users about the benefits of safer drug taking
Risk factors – informing service users about the risks in using drugs
Intentions – asking service users about their intentions regarding future use
Empathise – showing service user that you are non-judgemental and empathic
Feedback – advising services about their level of and/or route of use

Source: Hodgson (2002)

Exactly what constitutes a 'brief intervention' remains a source of debate (Howe, 2008). The appropriate intervention depends on the service user, on the severity of their problems with drugs, or has a co-occurring psychiatric problem. Brief interventions typically consist of 1–5 short counselling sessions with a social worker. Often, simply providing this space is enough to encourage those at risk to reduce their drug intake.

Brief interventions may include approaches, such as motivational interviewing (as discussed in Chapter 4), which are designed to persuade people who are resistant to moderating their drug intake or who do not believe they are using drugs in a harmful or hazardous way.

Regardless of the course of action chosen, it is fundamental that the social worker is involved at some point even if this is in coordinating services and ensuring the individual has the networks to maintain the effects of interventions. Lawson (1994) found that the most successful responses to problem drug use were those which involved input from the social worker as well as from one or more other agency.

Social work involvement

While it cannot replace the need for adequate training and support, the DECLARE Model (McCarthy and Galvani, 2004) below provides a very good 'process model' for working with substance users, identifying where individuals can deliver interventions within their competences, where and how to refer on, and what to do during this process. It highlights many of the issues: exploring the degree to which substance use may contribute to, or impact on, problems experienced in other areas of service users' lives; consulting and involving them; and providing adequate support during referrals.

DECLARE Model[19]	
Drug or alcohol use	Drugs or alcohol are identified as part of the service user's life and it may be that substance use is causing or contributing to the problems
Explore	Explore the issues of alcohol and drugs to see if the service user thinks substance use is part of the equation or if others involved are concerned about substance use
Consult	Consult the service user and their significant others. It may also be appropriate to discuss any concerns with colleagues, supervisor or other services
Liaise	Liaise with specialists who have greater substance-use knowledge and skills, to seek their advice, if, after consultation, alcohol or drugs are confirmed as an issue
Assess	Assess the next step, ideally with the service user, and seek guidance from any agencies to which it might be appropriate to refer

Refer	Referrals made 'cold', which are neither first explored with the receiving agency nor explained to the service user, are likely to fail. Always offer supported referrals
Evaluate	Evaluate: referral is not the last task: keep in touch during the early stages of contact to create a safety net in case the referral does not go smoothly

Source: McCarthy and Galvani (2004: 88)

Used in conjunction with the Six Cornered Addiction Rescue System (SCARS) below, the DECLARE model can assist social workers in providing a holistic approach to meeting many of the socio-economic needs which may contribute to problematic substance use and which may be highly influential on the success of referrals, treatment and support.

SCARS

Where the DECLARE model can be helpful in assisting social workers (and other professionals) in the assessment, referral and support process, SCARS can assist them in systematically analysing the wider support and resources (or the absence of these) before making treatment referrals (McCarthy and Galvani, 2004). 'Protective' or 'resilience' factors (McCarthy and Galvani, 2004) such as employment and residential status; social support and significant relationships; and psychological and physical health can be highly influential on treatment outcomes (Barber, 2002; Dobkin *et al.*, 2002; Powell *et al.*, 1998; Rasmussen, 2000; Rassool, 2009). These factors are also seen to offer protection against substance use becoming problematic in the first place (Warburton *et al.*, 2005b).

SCARS represents a six-cornered virtual safety net where, ideally, each corner is supported by a person or service representing one of six key elements, each of which represents one of these 'protective' or 'resilience' factors. In addition to the person or service offering support specifically related to substance use, the more effectively each of the other corners is supported, the greater the chance that the safety net will 'catch' the service user, and the greater the potential for positive outcomes (McCarthy and Galvani, 2004).

The five basic factors, in addition to *specialist addictions treatment*, are:

- *Securely accommodated* – the person has somewhere safe to live. They have somewhere to live that they can call their own. As long as they have a reasonable right to return each night and they are reasonably satisfied with the accommodation for the moment, this corner of the net is supported.

- *Satisfactorily employed* – the person has an acceptable structure to their day. They may be in paid or voluntary work; they may be a home carer or they may simply have a circle of friends and activities that provide structure and purpose to their daily life. So long as the daily 'employment' is satisfactory and does not revolve solely around drinking or other substance use, this corner of the net is supported.
- *Psychological health* – the person has reasonably good level of psychological health. They would be emotionally stable and in good psychiatric health, meaning that they would not be struggling with untreated mental illness such as depression, or with issues such as significant low mood, loss, repeated self-harm or suicidal thoughts and feelings. So long as there are no major unaddressed psychological problems, this corner of the net is supported.
- *Physical health* – the person needs to be in reasonably good physical health. This does not imply that they are at the peak of physical condition, merely that they should be in reasonably robust health, taking into account any physical disability or harm they may have experienced, whether as a direct or indirect consequence of substance use. In these circumstances, this corner of the net is supported.
- *Significant relationships* – there needs to be someone significant in the person's life. This may be a partner, close friend or friendship network, a parent or child. So long as this is a positive relationship, which is not predicated on substance use, this corner of the net is supported.

(McCarthy and Galvani, 2004: 90)

It should be noted that interpersonal relationships with significant others, especially partners, can also be negatively influential. Where service users are involved with drug-using partners, this can exert a negative effect on the process of change, and the possibility of assessing partner's motivation to change and referring them into treatment as well should always be considered.

Both comprehensive social work and substance-use assessments will commonly identify the existence or absence of these protective factors, but by using the SCARS model to overlay the information provided by these assessments, more rapid identification of unmet needs and prioritization may be enabled. From a social work perspective, the problem may be approached from almost any corner of the safety net (McCarthy and Galvani, 2004) and it is unimportant which corner or corners social workers are supporting, as long as all possible corners are supported. The SCARS model may also help to highlight the relationship between substance use and other identified problems which social workers may need to address, and if by the application of the model, service users feel that their substance use is being seen as one problem related to other socio-economic problems, rather than as the problem itself, this may lead to greater treatment involvement by service users and better outcomes. Conversely, where addressing substance use is seen as the only goal and in isolation to wider socio-economic issues, the service user may lack the protective factors to succeed in maintaining positive changes, relapse and return to their previous patterns of use and this can increase the length of time before return to services for support.

Cycle of change

Motivation, treatment engagement and readiness for treatment have found to be key predictors of outcomes. Motivation has been shown to predict both retention and engagement in treatment (De Leon and Jainchill, 1986; Hiller *et al.*, 2002). Studies have shown that motivation is essential for maintaining users in treatment and in helping them to become engaged with it (Hiller *et al.*, 2002). Motivational influences can be divided into internal (desire to change behaviour or readiness for treatment) and external motivations (such as family pressures or legal coercion). Motivation for treatment is commonly understood in terms of transtheoretical models. The most popular of these is Prochaska and DiClemente's (2009) 'stages of change' which describes the various stages of change through which the drug user is said to pass from precontemplation through contemplation, preparation, action, maintenance and relapse (Miller and Tonigan, 1996). The stages of change model has had quite an effect on policy in the UK with the advent of Models of Care and Integrated Treatment Pathways (Harris, 2007).

Significantly, the stages of change model seeks to understand the processes of drug treatment as well as the outcomes. Prochaska and DiClemente (2009) present five key stages of behaviour change in relation to addictive behaviours; precontemplation, contemplation, preparation, action and maintenance. They suggest that individuals at the precontemplation stage have no intention of changing their behaviour in the foreseeable future and many are unaware or under aware of their problems (Prochaska and DiClemente, 2009).

1   Precontemplation

Precontemplation is a stage where service users do not perceive they have a problem but others around them may be disapproving. At this stage although professionals may not be directly involved, they can undertake work within a harm reduction framework to enable the potential harm from the consumption of drugs to be minimalized, until the drug user is ready to attempt to change their lives and their drug use. This must be placed within a context which acknowledges that harm reduction is not necessarily aiming at abstinence, but also at reducing harm and the impact drug use has on individuals, their families and their communities.

In the precontemplation phase, thinking changes (through mechanisms such as rationalization and denial) to fit in with the drug-taking. At this stage the first task is to create conflict between the two, for without this there is little chance of lasting change. This may take one session or it may take many months. To create conflict you mainly summarize the service users' behaviour and reflect it back to them, to first elicit and then reinforce expressions of self concern.

Motivation for change arises when the service user sees their drug-taking behaviour as incompatible with their view of themselves or their feelings about what they should be like or should be doing. To reduce the resultant discomfort, either the drug-taking behaviour must change, or the service user must revise their thinking about themselves. Counselling intervention based on this conflict (or cognitive dissonance) is more likely to succeed in moving the service user through the stages in the process of change.

2 Contemplation

Contemplation is the stage where the service user is weighing up the pros and cons of their drug use. It is a time when, for whatever reason, the drug user is beginning to contemplate and consider changing their consumption. This may be the result of a range of events, illness, death of a friend, increased awareness about human immunodeficiency virus (HIV) or hepatitis C virus (HCV), arrest, or maybe the involvement of social services where the drug user is also a parent. They may be suffering financial hardship and deteriorating physical health but on the other hand may see their drug use as helping them cope with life's stresses.

In considering changing consumption patterns a whole range of emotions will become apparent; not least fear, worry and trepidation. The worker should be able to help address these issues and reinforce the positives and generally support the decision to change. This may involve a degree of directive and task-centred work to facilitate the process of change.

It is also important at this time to support the drug user in identifying and attempting achievable goals. If too high standards are set and the aims are unrealistic at this stage, it is very easy to undermine the good work undertaken in which case 'relapse' can occur; namely, a return to original patterns of drug use.

Once conflict is created (the contemplation stage) you can use positive feedback to raise the self-esteem and feeling of being able to control their own life. This may take the form of praise, or finding and playing back to them the positive achievements in what they may see as negative experiences – a version of finding the silver lining in every cloud.

Positive restructuring of, for instance, a return to drug use for a couple of days in the previous week might highlight the achievement of abstinence on the other days. Such positive feedback encourages the service user to end the decision stage with a change in drug-taking behaviour rather than return to rationalizing and denial to reduce conflict.

3   Decision

Decision is the point where the service user decides what to do about their drug use based on the previous stage of contemplation. Service users rarely stay in this stage for long and soon choose either to return to precontemplation, preferring to continue with their previous level of drug use, or alternatively, to move to change.

Active change is the process the service user takes to put their decision into effect. To do this they may use methods and goals negotiated with the social worker; for example, obtaining clean needles and syringes from the exchange scheme rather than sharing with friends. Is the stage when the decision has been made and things begin to take shape. Having made the decision to change levels and patterns of consumption, it may be that the worker needs to organize a detoxification programme (and possibly longer-term rehabilitation). It is also about continuing to reinforce the behaviour changes that have taken place. In acknowledging change of drug use, what 'help' needs to be offered to initially support this decision; maybe counselling, advice, health care and so on?

It is also important to begin to identify realistic alternatives to drug use. There is no point in simply stopping taking drugs and continuing with the same lifestyle. This will in all probability only lead to relapse. The drug user needs to acknowledge that aspects of lifestyle need to be changed. Therefore the wider context of consumption needs to be looked at and potentially reviewed and changed. Again this can be a traumatic time with a range of previously suppressed or ignored emotions coming to the fore. It is important to acknowledge that an individual's relationship with their drug of choice is a complex one. It is too simplistic to simply stop taking the drug, other aspects of life need to change and this is hard to change without support.

It has generally been acknowledged that coming off is hard, but staying off is a lot harder. This stage involves developing and building on the positive aspects of change, continuing to offer support and counselling while also acknowledging the change undertaken. It is a difficult time because it can often appear that nothing is happening, a time when people often begin to forget the initial reasons that led to contemplating change in the first place.

4   Maintenance

Maintenance involves the drug worker introducing and encouraging conscious coping to maintain the change already made, using relapse prevention techniques. The role of the social worker is absolutely crucial in supporting the individual as many service users need the social and psychological support to prevent relapse.

5 Relapse

Relapse is built into the Prochaska and DiClemente (2009) model and it may well be that the service user goes round the cycle several times. Collins and Keene (2000) identified that the majority of service users will relapse within one or two years and that this is often due to social and emotional factors. Marlatt and Gordon (1980) developed a model of relapse prevention which aims to teach the individual how to prepare for and cope with 'high-risk' situations which could potentially cause a relapse situation.

Relapse prevention can be used when the service user has stopped using and is in the maintenance stage no matter which treatment intervention they have used. Barber (1995) explains that Marlatt and Gordon (1985) make an important distinction between 'lapse' and 'relapse'. They explain that an individual having a single drug 'episode' after a period of abstinence is a 'lapse' does not mean that they have 'relapsed' and returned to their previous drug-taking behaviour. They emphasize that an individual can learn from such a 'slip' and on a cognitive level identify what coping response they could have used to manage the situation.

This relapse prevention model encourages the individual to anticipate situations which may act as a trigger to a 'relapse'. Cognitive behavioural approaches can then be used to teach coping skills and help develop lifestyle changes to plan coping responses to high-risk situations. If the individual is able to prepare coping responses to potential relapse situations then they are more likely to feel more confident and in control. Marlatt and George (1984) explain this by referring to Bandura's (1977) notion of self-efficacy in which the individual believes that they are able to cope with a future situation. This confidence in their own ability and sense of control is believed to reduce the possibility of a relapse.

Implications for social work practice

One of the central dichotomies of social work practice is actually set out quite explicitly by the GSCC (2002): social workers are expected to represent authority at the same time as addressing the welfare needs of their service users. This is a particularly challenging task in the light of the overarching social tensions described in previous chapters. Practitioners are responsible for balancing the needs of drug users against the risks posed by their behaviour. At the same time, social work values stress the importance of promoting individual rights, the need for understanding, empathy and non-judgemental attitudes and autonomy, while protecting service users (and others) from harm (Galvani, 2007). This means trying to negotiate accommodations between the interests and wishes of drug users and other people, including family members, the 'community' and their peers. The task for social workers is to resist defining drug users solely in terms of apparently neutral and external risk factors but to look for ways of exploring what these mean for service users and work with them to develop effective responses.

6   Recovery

Introduction

There are potentially a large number of individuals who have been stable in their drug use for a number of years, and who are well-motivated and committed to moving away from a drug-using lifestyle/culture. However, it is not easy for drug users to engage with wider society because of the process of marginalization and exclusion (Buchanan and Young, 1998). As a problematic/dependent drug user they experience marginalization which leads to social exclusion leaving the drug user isolated and constrained within a drug culture. Therefore, regardless of the motivation and commitment of the individual drug user to change, they are excluded from and unable to gain access to community resources and wider society generally. The damaging effects of this process cannot be underestimated as it leaves users vulnerable and reinforces their feelings of inadequacy and failure. No wonder then that so many drug users are caught up in a cycle of relapse.

However, a number of factors are coalescing which suggest the case for recovery-oriented initiatives and services that are more personalized and offer a better balance between psychosocial and medical interventions. The latest national drugs strategy seems to place greater emphasis on a holistic approach while the Big Society agenda calls for a community-led approach to the problem of drug misuse (Daddow and Broome, 2010). Allied to the vital role we emphasized in the previous chapter of the social worker being the link-pin regarding support and maintenance and in ensuring the individual has support networks mean social work is ideally placed to be at the forefront of the new agenda surrounding 'recovery' and problematic drug use. This chapter focuses on what is actually meant by recovery and as such adopts a more philosophic tone than other chapters in this book. We also offer some observations on the thorny topic of 'dual diagnosis' (in the form of an unreferenced commentary) which seems appropriate given the strong links to be found around the topic of recovery and mental health which have echoes in the discussion about drug use.

Recovery

Although undoubtedly drug services have been successful in attracting dependent drug users into service, once stability has been achieved there are few available options whereby users can move on, access and make use of community resources. Drug users having worked hard to achieve stability, where previously they would have been heavily involved in the process of procuring their daily supply of illicit drugs, are now faced with what seems like an excessive amount of 'free time'. However, suffering from a deficit of self-esteem and confidence and with little knowledge and/or experience of how to access and engage in community resources, the possibility of relapse into further periods of illicit and at times chaotic drug use is considerable. Thus begins the cycle of chaotic drug use – treatment – stability – relapse, and so on. Research indicates that this cycle can continue for many years.

As we highlighted in previous chapters, dealing with physical dependency and addiction are very different challenges. At the heart of that difference is the concept of 'recovery'. The idea of 'recovery' generally is a contested idea (e.g., Pilgrim, 2008; Spandler *et al.*, 2007), and a difficult concept to define (e.g., Jacobson, 2003). Nowhere does this debate about what we mean by 'recovery' exist more fiercely than within the UK addiction field (Best *et al.*, 2008). In other fields (i.e., mental health) the social work profession is considered to find particular alignment with ideas of 'recovery' (e.g. Social Care Institute for Excellence (SCIE), 2007; Care Services Improvement Partnership (CSIP), 2006).

Within the drugs field the 'recovery' literature attests to an emerging and complex field that is compromised by multiple definitions and meanings. It is a contested concept which prompted the UK Drug Policy Commission to circulate a discussion paper (UK Drug Policy Commission (UKDPC), 2008) which unfortunately did little to heal the rift. Indeed, Best *et al.* (2008: 6) commenting on the paper argues that it:

> not only misleads those entering treatment about what is on offer, it creates a self-fulfilling prophecy that may well act as a barrier to the more liberating (but riskier) recovery that is not reliant on the prescription pad and the concomitant therapeutic baggage.

The only thing about which most commentators seem to be able to agree on is that the notion of recovery has become the focus of a considerable amount of confusion and debate between and among various constituencies within the drugs field. In spite of the contested nature of 'recovery' (or possibly even because of it), discussions regarding 'recovery' are finding increasing resonance within the drug field.

Models of 'recovery' present a complex domain suggesting both consumer and scientific models. The former relates to modelling a way of living with drug use and the promotion of self-managed use. The latter finds orientation in its commitment to populating the evidence base with empirically sound 'recovery'-based interventions. Similar divides that relate to 'recovery' models are evident in the literature; between 'recovery' processes and 'recovery' outcomes and between 'recovery' *'in'* and 'recovery' *'from'* problematic drug use. However, these divisions are not neatly prescribed and there is considerable overlap and cross-pollination, both in terms of conceptual and empirical work, and in the positioning of service users and researchers in the field (White and Kurtz, 2005). Nevertheless, a 'tradition' is evident within the literature that strives to order the storied accounts of the lived experience of service users into a model of 'recovery' processes (e.g., McIntosh and McKeganey, 2002). An interesting point may be raised in the apparent contradiction between the unique personal nature of the 'recovery' process and the construction of 'recovery' models.

Reference to 'recovery' as a *philosophy* tends to operate either as an overarching umbrella term as in the approach of Alcoholics Anonymous (AA) (Kurtz, 2008) or *'system'* (McLellan, 2006) denoting all aspects of 'recovery'. A second association is that which links 'recovery' philosophy to ideas of 'self-management' or self-responsibility or 'natural recovery' (Burman, 1997). Some commentators (albeit those with no direct experience of drug treatment) have suggested that striving towards a sense of self *must* be made unfettered by external influences; a contentious area given some experiences of drug use.[20]

Self-mastery (or self-management) can be readily observed within the previous government policies not only, for example with respect to 'recovery' from severe and enduring mental illness (Department of Health (DoH), 2001a, 2003, 2004, 2006a) but across broader domains of health care in general (DoH, 2001b, 2005, 2006b).

Reflections on 'recovery'

The very notion of 'recovery' and its common-sense appeal to ideas of 'getting better' can be seen as powerful and emotive referents; after all, who could possibly deny the implied optimism of 'recovery?'

However, the subject area of 'recovery' is complex. Debate and tension are evident across many strands of the concept, including its definition, conceptualization and ultimately its meaning. The situation is undoubtedly magnified by the numerous stakeholders on the one hand (and their divergent political and organizational agendas) and the highly personal nature of the concept on the other.

The myriad of referents to 'recovery' may be partly due to a usage that is split between the objective (*'clinical or social recovery'* that is potentially amenable to measurement) and the subjective (*'existential and personalised'* accounts of the lived experience). The call to advance empirical knowledge of 'recovery' has necessitated the development of operational definitions in order for 'recovery' to be captured as a measurable outcome. From a 'recovery' orientation, what constitutes 'evidence' is debatable due to the division between 'recovery' as an outcome and as a process. It may be appreciated therefore that the urge to engage operational definitions of 'recovery' is met by a sense of frustration and leads some to question whether it can be defined at all.

The concept of 'recovery' is a complex process involving personal, interpersonal and interactive factors that are experienced by the individual through various nonlinear temporal stages. However, there is often a lack of clarity and a sense of contradiction surrounding the detail.

Even if specific 'elements' could be defined there is little evidence to suggest their relative weighting or importance in the lived experience. The extent to which this meshes with ideas of 'recovery' is contested within the literature.

However, such ventures are in their infancy and are made more complex by commentaries that indicate the imprecision surrounding the construction of operational measures of 'recovery'.

'Recovery' and spirituality

Harris (2007) in his engaging discussion of recovery from addiction writes of the 'much neglected' area of spirituality, in comparison to other areas (e.g., hope, self-identity and self-esteem). Fallot (2007: 262) makes a useful distinction between spirituality and religion. The former is described as '. . . that dimension of personal experience related to the sacred, ultimate, or transcendent'. The latter '. . . carries an organisational dimension, involving a community of believers with a shared set of doctrines or beliefs and ritual activities'. In a less informal manner, a participant in Russinova and Cash's (2007: 276) empirical study on the personal meaning of religion and spirituality suggested that: 'religion is for people who are afraid to go to hell and spirituality is for people that have been there already'. This is a frequent theme emerging from service user narrative that within the 'recovery' process, spirituality is seen as a source of moving forward or resilience and perhaps more centrally the acquisition of hope and meaning and purpose in one's life.

Several potential mechanisms may operate to bring about the positive benefits described above. Fallot (2007: 263) suggests that spirituality may serve to bolster a *'sense of self'* and *'self esteem'* through a sense of association or of being *'valued'* by a higher order.

At the same time, it may invoke a sense of 'community' and social support. Bussema and Bussema (2007: 304) argue that spirituality plays a positive role in what they term 'religious coping' by offering '. . . a frame of reference for understanding one's predicament . . .'.

Consideration of 'recovery' processes and subjective meanings place more traditional evidence-based practice (EBP) in some degree of turmoil by highlighting the insensitivity and inappropriateness of large-scale, positivistic research methods to elucidate complex social phenomena. Best *et al.* (2009) claim that 'recovery' does not represent a separation from drug services on the part of the service user, but a demand for a new response from services. Complementary to EBP, they argue that values-based practice (VBP) is compatible with 'recovery' for the following reasons:

- respect for the values of each individual
- focus upon strengths and positive values
- processes and outcomes are equitable
- options and choice in healthcare
- promotes service user decision making

As an *approach*, 'recovery' tends to be associated with service delivery agendas. In this context 'recovery' is seen as a mode of practice, a way of *'working with'*, relating or collaborating with service users. Although the 'recovery' approach extols the role of working in partnership with the service user, especially in order to achieve self-managed healthcare, the explicit nature of the 'partnership' role is contested.

The 'recovery' *model* has emerged from the service-user perspective and the lived experience and strives to relocate the individual as a self-determining agent of change. The element of the debate surrounding 'recovery', which generates the most heat, is around service users receiving 'medical interventions'; in particular, the maintenance prescribing of methadone.

This debate is not simplistically cast *between* service users and policy-makers, but also configured *within* diverse service user populations. Tension surrounds claims that the service-user-derived 'recovery' model has been appropriated by drug treatment providers – at least in the use of language.

As a movement 'recovery' is tied to the service user movement which is wedded to a civil rights agenda. Conceptualizations of 'recovery' as a movement illuminate the emergence of the individual as holding personal agency, and presents an alternative from which to articulate experiences of 'recovery' *'in'* drug use as opposed to 'recovery' *'from'* drug use; to talk of processes in 'recovery' (as opposed to outcomes) and to engage the politics of drug treatment provision.

The extent to which failure to 'recover' could be attributed to a 'negative attitude' is an interesting proposition and invites ideas of personal failure and says little about the structural inequalities that contextualize the issue. Harris (2007) poses the fundamental question of whose 'recovery' is it?

Dual diagnosis – an excursus commentary

The term 'dual diagnosis' is not particularly useful and it is arguably not appropriate for social workers given the heavy medical connotations surrounding it. However, given that it is has become so identified with the issue of coexisting problems we are sticking with it for the purpose of clarity.

Simplistically, dual diagnosis refers to the concurrent existence in an individual of substance misuse and a mental disorder. However, the complexity of problems experienced by service users belies the simplicity of the classification of merely the coexistences of problematic substance use alongside a mental health 'disorder'. Indeed, we must acknowledge that the actual concept of mental health disorder is a contested one, but even with definitions utilized within services, it is necessary to also incorporate wider social functioning such as personality disorder and learning disability. One only has to consider the legions of permutations of possible chemical and behavioural dependencies that could partner an equally diverse range of mental health disorders to comprehend the challenge that dual diagnosis poses to treatment services. The difficulty of working effectively and therapeutically with such service users leads many agencies to create boundaries based on single diagnoses, thus causing the rejection of those with more complex problems.

The variety of pathways resulting in a dual diagnosis, and the wide range of mental health symptoms and types and levels of drug use the term may encompass brings enormous complications to diagnosis and treatment. The general confusion about the whole concept of dual diagnosis has led to reluctance by any service to accept responsibility for this group. Consequently, there is as yet no concerted service response to dual diagnosis in the UK.

Many mental health agencies exclude service users who are actively misusing substances, and substance misuse agencies often cannot offer the levels of support needed to work with the more disturbed service users with mental health problems. Attitudinal barriers remain and are reflected in the reluctance of psychiatric services to embrace contemporary models of drug use such as harm minimization in favour of an insistence on abstinence with the threat of rejection from services if services are unable or unwilling to comply. The lack of integration between mental health and substance misuse services seriously compromises attempts to deal with the issue effectively. The difficulty in dealing with dual problems within separate specialized services results in many individuals 'falling between the cracks' or having one of their problems ignored. The fragmented package of care resulting from the involvement of two distinct services which tend to have conflicting philosophies, approaches and expectations exacerbates the difficulties in maintaining contact with a notoriously 'difficult to engage' group.

Drug use is becoming more prevalent in society generally and mental health services may need to accept that some drug use is inevitable and apply concepts such as harm minimization to people with dual diagnosis and relax their controlling and punitive attitudes towards drug use and aim to reduce their potentially deleterious effects rather than striving for the perhaps futile aim of ending drug use completely. Perhaps it is preferable to work with service users towards mutually acceptable goals rather than demand abstinence and risk service users disengaging and being lost from services.

Substance misuse services often feel that service users with additional mental health problems are beyond their remit and share with many mental health staff a perceived lack of expertise and confidence to deal effectively with the complex problems presented by prospective service users with a dual diagnosis. This is perhaps understandable from voluntary agency staff that tend not to have psychiatric training but somewhat perplexing with regard to community drug teams which are often staffed by nurses with mental health training. One would imagine that they would feel sufficiently skilled to support service users with a dual diagnosis.

There is a particular problem for service users with a dual diagnosis gaining access to residential treatment facilities which will often refuse to admit people with serious mental health problems because the treatment approaches used are seen as inappropriate for people who are psychologically more fragile. Specialist drug rehabilitation programmes are often too confrontational for the seriously mentally ill who may experience them as highly stressful since the emotional temperature of the group sessions can be high. The emphasis on group work in itself may prove difficult for people who find social interactions difficult. In addition, there is often a requirement for residents to abstain from all substances prior to treatment, including medication prescribed for the control of psychotic symptoms. This would obviously be unhelpful for a person with schizophrenia. Residential facilities often have strict limits on tolerance of relapse, and failure to adhere to the high expectations of the facility may mean that a person is discharged while in a psychologically vulnerable state.

One of the main challenges regarding work with dually diagnosed service users is that they are reputedly difficult to engage and retain in services and consistently fail to comply with treatment programmes. One might wonder how hard services have actually tried to 'engage and retain' service users since evidence suggests they are frequently passed between services who do not wish to accept responsibility for them. However, if service users with dual diagnosis do fail to engage with services, or disengage too quickly, it is important to examine the possible reasons why.

Disengagement from services while the person is still experiencing problems may mean the development or exacerbation of other social problems such as homelessness. In addition, disengagement from services at an early stage of treatment is likely to lead to a 'revolving door' syndrome whereby service users relapse periodically and require hospital admission. This may be the reason why people with a dual diagnosis are known to make heavy use of acute services compared with services who have a mental health problem alone. There seems to be an assumption that problems of engagement and treatment compliance are an inherent part of the complexity of the dual disorder. It is far easier to assume that unreliability is a feature of the chaotic nature of many service users' lives rather than consider the possibility that service users may disengage because they find current service approaches unacceptable.

There are many possible reasons why prospective service users might resist involvement with traditional services such as being aware of the potentially punitive responses (such as being reported to the police) they might face. Withdrawal of a person's drugs may be even more frightening for a person with mental health problems who may be using drugs in an attempt to alleviate psychological symptoms, pain or distress, or to provide a means of escape. Although service users may be aware of the destructive nature of their drug use in the long term, in the short term they may be too scared to lose the security of their chosen substance. Consequently, a service approach which is more accepting and understanding of the role of drugs in a person's life might be more successful in at least maintaining contact with the person with the long-term aim of helping them to develop healthier coping strategies and a more positive lifestyle to reduce their need for drugs.

If services are serious in aiming to engage and retain people with dual diagnosis, they need to adopt more flexible approaches or risk this highly vulnerable group being lost. Outreach with intensive case management is often needed on a long-term basis with the development of a trusting collaborative relationship is more likely to be facilitated by providing practical assistance with few demands for compliance or participation on the service user's part. This is a particularly relevant aspect of support required by many people with a dual diagnosis who often experience many complex and interrelated problems. An extension of outreach work should involve the provision of practical advice and assistance in overcoming social problems such as homelessness, financial difficulties, legal problems and so on.

Services often complain that people with a dual diagnosis are non-compliant with treatment programmes. If this is the case, one might wonder whether the aims and goals of the service were the same as the goals of the service user. If a truly collaborative working relationship is developed between service user and worker, it should be possible to arrive at mutually agreed goals; non-compliance ceases to be an issue if the service user makes their own decisions and goals. If services are to be 'needs-led' serious attempts need to be made to elicit service users' views about what they perceive their needs to be. They can then become active participants in their own recovery rather than passive recipients of treatment who are acted upon in their 'best interests' by 'expert professionals'. This passive paternalistic approach is not likely to enable service users to develop the skills to control their own lives in the absence of professional help in the future.

Motivational interviewing (see Chapter 4) is a useful method whereby service users can be assisted to make their own choices and identify goals based on their own perception of need. The method encourages recognition of the positive as well as the negative aspects of their drug use, and does not make assumptions that the negative aspects are necessarily a cause for concern for the service user. In discussing a person's hopes and plans for the future, the aim is to explore the role that the person's drug use might play in the achievement of these goals. If the service user begins to express a desire to change, they can be helped to choose goals by exploring the available options and their possible consequences.

Treatment would be individually tailored and would involve the attainment of the skills required to achieve the desired goals. For example, attention might be paid to finding alternative activities and networks which were incompatible with drug use. Relapse should be seen as a learning experience rather than a failure resulting in exclusion and withdrawal of support. Service users can be helped to identify 'high risk' situations where relapse is more likely, and generate ways to cope with these situations. For example, if anxiety provokes relapse, service users may be taught relaxation techniques; if people find it difficult to refuse drugs offered by peers, assertiveness techniques may be appropriate; if impulsivity is a factor, service users may be taught delaying tactics giving them space to think through the consequences of their proposed actions.

The central organizational challenge in working with people with dual or multiple needs is to develop a holistic service within a fragmented culture of care. Organization of services tends to be divided in terms of commissioning structures, professional disciplines and the specialization of service providers. These barriers affect service users with multiple disorders, a lack of integration between mental health and substance misuse services is seriously hindering attempts to support this service user group.

Some advocate specialist dual diagnosis services as the simplest way to provide continuity of care, but there are disadvantages to this approach. For example, if the rates of dual diagnosis are as high as published reports suggest, then substance misuse among people with a mental illness is usual rather than exceptional. A specialist service would quickly become swamped and would ultimately have to be very selective. Services would quickly develop barriers, taking on the most chaotic service users who have the greatest needs. Concentration of expertise within one specialist service may also perpetuate the already existing belief among both mental health and substance misuse services that people with a dual diagnosis are not their responsibility and therefore they do not need to develop the skills to deal with them. The perceived need for yet another specialism will further diminish the confidence of staff in existing services.

There are several issues services must address if they are to begin meeting the needs of people with dual diagnosis. First, services need to have an awareness of the widespread nature of a problem which is currently fairly well hidden. The possibility of substance misuse is not automatically considered in initial assessments despite the fact that statistics show that substance misuse is usual rather than exceptional. In addition, the punitive rather than therapeutic responses towards people who misuse drugs; for example, the threat of expulsion or even police involvement make it unlikely that service users will honestly admit they have a substance misuse problem. There is clearly a need for a change in attitude in mental health services. Its current standpoint on the issue of drug misuse is the expectation of immediate abstention from drugs or exclusion from service support. This contrasts starkly with contemporary models of drug use which emphasize harm reduction. Mental health services may have to accept the reality that many of their service users are using drugs and it is surely unethical to refuse to treat the symptoms of psychological distress for essentially moral reasons. There is a clear need for new assessment instruments which look at the impact of an individual's drug use upon their mental health symptoms rather than assessing the two disorders in isolation from the influences of the other. A person with a mental health problem may be affected by relatively small quantities of a substance which would not meet the criteria for a substance misuse disorder when taken in isolation. The interaction of the two disorders needs to be assessed.

Second, although causal factors are obviously important, these should not be attended to at the expense of immediately dealing with all the presenting problems. As the new model services are beginning to discover, causal effects in dual diagnosis are often difficult to untangle, and outcome of treatment is often the most reliable indication of causality. The high demands dually diagnosed people place on services are in many ways due to the revolving door syndrome. When service users are discharged early from services or disengage themselves because they do not find the approaches acceptable, there is a greater likelihood of relapse requiring regular acute admissions. Greater efforts to engage with this group through assertive outreach and long-term casework are necessary to engage and retain these vulnerable service users in services. This will only be possible if workers adopt a non-judgemental attitude towards service users, recognizing the important role drug use plays in their lives, often as a coping strategy or a means of treating symptoms of psychological distress. Non-compliance issues may be less of a problem if workers build relationships with service users based on empathy and respect, and work in partnership with them to define goals and achieve change based on service users' perception of their needs rather than the assumptions of service professionals. This contrasts with the current ethos of psychiatric units which make demands for compliance irrespective of the person's wishes or ability to immediately abstain from drug use.

The failure of services to integrate when necessary will only lead to more service users falling between the cracks as they are shuttled between services. Often dually diagnosed people who have the most complex needs and pose the greatest risks to themselves and others are the very people who are allowed to disengage from services sometime resulting in tragic yet avoidable incidents.

Risk

There is extensive literature on how knowledge and attitudes are formed and how they work in relation to risk-taking and health (see, for example, Brown and Horowitz, 1993; Compas et al., 1995; Klee et al., 1991; Labouvie and Pinsky, 2001; Rhodes, 2002; Rothman and Salowey, 1997). For example, previous work has looked at whether the impact of screening for hepatitis C virus (HCV) has impacted on risk-taking behaviour. Maher et al. (2004, 2007) found that attitudes and beliefs about HCV can be influenced by screening/testing but they concluded that knowledge, personality and stage of injecting career are more influential. Perception of status (in contrast to actual status) has also been found to possibly influence injecting risk behaviour. Best et al. (1999) found that participants' perceptions of their HCV and hepatitis B virus (HBV) status were often inaccurate; they tended to believe they were negative when they were positive. If injecting drug users (IDUs) mistakenly presume negative status this may have serious public health consequences.

The General Social Care Council (2002) recognizes that services users have the **right** (our emphasis) to take risks. In relation to drug users there are obviously other issues; as we have already discussed, they are often held to be responsible for a host of problematic or antisocial behaviour. At the same time, certain sub-groups of that population (e.g., sex workers, young people) are perceived as being particularly vulnerable to exploitation and abuse. It is perhaps unsurprising that much social work with drug users is driven by an emphasis on harm and the need to ensure that and the need to ensure that they do not put themselves at unnecessary risk.

Contemporary discussions of social welfare have increasingly been concerned with the concept of 'risk' (Webb, 2006). When discussing the field of drug use and the health problems that may be associated with it is interesting to look at the risk or propensity to develop certain health problems. These problems may only become apparent because of prolonged drug use or associated behaviours, so until one uses drugs on a regular basis the person is not aware of the potential risk. Corporeal or embodied risk describes the risk potential as actually being in the body; that is, the person has a propensity to a particular disorder or problem, immaterial of their lifestyle and environment (Kavanagh and Broom, 1998). This identified type of risk is prone to be possibly lost with such overlaps with lifestyle and environmental influences. But is an important part of the risk theory jigsaw. A good example of this could perhaps be that as yet an unidentified corporeal risk lies undiscovered, which may be able to explain why 20 per cent of those infected with HCV will naturally clear the infection and others do not.

A tension may exist therefore in the interplay between meeting the personally unique needs of 'recovery' at the level of the social worker and service provisions that are increasingly driven by '*new managerialism*' approaches (Harlow, 2003).

Consideration of the relationship between 'recovery' and risk necessarily involves discussion of the '*dignity of risk*' and the '*right to failure*'. 'Recovery'-oriented background to dignity of risk flows from the argument that in order to support service user's, 'recovery', drug services need to step back and 'allow' service users the opportunity to fail. Only by doing so will a process of learning and self-determined 'recovery' occur.

The 'ordinary' everyday failures that we all experience are one thing but couched in terms of drug use they represent 'relapse' and/or 'poor risk management.'

Achieving the professional balance between positive risk-taking and risk management is frequently linked to ideas of collaboration between service user and practitioner. However, all is not collaborative. An assumption is being made that 'recovery' meant ideas of '*movement*', '*progress*' and '*getting better*' when, in fact, it had little meaning outside of subjective experience. A critique emerges that not only demands greater clarity between conceptualizations of 'recovery' *from* and 'recovery' *in* drug use, but between the meanings held by service users and social workers.

At some stage in the recovery process the service user is going to have to confront and overcome risk factors (Harris, 2007). An increased risk of service user neglect; for example, in context of the service user exercising their 'dignity of risk' and opting against professional advice.

Masterson and Owen (2006) revisit issues regarding 'recovery', power and colonization in their consideration of service user empowerment. They maintain that not only is '. . . there is some evidence that professionals have softened the more provocative aspects of the empowerment perspective . . .' (p. 30), but that if left to professionally defined criteria, then an underclass of mentally ill people could be created who '*do not recover*' (p. 30). Thus, to adulterate Roberts and Wolfson's (2004) subtitle; 'recovery' would *not* be '*open to all.*'

Implications for social work practice

'Recovery' is unquestionably a complex and multifaceted phenomenon. Recovery may mean in actuality that while one size does not fit all, it may fit some better than others. Hence, a question emerges surrounding the ability of the 'recovery' vision to focus drug use in a culturally equitable manner. Nevertheless, it does seem that the largely unchallenged introduction of the 'recovery' vision and the observed sanguinity from within the literature may usher a different 'turn' for 'recovery' especially in the context of a growing rights-based and citizenship agenda.

According to Best *et al.* (2009: 14) the recovery agenda is about: 'positive work or relationship experiences and the building of personal resources and supportive networks . . . empowerment of users'.

In terms of professional practice, social work is particularly aligned with 'recovery' (Ranon *et al.*, 2007) and its relationship to related themes such as social models (Beresford, 2002) and person-centred planning (Social Care Institute for Excellence (SCIE), 2007). The challenge, according to Best *et al.* (2009) is to shift the emphasis from stigmatization of drug uses to one which is embedded in 'notions of citizenship, social capital and community growth' giving recovering drug users a place in the wider community. This clearly has echoes in social work commitment to social justice (e.g., Bradshaw *et al.*, 2007: 41; British Association of Social Workers (BASW), 2002; Fraser, 2009: 87) and its promotion of a service user-centred approach which we explore in the next chapter.

7 Involving service users in services and interventions

Introduction

The term 'service user'[21] has increasingly been used to describe people on the receiving end of health, welfare and social care policies and services. However, such language is often criticized for many reasons including ignoring individuality and identifying people by common service consumption, portraying people in passive, consumerist terms, and because there is a stigma attached to the term, not least because it is often associated with drug users (Beresford, 2005). Beresford questions though whether the problems lie predominantly in the term 'service user' or in the status of needing or being at risk of needing to use such services. Despite this many people who are not happy with the terminology continue to use it to describe themselves and for the purposes of this chapter the terms 'service user' and 'service user involvement' will be used, while recognizing that the terminology is problematic and not universally accepted. This chapter explores how increased service user involvement in the planning of treatment can remove some of the barriers to engaging service users in treatment and empower them, giving them greater ownership of the treatment process and increasing the potential for positive change.

Service user involvement

In recent years service user involvement has become a key principle in the delivery of health and social care in the UK (Fischer *et al.*, 2007, Fischer *et al.*, 2008; Garret and Foster, 2005) and is a key feature in the current government's agenda to develop more participatory forms of governance (Hodge, 2005). Section 11 of the Health and Social Care Act 2001 places a duty on National Health Service (NHS) organizations to consult and involve patients and the public in the processes of planning, developing and delivering services (OPSI, 2001). The National Treatment Agency (NTA) recommends that practitioners should factor patient choices into their decisions wherever possible (NTA, 2006c). Service user involvement is seen as important because it is linked to improved retention in treatment (Simpson and Joe, 1993, Simpson *et al.*, 1997a, Simpson *et al.*, 1997b), enhanced service user satisfaction and positive treatment outcomes (Neale, 2006). It also empowers individuals by giving them greater control over their treatment, may make them less resistant to treatment (Fischer *et al.*, 2007) and it has been suggested that as well as a democratic right, service user involvement is an ethical requirement (Crawford *et al.*, 2002).

What is service user involvement?

This chapter focuses on service user involvement in the planning and delivery of their own treatment. However, service user involvement is much broader than this and can include service users contributing to strategic planning at Drug Action Team (DAT) level, their involvement in the commissioning and running of drug (and alcohol) services, ex-service users working in a paid or voluntary capacity in such services, and user rights and advocacy groups and forums (Fischer and Neale, 2008; Hodge, 2005).

What is desirable about service user involvement?

Increased service user involvement is seen as an important feature of social care for many reasons: service users may be the best placed to provide relevant information about their reasons for using drugs and about their needs, wants and motivation which is information that could lead to improved outcomes (Montagne, 2002); it provides important opportunities to empower service users through providing choice and increased feelings of ownership; where service users feel empowered and that their views are being listened to, they are more likely to engage with treatment and feel more satisfied with it. Better engagement can increase retention (Meier *et al.*, 2006), especially in new service users (Fischer and Neale, 2008) and retention is seen as a measure of treatment success (Simpson *et al.*, 1997a).

Active participation versus Informed consent

It is argued that in reality, some service user involvement initiatives are little more than a mechanism by which agencies give legitimacy to the decision-making process and often exclude voices that are deemed not acceptable (Hodge, 2005). The NTA reinforces the concept that service user involvement is not about 'ticking boxes', but it is about developing constructive relationships and communicating with service users effectively in order to: involve service users in all key aspects of treatment decisions; learn more about service users' experiences of treatment providers (both past and present); encourage closer and more productive relationships between service providers and service users; identify the most appropriate ways to meet service users' needs; and improve the quality of support and treatment provided (NTA, 2006c).

Service user involvement is also about more than just gaining informed consent. Services certainly need to provide sufficient information about the possible options available to service users to allow them to formulate their own decisions and give informed consent, as without a certain degree of user involvement informed consent is not feasible. However, as Fischer *et al.* (2007) describe, informed consent to treatment decisions does not necessarily equate to service user involvement; it entails active participation by the service user in all aspects of treatment decisions. The extent to which service users can be involved in treatment decisions will vary with the job role and the function of the service provider. Where the latter is the primary provider or coordinator of treatment then the degree of service user involvement possible will be substantially greater. However, if the primary function is to evaluate possible options and refer on to more intense or structured services, then service user involvement may be restricted to their discussing and evaluating the options, deciding on the most suitable and providing informed consent to the referral. Effective and sufficient communication between the referrer and the service user is still an important feature during this transition though, especially concerning the progress of referrals and information about any possible delays in accessing treatment. It is also important for referrers to explore with service users the degree to which they anticipate that treatment may be a difficult and challenging experience (Fisher *et al.*, 2007) and service providers may need to provide sufficient support to service users to maintain their motivation during the referral process.

Barriers to service user involvement

While active and extensive service user involvement may appear to be an ideal scenario, the extent to which it can actually be achieved will be influenced by a wide range of factors including current and historical user–provider relationships, service user expectations, budgets and resources and the capacity of the service user to participate in the decision-making process, especially in terms of stability and motivation.

Professionals may have different views from their service users about the extent to which service user involvement is appropriate and this can lead to a resistance among service providers to involve service users. This may be more commonly encountered in services to drug users than in other services offering health and social care because of the nature of the problems and the stereotypical perceptions of the service user group. Where professionals implicitly or explicitly blame drug users for their problems, disregard the nature of their problems or treat them with contempt, the service users' confidence and self-worth may be undermined and this can create further barriers to seeking and engaging in treatment (Fischer and Neale, 2008).

The legal status of the drugs used and perceptions of drug users can also act as a barrier to service user involvement. Many of the drugs with which such service users experience problems are illegal, meaning that most users are at least committing the primary offence of possession of drugs that are illegal under the Misuse of Drugs Act 1971 (MDA) and some may be committing secondary offences in order to fund their drug use. This not only reinforces negative stereotypes of substance users but may also be seen by some as undermining their democratic right to be involved in decisions relating to service provision (Fischer et al., 2007, Fischer and Neale 2008). This is even more apparent when working with service users within the Criminal Justice System. Where service users have been referred into treatment via the Criminal Justice System, there are questions about the rights of the individual to have an extensive degree of input into their treatment plans, especially where this forms a part of a community sentence. In addition to this the perceptions of substance users as undeserving and treatment-resistant, discussed in Chapter 4, may also undermine the belief that service users know what is best for them and that they should play an active role in the planning of suitable and appropriate interventions. Crawford et al. (2002: 1266) argue that 'involving patients has been viewed by many as a democratic or ethical requirement: because patients pay for services they have a right to influence how they are managed'. However, the perception of problematic drug users as welfare-dependent, undeserving and a drain on society may be perceived as negating this right.

The perception of drug users as dishonest, manipulative and untrustworthy can also be a barrier to service user involvement where it is believed that service users will manipulate the involvement process to their own ends; for example, by requesting higher doses of medication than is necessary (Fischer and Neale, 2008; Griffiths and Pearson, 1988). It is, however, very important not to 'throw the baby out with the bathwater' and there is a strong case for the role of professional judgement in such situations, and scope for exploration about why, for example, the service user believes they need a higher dose. While some service users may well seek to manipulate the process, this is certainly not the case for all, and involving drug users in prescribing decisions and allowing them to feedback whether a methadone prescription is high enough to stabilize them or a reduction programme is proceeding too quickly, increases their perception of choice in decisions, empowering them and reducing resistance which in turn can lead to greater compliance (Montagne, 2002).

The service provider–service-user relationship is also not an equal one and this power imbalance means that service users' views may be overruled. This can lead to conflict where service users feel that they are not being listened to, or that their views are not being taken seriously, or where the service provider perceives the service user as poorly motivated, treatment-resistant and in denial. As Fisher *et al.* (2007: 16) describe, conflict is often resolved 'by client conversion to the staff point of view'. Beyond this the power of service providers to terminate treatment for service users whom they perceive as unco-operative may also dissuade service users from requesting a greater degree of involvement in treatment decisions (Fischer and Neale, 2008, Fischer *et al.*, 2008). Service user dissatisfaction and conflict between service users and service providers may be seen as an inevitable part of service user involvement (Carr, 2007). However, the process of exploring and discussing sources of conflict and seeking resolution may enhance service users' perceptions of involvement and as such conflict should not necessarily be avoided but neither should it be resolved solely by service user conversion to the service provider's point of view.

Disagreement over appropriate sources of support, interventions and treatment pathways may also be compounded by service-users' unrealistic expectations about how achievable their ultimate goals are, or how quickly they can be achieved, especially in the short term. For example, some service users may seek outright abstinence straight away. This always remains the ideal goal, but smaller more achievable short-term objectives such as cutting down on use or changing to a safer way of using drugs (switching from injecting to smoking a drug, for example) while other social and environmental issues are simultaneously addressed may be a more realistic target. Where service users request treatment for which the service provider does not feel that they are ready, but that the service provider agrees to, then this may set them up to fail. Service users may also have unrealistic expectations about how quickly treatment can be accessed and what treatment is available.

Beyond this Fischer and Neale (2008) suggest that some service users' expectations of, or desires for quick solutions to their problems, can mean that they do not try to become overly involved in treatment decisions in case questioning professional judgement or asking for particular treatments slows down the treatment process. There is also the possibility of service users not seeking the treatment they feel would be most beneficial for fear of the delays it may cause in getting into treatment. However, this can be overcome by ensuring that support is available during the waiting period.

What has been discussed so far may suggest that all service users desire and expect to be actively involved in all aspects of their treatment and support. However, research by Fischer *et al.* (2007) indicates that some service users do not expect services to be user-led. Instead they expect to be passive recipients of treatment and support, though many who were initially content with a low level of initial involvement often desired a greater degree of involvement at later stages. This may be because many, at least initially, view service providers as the 'experts' who will guide them through treatment, or because they view their problems solely in terms of dependency, and thus they view the solution medically in terms of a 'cure' that is 'done to them' (Griffiths and Pearson, 1988).

Budgets and resources

In an ideal world, where resources are infinite and all potential treatment and support is available, meeting the service users' desires might more easily be achieved. However, limited resources and options may restrict a service provider's ability to meet all the demands of users (Fischer *et al.*, 2007). For example, access to residential services may be constrained by available funding, availability of places and local protocols favouring greater provision of structured day care over more selective provision of more expensive residential services. Even where choices are limited, however, either due to budgetary constraints or service availability, the notion of choice, albeit from a limited range of options, may still be very empowering and enhance service user involvement in treatment itself.

There are also issues around whether service users understand their needs better than service providers. The substance-using service user may have limited understanding of the nature of the potential problems and the possible solutions, whereas the service providers will often have a wealth of experience in terms of what works and what does not. It is also possible that service users and service providers will have different perceptions of the nature of the problems, the nature of the solutions and the desired outcomes. Services may expect service users to seek abstinence or changes in their substance use, whereas service users may be seeking better relationships with close and significant personal others, getting a job, or achieving a more stable and 'normal' life (Fischer *et al.*, 2007).

Service-user factors

The nature of the problems related to substance use may mean that, at least initially, service user involvement may prove complex. Interventions such as detoxification that are ultimately aimed to enhance stability may initially make it harder for service users to retain information and make informed choices or be more stressful than constructive at the start of treatment (Fischer and Neale, 2008). The degree to which service users can be involved may also relate to their readiness for treatment and their level of motivation. In order to be involved in the planning of service delivery, service users need to be sufficiently motivated to engage with services and actively participate in the treatment and support that has been agreed. While service user involvement may enhance motivation, involvement may prove impossible where the service user does not engage at all.

Welfare and control

It is interesting to note that the rise in the 'consumerist' approach to health and social care, including drug treatment and support, has been paralleled with the move towards more criminal justice-oriented responses to drug treatment involving quasi-compulsory treatment and treatment as punishment, where participants may have little or no control over their treatment. Increasingly, service users are entering drug treatment through the criminal justice system and as such may be perceived as having been coerced into treatment (Fischer and Neale, 2008; Bean, 2002). However, as several commentators including Wild *et al.* (1998) and Longshore *et al.* (2004) note, it is not possible to determine the degree of coercion a service user feels from their referral source. Coercion is seen as more complicated than merely a route of entry into treatment (Stevens *et al.*, 2006): within service user groups sharing the same referral source there is considerable heterogeneity in terms of perceived levels of coercion (Wild *et al.*, 1998), in drugs used, and in physical, psychological and social factors (Klag *et al.*, 2005).

Coercion can also come from other sources such as those with which the service user has a close personal relationship, such as family members or partners, and some of those who have been referred by the criminal justice system may welcome the opportunity to access treatment and support. Despite compulsory criminal justice interventions, such as Drug Treatment and Testing Orders (DTTOs), Drug Rehabilitation Requirements (DRRs) or Arrest referral schemes offering comparatively little scope for service user involvement in treatment decisions (Fischer and Neale, 2008), findings suggest that drug users subjected to DTTOs experience similar retention rates and outcomes to those who appear to have entered treatment voluntarily, and that two-fifths of them did not feel that they had been coerced into treatment (McSweeney *et al.*, 2007). Beyond this, coercion from whatever source, criminal justice or other more informal, extra-legal sources may provide the necessary extrinsic motivation for service users to engage with and participate in treatment, and several studies have found that a combination of strong external coercion and strong internal motivation may lead to the best outcomes (Longshore *et al.*, 2004; Simpson and Joe, 1993).

A policy emphasis on criminality is likely to promulgate notions of deviance and lead to the stigmatization and social exclusion of drug users. The stigmatization of drug users has implications for availability of support networks and for users' help-seeking behaviour. Additionally, users may become part of subcultures where they are more difficult for services to reach. This highlights the conflict between welfare and social control functions of work with drug users and the uncertainty that workers are likely to feel about their role in light of an increase in compulsory referrals to treatment.

A further example of an integrated approach between criminal justice and treatment agencies is the Drug Intervention Programme (DIP). In 2003, the government introduced the DIP (originally called the Criminal Justice Interventions Programme), initially in a limited number of pilot areas, and subsequently rolled out across England. DIP represents a crucial part of the Government's strategy for tackling drug-related crime. It seeks to use every opportunity from arrest to sentence to direct drug-using offenders into treatment by integrating work in police custody, the courts and prisons with treatment agencies.

With the introduction of DIP, it is inevitable that social workers will come into contact with an increasing number of involuntary service users. Trotter (1999: 48) highlights the uncertainty workers may often feel about the 'welfare versus social control' dilemma. Workers are likely to question whether the primary purpose of their work with involuntary service users should be to administer court orders and control antisocial behaviour, or whether they should maintain their traditional social work values and focus primarily upon service users' welfare. There is some research evidence which suggests that an approach to practice which achieves a balance between social control and welfare functions is likely to be of more benefit to service users than interventions based solely on one approach or the other (Trotter, 1999). Trotter suggests that practitioners should make clear their dual role from the outset of the intervention.

The intervention model presented by Trotter (1999) highlights the importance of a collaborative approach to problem solving which seeks to identify and address issues that are pertinent to the service user. In working with the service users' definition of problems and the service users' goals, the intervention is less likely to be perceived as an imposition of the worker's or court's goals upon them. In working collaboratively, Trotter suggests that service users may come to view the worker as an advocate or facilitator rather than an agent of the legal system *per se*, and thus the likelihood of compliance with the requirements of the intervention is increased.

Others (Marsh, 2002; Doel, 2002) endorse a task-centred approach to working with involuntary service users. Task-centred work is considered particularly useful where there is a clear mandate for action either from the user, the courts or both. The aim of task-centred work is to move from agreed problems to agreed goals in a set period of time via a series of tasks (Marsh, 2002). The task-centred approach may be particularly useful in work with drug users as it does not place value judgements upon service users or their behaviour, but rather focuses upon goals to be achieved. This particular approach places the problem 'centre-stage', so that it is the problem rather than the person that is 'the client' (Doel, 2002: 197).

Additionally, the task-centred approach is based on a strengths model which recognizes the user as the 'primary expert' regarding their problems and solutions to them, and seeks to utilize the user's own strengths and capacity to help themselves thus encouraging the user to take greater ownership of the intervention (Marsh, 2002).

It stands to reason, however, that the effectiveness of a collaborative approach to problem solving is largely dependent upon the service users' perception of their behaviour as problematic.

Social work and coercion

There is also an assumption that individuals who enter treatment involuntarily will be unmotivated or resistant to change due to their experience of coercion. The debate continues as to the potential effectiveness of coerced treatment with the question remaining as to how external motivation can lead to an increase in internal motivation. It may be that criminal justice sanctions signal to the individual that they have reached 'rock bottom' often understood to be a necessary precursor to seeking treatment. External motivations may have an effect regardless of whether that pressure is negative (as an alternative to prison) or positive (as an incentive to maintain employment) depending on whether the user sees external pressure as a product of their own behaviour or not (Longshore *et al.*, 2004).

The exact roles of internal and external motivation in the treatment process are complex. Knight *et al.* (2000) found both legal pressure and readiness for treatment were shown to exert significant but independent influences on retention in residential programme. There is also some evidence that a combination of internal and external motivation may lead to better outcomes than those produced by either factor alone. De Leon *et al.* (1994) demonstrated that internal motivation had more influence among persons experiencing stronger external pressure for treatment, while Wild and Enzle (2002) argue that negative external motivation could undermine internal pressure to produce worse outcomes.

It is important, however, that the concept of coercion does not become oversimplified. There is a tendency to view the source of referral to treatment and the experience of coercion as synonymous. Voluntary entry into treatment is commonly considered to be non-coerced whereas involuntary entry is seen as coerced. Critics suggest that this represents a misuse of terminology, emphasizing that the source of referral and the individual's experience of coercion are independent variables (Prendergast *et al.*, 2002). For example, individuals who enter treatment via the criminal justice system will do so under varying degrees of legal pressure and will have differing experiences of coercion. Coercion is not a dichotomous variable but, rather, represents a range of degrees of force used across various stages of the treatment and criminal justice system (Paylor, 2008). Indeed, research by Wild *et al.* (1998) found that a significant proportion of individuals referred to treatment via the criminal justice system perceived no coercive pressure at all. Nor is the individual's perception of coercion determined solely by legal pressure. As Marlowe *et al.* (1996: 81) found in their study, individuals in treatment perceived entry pressures as stemming predominantly from psychological, financial, social, familial and medical domains; and these findings were independent of whether they had been referred to treatment by legal authorities. Wild *et al.* (1998: 81) suggest that such findings are inconsistent with prevailing beliefs regarding the link between compulsion and perceived coercion but rather 'support a "self-determination theory" (Deci and Ryan, 1985), which proposes that multiple social and psychological events promote perceived coercion by undermining personal autonomy'. It would be erroneous then for workers to assume that all individuals who enter treatment via the criminal justice system will have experienced equal coercion and will therefore lack motivation or be resistant to engagement with treatment.

Varying degrees of coercion may be applied to individuals referred to treatment from the criminal justice system and the extent of this coercion may vary over time. Entering treatment under compulsion does not necessarily imply that the individual cannot become an essentially 'voluntary' participant at some later stage. It is possible for an initially 'voluntary' patient to become 'coerced' at some stage in the treatment process (Longshore *et al.*, 2004). This is one reason why it is essential not to confuse the experience of coercion with the source of the referral into treatment, although this is commonly done (Marlowe *et al.*, 1996). This is particularly important given the huge variation in the nature and application of legal treatment mandates between time and place (Anglin, 1988; Stevens *et al.*, 2005).

The other major assumption that social workers should guard against is that 'coerced' service users are under greater pressure and are less motivated or ready for treatment than voluntary service users. Yet, it is by no means clear that there is a direct relationship between a criminal justice referral into treatment and the service users experience of 'coercion'. In reality, there is a divergence between the way 'coercion' is applied and the perception of it by the individual drug user. This has led recent research to emphasize the importance of the individual drug user's perceptions. If coercion is experienced differently by different people, examining 'coerced' treatment solely by referral source is not very helpful. Wild *et al.*'s (1998) study of perceived coercion among drug users in treatment, revealed that 35 per cent of those who had entered treatment under legal mandates did not perceive any coercion. Other studies have shown that even those who do perceive legal coercion may rate other coercive factors, such as family pressure, as more relevant to the treatment experience (Marlowe *et al.*, 1996). Furthermore, it is incorrect to assume that users who have been 'coerced' into treatment are not motivated or 'ready' for treatment. Work by Farabee *et al.* (2002) found no statistically significant correlation between perceived coercion and perceived need for treatment. This brings into question whether researchers measuring 'coerced' treatment by referral source are, in fact, measuring the correct variable. Studies that fail to distinguish between referral source, extent of compulsion, perceived coercion and readiness for treatment fail to examine the concept in a meaningful way.

It is inaccurate to assume that those entering treatment through the criminal justice system are under greater coercion than others (Longshore *et al.*, 2004). Even voluntary treatment participants often enter under some form of social or pharmacological pressure (Maddux, 1988). Work by Wild and colleagues stresses that those who have entered treatment under legal pressure do not necessarily perceive a greater level of coercion than those who have not (Wild *et al.*, 1998; Wild, 2006). In Wild *et al.*'s (1998) study, 37 per cent of self-referred participants reported being coerced into treatment. Wild (2006) pointed out that social pressures are commonly an integral part of the process of seeking treatment and outlined a typology of coercion. Borrowing from Room (1989), he divided coercion into legal social controls such as court-ordered treatment, formal social controls such as mandatory referrals to employee assistance programmes through work and informal social controls such as pressures from family and friends. Each of these, he argues, may play a significant role in accessing and remaining in treatment (Wild, 2006). Thus, it may be incorrect to assume that criminal justice service users have been coerced while 'voluntary' service users have not.

Hence, there is no clear division between 'voluntary' and 'involuntary' treatment participants. The use of the term 'coercion' as a proxy for 'criminal justice referral' is insufficient. Rather the exact level of compulsion, the effect on the subject and its interplay with other factors is highly relevant.

The complexity of the treatment experience is well understood, and it is essential to apply this to our understanding of the concept of 'coerced' treatment. The significance of the user's internal and external motivation has been described above. Thus, 'coercion' must be understood with reference to its role in this wider process, as opposed to a variable in its own right. The relevant question is not whether 'coerced' treatment can be successful but what role 'coercion' can play in creating, sustaining or, potentially destroying a user's motivation to engage in treatment (Prendergast *et al.*, 2002).

Facilitating service user involvement

A fundamental aspect of service user involvement relates to communication and agreement on roles and responsibilities. Fischer *et al.* (2007) identified that service users' overwhelming focus on the importance of service providers listening to their concerns, empathizing with their problems, making them feel valued, and taking the time to explain treatment procedures to them in sufficient detail. Service users report that this cannot happen unless they are listened to and taken seriously, provided with information about treatment options, informed about referral progress and that problems and differences of opinion can be overcome by negotiation. Prescriptive or didactic approaches where the service user is told what is best for them will not enhance feelings of service user involvement unless they desire this kind of approach, and this understanding can only be achieved through communication. Conversely, the service users need to appreciate that they also need to participate fully in the communication process, be honest, explain what they want and what they are willing to do to achieve their goals and be prepared to make compromises themselves, otherwise it will prove hard for service providers to match service users' expectations to possible treatment services.

Implications for social work practice

Service user involvement in treatment decisions is increasingly seen as a funda-mental principal in service delivery in the health and social care sectors, and certain agencies such as the NHS perceive service user involvement as a part of their duty of care. It is widely suggested that service user involvement in substance use support and treatment lowers resistance in those who are ambiv-alent about change, empowering them, improving engagement and retention and leading to more positive treatment outcomes. This may be because service users themselves are best placed to provide input about their needs, motiva-tions and the changes that they wish to make, and that participating in treat-ment decisions gives them a feeling of ownership of the process, increasing motivation and treatment satisfaction and thus improving treatment outcomes. Put simply, active participation in treatment decisions increases active participation in treatment, though only where suitable treatment and support is offered.

However, involving substance-using service users can require a range of skills in terms of identifying and assessing substance use, and in assessing service users' needs, motivations and desire to be involved in treatment deci-sions. For those for whom working with substance users is a core part of their job role, these skills may already be evident; for those for whom it is not, acqui-sition of appropriate skills may be identified as areas for professional develop-ment at a later time. Beyond this, a range of other barriers to service user involvement also exist. Failure on the part of the service user to explain what they want and what they are willing to do to achieve desired change can be compounded by services failing to discuss and explain available options or failing to listen to the service user, sometimes driven by stigma, prejudicial perceptions of the service user group, and a belief that 'the professional knows best'. A cycle can occur in which service users are perceived as poorly motivated because appropriate and attractive treatment and support options are not made available to them, and services then passively wait for their service user to become motivated instead of exploring ways in which motivation can be improved and service user engagement in treatment increased. Beyond this time and resource constraints may mean that a service user's preferred treatment or support is not available and alternatives may need to be explored. There can also be a tendency for services to view substance use problems in isolation and separate to wider socio-economic problems, and by failing to address a service user's substance use-related needs within a broader context of these socio-economic issues, that service users can be set up to fail, reducing the chances that they will actively involve themselves in services in the future.

8 Networking, advocacy and empowerment

Introduction

The National Treatment Agency (NTA) (2006a) refers to the need to identify child protection issues and share information around these. The Drug Intervention Programme (DIP) focuses on drug-using offenders in contact with the criminal justice system and brings together a number of existing initiatives with a new focus on throughcare and aftercare, in order to provide coherent and ongoing support and intervention for service users. All Alcohol and Drug Action Teams and Child Protection Committees should have in place local protocols and policies for joint working across agencies with children and families affected by substance misuse. Underlying much of the *Hidden Harm* (Advisory Council on Misuse of Drugs (ACMD), 2003) report is the need for joint working across different disciplines and agency boundaries.

However, one of the factors that makes multidisciplinary partnership hard to address is the lack of attitudinal common ground, a difficulty that arises from the differing theoretical and experience bases of the myriad services on offer. The purpose of this chapter is to explore the potential for rather more systemic approaches to practice, which ensures that comprehensive solutions can be found.

Parental drug use

Parental drug use as we have discussed previously can have serious negative effects on the user and on those around them leading to psychological, social and interpersonal, financial or legal problems. Due to the stigma that surrounds drug use, parents and children are often reluctant to share their problems, due to a fear of social isolation or concern that a child may be taken away from the family home (ACMD, 2003).

Substance use and indeed family life are private activities (Murphy and Harbin, 2000) and the deeper one goes into the intricacies of family life, the more interfering and invasive it can feel for the parents and children involved. The difficulty for social care workers in practice can be in creating the right skills, context and environment for that exchange of information to take place. Forrester (2004) found in his research that one of the biggest problems social workers described was *how* they could collect the information needed for assessment rather than knowing *what* information was needed. This issue of how to collect information also emerged in Kroll and Taylor's (2003) interviews with social care workers (1999–2001).

Forrester (2004) found in his interviews with social workers that the most common problem that they discussed was how to deal with parental denial or minimization of their substance use. A crucial part of social care workers over-coming problems of parental denial or lack of engagement and developing more sympathetic ways of listening to service users is to recognize their own values and judgements and how these can affect the assessment process (Forrester, 2004). Self-awareness of the values that social care workers bring to their practice is particularly important in a social and political context where people who use substances are viewed so negatively (Forrester, 2004). Judgemental attitudes towards parents have a crucial impact upon parental engagement with social services (Klee *et al.*, 2002).

Parents fear judgemental attitudes and that seeking help may risk their children being taking away and some have bad experiences of past engagement with social services so getting it right is very important and getting it wrong has real consequences. Decisions and assessments of families in cases of concern about the child have found that the dynamic between the professional and the family play a crucial role in what happens with cases. Research shows that people's experiences of attitudes towards drug use by practitioners or expecta-tions of what they might encounter can seriously impact upon a drug user's willingness to engage with services (Klee *et al.*, 2002). For women there can be the added burden of gender differences in the way in which substance use is perceived, in that women who use substances are viewed even more negatively than men and mothers are particularly vilified (Klee *et al.*, 2002).

Pregnancy and substance use

The effects of parental substance use on children can start from the moment of conception. Many problem substance users are unaware of the possible conse-quences that using while pregnant can have on the unborn foetus. This is largely down to the fact the majority of the women have little contact with antenatal services through fear of stigmatization or having their babies removed from their care. It is also the case though that many substance-using women have irregular periods and therefore do not find out about their pregnancies until late on, in which circumstances they would have made little opportunity to reduce or refrain from taking substances to prevent future damage to the baby. Mothers who continue to use a substantial amount of substances during pregnancy do put the health of their babies in increased danger. The most likely side-effect the baby will suffer is neonatal abstinence syndrome or fetal alcohol syndrome. Not only are such newborns subject to withdrawal, more susceptible to sudden infant death, they are more at risk from low birth weight and premature delivery. That the babies of substance-using mothers can experience various health implications, it is not surprising that along with their symptoms come the intense and often diffi-cult task of caring for them. As a result of such difficulties it can make parenting less rewarding and can compromise mothers' parenting ability. Unfortunately, this puts substance-using mothers at a disadvantage from the outset, as their parenting abilities will immediately be put to the test.

The issue that lack of engagement by parents who use substances is not merely due to the fault of parents but the stigma that they face is particularly important given that research suggests that drug-using parents are more likely to reject court-ordered services, make service delivery difficult and conse-quently have their children removed permanently (Harbin and Murphy, 2006). So it is very important that this reflexivity is an ongoing and important part of assessments and work with parents who use substances in social care services. A crucial aspect of this reflexivity is for social workers to confront their own fears in handling difficult emotion or conflictual situations with parents, and having proper training and support in doing that, so that they do not avoid situations and thus get more detailed assessments (Kroll and Taylor, 2003; Klee *et al.*, 2002).

Since the Children Act 1989 legislation, policy and guidance has supported the principle that children should remain within their family home wherever possible. No law can ensure that a child can be safe from risk (Thom *et al.*, 2007) but since the implementation of the Children Act 1989, the policy that children should remain within their family home wherever possible has fared well (Allen, 2005). This policy must also be considered by social workers when dealing with parents who use drugs (Kroll, 2007).

The key to this we are told by various bodies (both inside and outside government) is 'partnership'. Hidden Harm Three Years On pinpoints various conclusions drawn by The Children of Drug Misusing Parents Project, in its efforts to identify and develop 'a good practice model relevant to all front-line practitioners' (ACMD, 2007: 36). These include the need to develop 'a multi-agency response', to promote practitioners' 'confidence and competence' by improving child-care workers' understanding of substance use and substance use workers' knowledge of children's needs and to develop a range 'of family focussed services' incorporating 'direct work with children' (ACMD, 2007: 37). The Commission for Social Care Inspection (CSCI) (2006) report stresses the need for 'joint assessments between adult and children's services and the need for inter-agency protocols to support this'.

Social services departments have a lead responsibility for the assessment of children who are deemed to be suffering significant harm; but under section 27 of the Children Act 1989, other local authority organizations, such as health, have a duty to work together with social services to provide such support (Waller, 2005; Jones *et al.*, 2005). The Children Acts (1989, 2004) place local authorities under a duty to support children and families by offering them a range of services appropriate to their needs; however, this always depends on the services and resources available. The Children Act 1989 places requirements on local social services authorities to bring together child protection agencies who work with families in crisis situations, and to combine this with preventative work with the families of children in need (Howarth and Morrison, 2007).The initial consideration is whether the child is safe while in the care of their parent or parents (Jowitt and O'Loughlin, 2005) and agencies should cooperate around this consideration.

The implementation of the Children Act 2004 and the policy developments that accompanied the new legislation heralded major changes in the structure and presentation of children's services (Jones *et al.*, 2005). The background of these changes included the Victoria Climbie inquiry (Waller, 2005; Jones *et al.*, 2005) which criticized the lack of inter-agency working. The inquiry also influenced the proposals set out in *Every Child Matters: Change for Children* (Department for Education and Skills (DFES), 2004) which contained much detail on the problems faced by some local authorities in the late 1990s.

The initiative stresses the importance of an increasingly holistic approach to working with children and families. The new children's agenda highlights the potential impact that good partnerships between agencies can have on the services they offer to children and parents (Tunstill *et al.*, 2007). The concept of agencies working together is not new (Waller, 2005) with government advice on partnership working dating back to the early 1990s (Smith *et al.*, 1993).

The absence of inter-agency collaboration causes a breakdown in communication, delays in service delivery and general confusion and dissatisfaction with service users (Weinstein *et al.*, 2003). Taylor and Kroll (2004) raise the issue of the differing 'timescales' under which professionals in adult and children's services operate. They indicate that the former take a longer-term approach to their work than the latter, reflecting their opposing concerns that, on the one hand, substance abuse is a 'chronic condition' and on the other, that the welfare of children can be seriously compromised. They also highlight practitioners' worries regarding the 'different agendas' and 'at times . . . . . polarisation', which can occur within adult and children's services, which has sometimes 'significantly affected the assessment process' (Taylor and Kroll, 2004: 1122).

Sharing information across agencies is an integral part of child protection work and deemed essential for effective practice (DoH, 1999b; Waller, 2005). Although information sharing is vital, it also causes challenges and privacy issues with regard to confidentiality (Richardson, 2003).

Confidentiality – some notes

The Human Rights Act 2000 implements provisions of the European Convention of Human Rights. Article 8 of ECHR guarantees respect for a person's private and family life, his home and his correspondence. Disclosure of health related information would breach that right unless it is in accordance with the law and necessary for the protection of health. Unless there is a lawful basis for disclosing health information, such as the subject having given consent, compliance with a legal requirement to disclose, or the need to protect life, the information should not be shared.

Disclosure of personal information is governed by the Data Protection Act 1998. The provisions of the Data Protection Act 1998 ensure that personal information held about any individual cannot be used for purposes other than those for which it was originally supplied without the individual's consent. There is however a number of important exceptions to this set out in the Act.

People with drugs related problems may be particularly concerned about their support services sharing information with other professionals. They may fear that they will be denied help, disadvantaged, stigmatised or blamed if other professionals or agencies are given any information about them. They may also fear investigation by the police about illegal drug misuse or child protection agencies making inquiries. Contact with these agencies may be stressful even if there is no cause for concern. In most circumstances users of treatment and support agencies can rely on confidentiality as their guiding principle. But there are important exceptions to this.

If there is reasonable professional concern that a child may be at risk of harm this will always override a professional or agency requirement to keep information confidential. Professionals have a responsibility to act to make sure that a child whose safety or welfare may be at risk is protected from harm. They should always tell parents this.

Confidentiality is an important factor in enabling service users to engage confidently and honestly with treatment and support agencies and this is an essential requirement for successful rehabilitation. All agencies should tell service users about the kinds of situations where they may have to share information. If there are worries about a child's care, development or welfare, professionals in touch with the family must co-operate to enable proper assessment of the child's circumstances, provide any support needed and take action to reduce risk to the child.

Source: Scottish Executive (2007) *Getting our Priorities Right: Policy and Practice Guidelines for Working with Children and Families Affected by Problem Drug Use.* Edinburgh: Scottish Executive

The issue of confidentiality is directly relevant to the issue of stigma and disclosure discussed in Chapter 3 because individuals may be afraid that their status will be disclosed without their consent to other professionals, or accidentally because of their association with HIV/AIDS services, making them less likely to disclose and/or access services. This is therefore an important area that needs to be addressed by statutory and voluntary agencies, whether specialist or generic, and also by health professionals that come into contact with children and families in relation to HIV/AIDS. Once a person discloses their HIV status their personal information is restricted under the Access to Personal Files Act 1987 and also the Data Protection Act 1998 unless requested by a court or if a HIV-positive person is thought to be a danger to others. Information can also be accessed if a HIV-positive child is to be fostered or adopted (Children in Scotland, 2002: 10).

However, it could be argued that confidentiality relies on the integrity of each worker; therefore, it is important that agencies have relevant protocol in relation to this issue. As highlighted in the Children in Scotland report (2002: 10) 'agencies should develop written statements on confidentiality and information-sharing'. This would then clearly set out 'how information may be shared by workers and also how information may be shared with others outside the agency'. This is important as it then makes clear to both service users and all members of a multidisciplinary team that information will be shared as required.

The 2002 report also suggested the importance of workers asking service users from the start who they are comfortable with them contacting, and from this gaining written consent. It is also about understanding that people's lives are not static and that consent should be gained throughout, as aspects of people's lives will change. Individuals need to trust workers, which means that there has to be an understanding that workers will only divulge information when absolutely necessary. As the report shows, workers can be selective with the information that they give other agencies. For example, it would be enough for housing agencies to be made aware that 'a parent has a serious health problem' without full disclosure (Children in Scotland, 2002: 11). Additionally, service users need to believe that information will be held securely. How this should be carried out could be developed as a protocol, to be followed by all professionals involved with HIV/AIDS-infected and affected service users (Children in Scotland, 2002: 11).

The 2002 report also highlighted that many workers think they should know if there is HIV in the families they are working with so they can do their job more effectively. However, it is additionally highlighted that the 'need to know' is not important as long as the services and support that are needed are put in place. The key factor is that workers 'are open, flexible and ready to listen, so that children are helped whatever their specific issue or problem' (Children in Scotland, 2002: 10). Disclosure, it could be suggested, is more likely to occur when there is a relationship developed on trust. It has been suggested that whether specialist or generic workers, balancing a child's right to know with a parent's right to confidentiality can only be achieved by building a trusting relationship and disclosure is part of that process (Knight et al., 1999: 3). In relation to services it should be noted that 'the majority of service providers and users interviewed felt strongly that children affected by HIV, while needing a sense of "normality" in their lives, also needed specialist provision; again this was linked to issues of stigma, secrecy, disclosure and confidentiality' (Knight et al., 1999: 2).

Knight et al. (1999) showed that all the statutory and voluntary agencies that took part in their study were aware of issues and concerns individuals had in relation to confidentiality and the effect this had on the uptake of services. The study acknowledged that the measures that had been put in place to protect service users were effective in such a way that gaining access to them for research purposes was difficult. The study additionally highlighted that service users were so afraid that people would find out that they were accessing HIV/AIDS services that certain service providers adopted a policy of using plain notepaper, rather than headed paper when writing to service users, in case written material was inadvertently mislaid (Knight et al., 1999: 24). Also highlighted from the research was the fact that many black African families had specifically requested that they did not have a black African worker for fear of their status being disclosed among their community (Knight et al., 1999: 24). Lewis (2001: 15) also found that black African families preferred a researcher 'that was not part of their cultural group' because service users believed it 'would ensure greater confidentiality'. That is not to say that all black African families feel the same way, but it does highlight the additional worries of some service users accessing HIV/AIDS services (Knight et al., 1999: 24). Lewis (2001: 15) additionally highlights 'the implications this has in relation to the accessibility and provision of service' which therefore needs to be taken into account by service providers. However it is also important that 'while ensuring the voices of minority groups in London disproportionately affected by HIV are kept on the agenda that target support incorporates all infected families' (Lewis, 2001: 129).

Although confidentiality is needed to protect those with HIV/AIDS from the stigma that is so evident in society, it could be suggested that the way it is used veils the disease to an extent, perpetuating the stigma of those it is intended to protect. Obviously, this is not something that can simply be changed immediately. However, if as much time and effort went in to highlighting the destructive nature of stigmatization as is invested in the development of laws and protocol in relation to confidentiality, it is suggested that the campaign against preventing HIV/AIDS would have progressed in a more positive direction than has so far been the case. Adults, young people and children, whether infected or affected by HIV/AIDS should not have to worry about issues relating to HIV/AIDS stigma in addition to all their other concerns. A specific adverse consequence is the negative effect on their mental health, which is an important part of maintaining physical well-being. A chronic life-threatening illness causes sufficient problems in relation to changes in lifestyle, appearance and confidence without people having to worry about rejection, disclosure, discrimination and secrets (Dodds *et al.*, 2004). If a cancer sufferer was asked to hide it from their family, friends and colleagues and to try and hold down their job while they had treatment it would be perceived as barbaric. Yet that is what most people with HIV face on a daily basis, or have faced at some time, and not because they choose to, but because they are forced to through the stigmatizing society we live in.

Inter-agency communication

Consistent messages concerning factors that help and hinder inter-agency communication within child and family services are well-documented (Moran *et al.*, 2006; Mason, 2006). Different treatment systems that seeks to address these issues are often not integrated (Stanley, 2007). The fact that these problems can be detrimental for a child's well-being shows the need for children's and adult's services to work together. Unfortunately, it is still the case that this does not often happen (Stanley, 2007).

Collaborative practice is essential to the effective safeguarding of children and the promotion of family care. Social workers require skills that enable them to offer effective interventions and to make realistic judgements about a family's situation while working effectively with all the practitioners involved and, most importantly, the parents. Thus, greater emphasis needs to be placed on communication skills and understanding the barriers to effective working as working together is a vital contribution to change (Hall, 1999; Waller, 2005; Warrin, 2007).

As suggested above, the art of inter-agency is essential for effective practice, but is not always achieved. The absence of inter-agency collaboration causes a breakdown in communication, delays in service delivery and general confusion and dissatisfaction with service users (Weinstein *et al.*, 2003). Research (Kroll and Taylor, 2003) suggests that there is often no cooperation between agencies due to the variety of support being offered by drug use workers and children and family social workers. Such inter-agency working, however, is vital to ensure all bases are covered (Hobart and Frankel, 2005). Problems regarding collaboration have existed within child protection since the 1960s (Howarth and Morrison, 2007), and surrounding issues have been well-documented (Milbourne *et al.*, 2003; Howarth and Morrison, 2007). These problems include: communication problems, poor understanding of roles and responsibilities, hierarchical issues and mistrust among professionals in sharing information (Howarth and Morrison, 2007).

Child protection is seen essentially as a team task; it is the issue of collaboration that is key to success (Murphy, 2004). In addition to inter-agency collaboration and assessment of an individual family's situation, partnerships between parents and practitioners are a vital aspect of social work practice. Hence, communication skills are essential to working together effectively with parents.

It has been recognized that the extent to which a social worker understands a family's situation enhances cooperation from parents (Cleaver *et al.*, 2003; Krane and Davies, 2000; Platt, 2006). The relationship between social workers and parents is vital to successful interventions (Ruch, 2005); in particular, the consistency between a social worker's understanding of a family's situation and the understanding of the child and parent (Platt, 2006). There may also be other issues that need addressing; for example, economic and environmental factors (Cleaver *et al.*, 1999). Drug use may be a result of additional stresses on family life, therefore, it must not be seen in isolation (Phillips, 2004). Service users are the most important participants in the collaborative process; they are the experts on their own individual situations and they have an opinion to give (Weinstein *et al.*, 2003). One way of preventing carers from feeling marginalized is to utilize the special understanding they have on their situation so as to engage them fully. However, it must be recognized that some professionals can feel threatened by this process and some service users may feel uncomfortable (Weinstein *et al.*, 2003). In these circumstances the relationship between service users and practitioners may take the form of a *defined partnership* with professionals acknowledging the need for expertise and understanding necessary to promote effective relationships and to be able to communicate successfully (Kirkpatrick *et al.*, 2007). Moreover, practitioners need to be able to provide an environment where parents feel comfortable to share, admit any difficulties, and feel empowered and supported. Parents deeply value trust and a non-judgemental attitude from practitioners (Kirkpatrick *et al.*, 2007).

Tackling the issue of *how* to engage families and conduct more detailed assessments is also a practical one in that services need to be delivered with proper provision for families. Part of this aspect would be thinking through where the best place is to 'enter the world' (Aldridge, 1999: 9) of families where parents use substances and how the needs of the family can be best met during that process. This aspect of the assessment process is about thinking through how it might feel as a parent to be subject to the kinds of detailed investigation that Aldridge suggests and how that process can best be made easier, which is particularly important in terms of making observations of families. Parents can be reluctant to attend substances services or social work buildings because of the lack of childcare facilities, stigma, perceived risks to children in waiting rooms and the difficulty of travelling to locations with children. These sorts of practicalities can particularly impact upon women's access to services as they are often the main carers of children (Harbin and Murphy, 2006; Klee *et al.*, 2002). These practicalities can have important effects; for example, Harbin and Murphy (2006) report on the 'Safer Families Project' in Bolton (2000) which had a parents' drop in group but despite offering transport and refreshments no one attended. The feedback was that the taboo of drug use and it being a group for parent drug users would put people off with fears also of confidentiality and meeting people they know. Evidence shows treatment and retention outcomes are better within those services which offer childcare provision (Klee *et al.*, 2002).

Crucial to assessments of families with parent(s) who use substances is the need to keep the child at the centre and any actions taken in relation to the parents' substance use need to be assessed in relation to the potential impact upon the child. A crucial and often overlooked source of information on the child's needs is the child itself (ACDM, 2003; Harbin and Murphy, 2006; Kroll and Taylor, 2003; Murphy and Harbin, 2000). Kroll and Taylor (2003) highlight that lack of child engagement in the process of assessment is due to workers' avoidance of a difficult and emotional task (often due to lack of training and confidence), children's loyalty to parents, fear of speaking out and mistrust of services, or difficulties in accessing children. These issues highlight the need for social workers to create the right context and relationship through which the child's views can be elicited.

Social workers should spend more time understanding a family's situation rather than feeling under pressure to follow procedures and to meet targets (Krane and Davies, 2000; McKeganey and Barnard, 2007). The relationship between the parent and social worker is important so they are able to work together. A parent needs to feel valued rather than feeling worthless, otherwise they are unlikely to engage and cooperate (Thom *et al.*, 2007). It is essential that agencies are in touch with a child and his or her parents (Warrin, 2007). Under the Children Act 1989, it is ultimately the need of the child not the parent that is the priority, but in practice the needs of the parent often coincide (Beckett and Maynard, 2005).

Drug use may not be particularly troublesome if it is limited, not chaotic and not necessarily weakening to a parent's ability to care for their child (Humphreys and Stanley, 2006). However, as we discussed earlier, parental drug use is now a significant feature in relation to children in need, and challenges professionals from child and family social work (Kroll, 2004). Social workers require skills that enable them to offer effective interventions and to make realistic judgements about a family's situation while working effectively with all the practitioners involved and, most importantly, the parents. Greater emphasis needs to be placed on communication skills and understanding the barriers to effective working, as working together is a vital contribution to change (Dixon, 2006; Hall, 1999; Waller, 2005; Warrin, 2007). Therefore, in order to learn from previous research, and not to replicate the well-established barriers to successful intervention, partnership working must be achieved (Warrin, 2007). There also needs to be a supportive environment established for individual practitioners to have ongoing training and practical support so they are able to offer the best services to families (Brandon *et al.*, 2006; Gupta and Blewett, 2007; Philips, 2004).

Implications for social work practice

Assessment is a major part of social work (Mantle *et al.*, 2008) and assessment and decision making are complex issues in child protection cases. Although social workers have become increasingly good at collecting information, often adhering to agency policies and procedures (Howe *et al.*, 2000), they still need to look at individual factors pertaining to families, especially when making decisions (Phillips, 2004). The concept of collaboration is vital to inter-agency working and the working together of parents and professionals. Emphasis should be placed on the establishment of a close and trusting relationship between parents and social workers which focuses on the ecological impact of parental drug abuse on individual families. Shared training and multidisciplinary teams may help to address the problems inherent in this process but practitioners should also reflect on their own practice: gaps in knowledge, judgements exercised, efforts made to engage with children and the procedural and resource limitations within which they work and seek to address all issues which currently prevent them from meeting families' holistic needs.

Aldridge's (1999) argument about the need to move beyond simplistic assessments of parental substance use in instances of concern for the child fits in well with both academic literature and the tone of recent policy documents and guidelines but the question remains as to how social care workers on the ground put his ideas into practice. While more holistic assessments are an important way forward, particularly in terms of better meeting the needs of the child, they also require shifts in practices around family engagement, inter-agency working and involvement of the child. The fleshing-out of a holistic assessment in terms of what it means to do that work in practice needs a lot of work. There is also an important and ongoing need for training and support for social care workers in this work. However, as Forrester *et al.* (2008: 1304) argue:

'The increasing emphasis on tight timescales and rapid turnover in carrying out assessments in social work may make using any person centred style of work difficult'. The shortage of resources is also, as Taylor and Kroll (2004: 1117) argue, it is 'a critical practice issue', getting in the way of holistic assessments of the family.

Organizational, resource and skills issues constantly threaten to interfere with this type of work being done but we must not lose sight of the importance of working with families, where the parents use substances, in a compassionate and holistic way understanding the positive impact it can have on family life and therefore the well-being of the child who should be at the centre of all assessments.

9 Meeting the challenge

It is the nature of the social work task that the starting point for most interventions will be a 'problem' of one sort or another. This may be compounded by those processes which tend to highlight the problematic aspects of certain substance users' characteristics, or behaviour, or their circumstances, or possibly a mixture of all three, and in the case of the use of illegal drugs the matter of actually breaking the law. Social workers may find themselves having to deal with these issues in order to achieve a proper focus on needs and expectations from their own perspective. They have a role in seeking to understand, then interpret and provide legitimacy for the judgements made about drug users, and their risks and needs. Those decisions will have a significant effect on the nature and extent of any future services or resources provided, as well as shaping the drug users' view of the service and their place in relation to it.

Distinguishing between what are normal, acceptable and manageable risks and those that need to be controlled in some way or removed is problematic. Allied to this is the use of authority and the impact this will have on relationships, where trust and a sense of mutuality may be difficult to achieve and even harder to sustain. The use of that power, even when you feel it is in your service user's best interest, will have consequences and may impact on your overall intervention strategy.

Working with illicit drug users in whatever setting will provoke management problems. These are the problems that drug use can cause you as a social worker; most noticeably legal problems. Under Section 8 of the Misuse of Drugs Act (MDA) 1971, it is an offence for a person responsible for a premise or service to knowingly allow drugs to be used or administered on those premises.[22] This was the legal provision used to prosecute John Brook and Ruth Wyner (the so-called Cambridge Two) who received long prison sentences in 1999 when it was found that heroin was being dealt at a day centre for the homeless that they ran in Cambridge.

Management problems are your problems. They may be cause or provoked by the person's use of drugs but they give you problems only you can deal with. Drug users will rarely recognize management problems as their problems. Most problematic, but arguably most crucial for drug users, is the question of how social work addresses the type of problem they encounter, which originates in inequality, discrimination and disadvantage. We know that social work typically engages with service users whose background and experiences often reflect a history of social exclusion, and that this forms the context for any practice intervention. It is therefore crucial that practitioners do not overlook this, or fall prey to 'victim blaming', by applying standards and norms which are simply unrealistic in the light of drug users' circumstances.

It may also be part of the social work task to challenge the ways in which drug users are seen. Legal issues create barriers to appropriate care, support and treatment for HIV-positive and HCV injecting drug users (IDUs), and the prevention of HIV and HCV infection among IDUs as discussed in Chapter 3. In particular, service providers may be caught between legal constraints and ethical demands in providing services to IDUs. The legal status of drugs contributes to the difficulties encountered in addressing HIV and HCV among IDUs. However, analysis of legal and ethical issues related to HIV/AIDS and HCV and IDU has shown that much can be done now, without waiting for much-needed legal changes, within the current legal framework; indeed, much must be done, as ethical analysis reveals, because current approaches do not withstand ethical scrutiny.

This obviously has a number of significant implications for practice. It may well necessitate taking a positive position in relation to substance users whose behaviour is viewed as unacceptable or worthy of condemnation, such as parents who continue to use substances as discussed in Chapter 8. It is important to distinguish clearly between behaviour which will not be tolerated and the substance user who should none the less be treated with respect and valued.

An important part of the social work task is to work with the substance user to deal with the implications of being labelled or defined in purely negative terms. The influence of others' attitudes and characterizations may confirm individuals' perceptions of themselves as having limited self-worth. As highlighted in Chapter 3 the stigma attached to drug users and in particular those who have contracted HIV/AIDS and/or HCV sits at the heart of the problem. A vicious circle has been established, with the prevalence of discrimination and prejudice found in all spheres, both formally and informally.

As we discussed in Chapters 4 and 8 the issues of disclosure and confidentiality are closely linked with stigma; that is, it has been shown here that the above-mentioned issues serve to reinforce a blame culture. The prohibitive effects of the stigma related to HIV/AIDS and HCV are generally not found with any other life-threatening illness, which usually elicit sympathetic responses both at a societal and professional level. Chapter 3 identified that fundamentally there is a lack of understanding in relation to stigma and the real effects this has on the children and families affected by HIV/AIDS and HCV. Issues of confidentiality and disclosure, necessary mechanisms for the protection of individuals' privacy and well-being, none the less serve to reinforce and maintain the invisibility of the affected. It is necessary for understanding, across the social and professional spectrum, to be promoted and a healthy balance made between individuals' rights and the short and long-term well-being of the children and families affected.

In order to avoid the negativity attached to drug use those affected through fear of discrimination prevent themselves from seeking the help they need. This, in terms of social service provision, policy decisions and funding allocation indicates that there is no need to be met, and therefore to a certain degree, the extent of the problem remains hidden. And so the cycle continues.

The aim should be to generate a more open understanding of different and possibly competing accounts of drug users. The distinction between 'deserving' and 'undeserving' cases should be questioned and unacknowledged processes of discrimination and selection made clear. Effective practice needs to be self-conscious, and to take an actively critical view of the impact of language and narratives on outcomes for drug users. It is a continuing task of social workers to test assumptions, including their own, especially where these are linked to popular and powerful beliefs about drug users, in general, or certain sub-groups in particular.

However, meaningful and progressive social work practice also has to deal with a number of professional uncertainties and institutional constraints, especially for those working in statutory settings. One of the key roles of social work is to develop effective therapeutic relationships with service users within these structural and organizational restraints (Wilson *et al.*, 2011). It is very difficult to balance these complex and at times competing perspectives especially when working with people engaged in an illegal activity such as illicit drug-taking.

Social workers have to make assessments of people's lives, often at times of major crisis. Assumptions about what is normal behaviour underpin professional judgements about what are the limits of acceptable and appropriate behaviour. It can be very hard to challenge our basic values and perceptions. Yet it is essential that we as social workers challenge our definitions of 'normal' and 'good enough' before we start to make judgements about other people's lives.

Social workers have the power to act on their judgements and alter people's lives in far-reaching ways. It is our professional responsibility to become conscious of how we make judgements. This is not a once and for all task, but a process which needs to be kept under scrutiny throughout our working lives.

There is a relationship between attitude and behaviour. The General Social Care Council (GSCC) (2002) quite rightly requires social workers to be aware of discrimination and develop a practice style which challenges it. All of us carry some kind or level of prejudice. Prejudice works at the level of attitudes and feelings. Prejudice is learnt, it is not innate. It consists of prejudgements based either on internalized stereotypical misinformation or correct but selective facts (Stern with Clough, 1996).

Stereotypes have an important function in the transmission of ideologies which maintain inequalities. Ideas and ideologies are important in establishing what is considered to be 'normal' and 'natural' and therefore what is thought of as 'deviant' and 'abnormal'. Most of the stereotypes we hold relate to groups to which we ourselves do not belong. There is a tendency for us to see our own group as individuals rather than stereotypically. Categorizing people on the basis of limited information is unfortunately a practical necessity of everyday life. The key factors are whether the classification is based on accurate information in the first place, and how such material will be used (Stern with Clough, 1996).

Antidiscriminatory practice (ADP) developed from the growing recognition of the discriminations and oppressions derived from the inequalities of gender, race, class, age, disability and sexual orientation. Antidiscriminatory practice (ADP) as defined by the GSCC does not mean that everybody is to be treated the same in all circumstances. Treating people as individuals properly will mean treating them differently. In essence, this is an aspect of recognizing 'to each according to need'.

It is essential to distinguish between treating people as individuals (and therefore differently – with not everyone getting the same service) from discrimination between people (as individuals, or groups) on the grounds of stereotypes: the latter means treating a person differently because of stereotypes attached to membership of a particular group.

Dependent on which of Dominelli's (2009) schools of social work, which we discussed at the beginning of the introductory chapter, you most identify with, there is a division between those who see social work as part of a movement which aims to transform the social structure and those who consider that ADP can be achieved within existing liberal capitalist societies. This is one of the most underdeveloped aspects of ADP writings. Nevertheless, despite such disagreements, there are a set of common themes which run through the progressive social work literature and which are useful as ways of starting to think about antidiscrimination.

Antidiscriminatory practice (ADP) philosophy is predominantly about the recognition that social work is deep-rooted within a complex set of power relations. First, there is the power imbalance between social groups which is institutionalized as the unequal distribution of power and opportunities within social relationships and institutions which comprise the social structure (Thompson, 2008).

Second, it relates to the way in which professional power has contributed to discrimination towards service users (Hugman, 2007). Antidiscriminatory practice (ADP) acknowledges this and seeks to use professional power differently – not to assume you always know best and impose action without consultation, but to promote participation and self-direction for those you work with wherever possible.

Social work might not be able to compensate for all the structural power inequalities in society but social workers can avoid reproducing them in their practice and contribute to and help to shape good practice. Although social work represents the exercise of professional and legal power as it resides in one arm of the state, ADP is about changing the way in which that power has traditionally been exercised.

Power and empowerment are key themes in ADP philosophy. As discussed in Chapter 7, empowerment is the philosophy underpinning the 'user movement' and refers to the collective voicing of need in order to increase people's power, resources and control over life. It is about overcoming powerlessness and marginalization in all aspects of service delivery. Empowerment is both a goal and a process for overcoming oppression, and contains a view of people as being able to act positively to change their circumstances given the opportunity.

Chapter 7's emphasis on collective action is echoed in much literature which promotes the use of group work – self-advocacy groups, support groups, groups for raising self-esteem, self-help groups, tenants' groups, food co-ops and a whole range of others. In Chapter 8 we discussed the importance of working together which sets the backdrop for both the Children Acts 1989, 2004 which is seen as vital to achieve an effective outcome for families: inter-agency collaboration and communication is essential to effective working. Such methods involve developing appropriate services in consultation with users. The injunction for social workers to build upon the strengths of individuals and communities derives from the recognition that while people may be marginalized and victimized, this does not make them passive victims unable to do anything for themselves.

Clearly, this is a complex and difficult area and there is still much confusion over the basic premises of ADP, its theory base and what constitutes principles of good practice but fundamentally ADP is centrally concerned with challenging oppression in its various forms. Even the most committed social worker recognizes that ADP is hard. Social work itself is difficult, and challenging established practices, policies and attitudes adds to the burden. Antidiscriminatory practice (ADP) is possible and is being carried out creatively in many situations, establishments and agencies but it requires skill and certain working conditions for effective work to take place (McPherson, 2010; Thompson, 2009).

An important focus of ADP work is recognizing the relationship between private problems and public issues – between private problems and the processes of disadvantage and discrimination which impact on an individual's life.

We need to consider the individual in the social context of their experiences. The unit of social work analysis becomes not the inadequacy of the individual or family, but the structures which shape their lives. This does not mean that social workers ignore individual problems; rather, that these problems are located within the social arrangements which often give rise to them. Individuals do not exist in social vacuums; their experiences and opportunities are structured by the organization of the society they live in, and it is this organization which gives rise to most of the social problems experienced by those who end as social work service users (Stern with Clough, 1996).

This is overlaid with the avoidance of 'hierarchies of oppression' (i.e., questioning who is more oppressed than whom, and according to what criteria) and that we must have an integrated approach and recognize the connections between oppressions. This poses many problems, not least because each oppressed group is implicated in the oppression of other groups. It is not the case that there is one dominant group which oppresses all others but that there are networks of oppressions criss-crossing various social groups in complex ways.

Almost by definition, substance users who become service users will be marginalized in one way or another, and sometimes they will experience multiple discriminations. The commitment of social work to anti-oppressive practice requires the profession to adopt a critical view of those attitudes and beliefs which misrepresent drug users, both individually and collectively (Thompson, 2008).

Social work with drug users is significantly influenced by many of the wider tensions and challenges encapsulated within the relationship between the wider society and its drug-using members. That this is the case for many, if not most, drug users, only generates a more acute sense of challenge and discontinuity for drug users who are marginalized in one or more senses; that is, the population with whom social work is most likely to engage.

Social work is expected to adopt a commitment to 'human rights' and to pursue social justice and to challenge 'discrimination and exclusion' (GSCC, 2007: 7). To that end it is the place of social work practice to achieve social justice for drug users, especially those who are excluded in some way. In acknowledging the importance of structural factors and societal attitudes, social workers should explicitly 'side' with drug users who use social work services, in the sense that they are likely to be experiencing disadvantage, or victimization by virtue of their position as service users. In contrast to widely-held concerns about the 'threat' represented by drug users, the aim of social work should be to restate the importance of listening to them, taking their concerns seriously, and challenging the discrimination they encounter. A necessary feature of social work practice with drug users is, indeed, a commitment to social justice.

Glossary

Abstinence   refraining from licit and/or illicit drug use.

Amphetamine   one of a class of drugs with a powerful stimulant action on the central nervous system.

Amyl nitrite   part of the nitrites drug group. Known as 'poppers' – 'rushing' effects when inhaled.

Benzodiazepine   a group of structurally related drugs used mainly as sedatives/hypnotics.

Cannabis   derived from the cannabis plant. The most important psychoactive ingredients are the tetrahydrocannabinols (THC). Cannabis with very high THC content ('skunk', 'northern lights') is increasingly being grown in the UK.

Class of drug   a system that defines legal penalties for the possession, cultivation and trafficking of different drugs (*see* MDA 1971).

Cocaine   a powerful central nervous system stimulant.

Crack/rock cocaine   highly pure form of the freebase of cocaine.

Dependence   a cluster of symptoms that indicate a person has impaired control over their psychoactive substance use.

Ecstasy   *see* MDMA.

GBH and GBL   Gamma-hydroxybutyrate (GHB) and Gamma-butyrolactone (GBL) Originally synthesized for use as an anaesthetic, they are used recreationally for their sedative and anaesthetic effects.

Heroin   a simple derivative of morphine. Heroin is the most widely used illicit opioid because of its potency, availability, solubility in water and speed with which it crosses the blood-brain barrier.

Illicit drug   a psychoactive substance, the production, sale, possession or use of which is prohibited.

Ketamine   a dissociative anaesthetic with central nervous system depressant, stimulant, analgesic and hallucinogenic effects. Some ketamine users may experience a feeling of almost complete sensory detachment that is likened to a near-death experience; known as the 'K-hole'.

Legal highs unregulated psychoactive substances. New and emerging synthetic and plant-derived substances and products, including 'research chemicals', 'party pills' and 'herbal highs', which are usually sold via the Internet or in head shops.

Licit drug a drug that is legally available with or without a medical prescription.

LSD (Lysergic acid diethylamide) a semi-synthetic product of lysergic acid, a natural substance from the parasitic rye fungus that induces alterations in perception, thinking and feeling.

Magic mushrooms the effects of psilocybin-containing mushrooms are similar to a mild LSD experience.

MDA 1971 (Misuse of Drug Act 1971) legislation that aims to control the possession, cultivation and trafficking of certain psychoactive substances.

MDMA (methylenedioxymethamphetamine) a synthetic derivative of amphetamine, exhibiting both stimulant and mild hallucinogenic properties. Effects include feelings of euphoria and solidarity, heightened sensory awareness and ease of contact with others. Commonly known as ecstasy, a wide range of substances may appear in varying concentrations in ecstasy tablets. Most ecstasy tablets now available in the UK no longer contain MDMA.

Methadone a synthetic opioid drug.

Opioid the generic term applied to alkaloids from the opium poppy, their synthetic analogues, and compounds synthesised within the body.

Over-the-counter products drugs that are available from a chemist without prescription.

Polysubstance use the use of more than one drug or type of drug by an individual, often concurrently or sequentially.

Psilocybin a naturally occurring hallucinogen found in certain species of mushroom.

Psychoactive drug or substance a substance that when ingested affects mental processes.

Relapse a return to drinking or other substance use after a period of abstinence.

Stimulant any agent that activates, enhances or increases neural activity.

Withdrawal a group of symptoms of variable degree of severity which occur on cessation, or reduction of use of a psychoactive substance that has been taken repeatedly, usually for a prolonged period and/or in high doses.

Contacts

There are several easy ways to access substance use specialists in your local area or geographical region:

Local (or national) agencies

- Contact your local **Drug and Alcohol Action Team (DAAT)**. Each region in England has a DAAT (or DAT – Drug Action Team) – a statutory service that provides a range of drug and alcohol services in the region. To find your local DAAT/DAT, go to the National Treatment Agency website (see below) and look under the drop down menu 'About Treatment' for 'Treatment Directories'. Click on 'Local DAT Directories', find your region and nearest town and email or telephone the contact listed. Most DAATs will offer free training for social work professionals as well as training student groups.
- **Helpfinder** is a database of drug agencies (some of whom will accept both alcohol and drug-using service users) provided by Drugscope, the UK's leading charity on drug use and related policy matters. Click on the 'Search Helpfinder' hyperlink then complete the search form with as much or as little data as you can. For example, you could search by town or by drug or by the type of treatment offered. Summary details and contacts are given and can be found at www.drugscope.org.uk/resources/databases/helpfinder.htm.
- Services in **Scotland** can be found on the *Scottish Drugs Forum directory* at www.scottishdrugservices.com/sdd/homepage.htm.
- Services for **Northern Ireland** can be found at www.drugsalcohol.info/.
- Services in **Wales** can be found at www.dan247.org.uk/Services_Drugs_Alcohol.asp.

For local (or national) service users

- Most DAATs or DATs will have a **service-user coordinator** whose role is to facilitate service user involvement in the design, delivery and evaluation of services. Some will also have or want experience of public speaking or training. Contact your local DAAT/DAT (see above) and ask for the service user coordinator's details.
- Many voluntary sector alcohol and drug agencies now have **service user groups** established to support the development and evaluation of the service and/or to provide a supportive peer group for those attending the service. Call your local alcohol or drug agency and ask if they have a service user group or, if not, any service user representatives they could approach on your behalf to ask about taking part in training.
- **Black Poppy** is a small voluntary sector organization that produces a website and magazine run by drug users. It has a contacts and links section that lists drug-user forums and groups and special interest groups; for example, women's groups, as well as listing other links and useful resources and can be found at www.blackpoppy.org.uk/blackpoppy/contacts.htm.

Useful websites and other sources of information

SWAP   SWAP is the UK subject centre for social policy and social work, and is one of the Higher Education Academy's 24 discipline-based centres. SWAP aims to enhance the student learning experience by promoting high-quality learning, teaching and assessment. SWAP produces many publications which you can view and/or download. There is material specifically about social work and drug use but have a look at the site generally at www.swap.ac.uk/index.html.

Social Work, Alcohol and Drugs   This is a very good introductory website developed by *Sarah Galvani*. The objective of the website is to provide social workers with accessible information on substance use that is geared specifically towards the social work profession, its roles, values and responsibilities. Social work and social care practitioners and academics who wish to share information, exchange ideas, seek views and advice, or learn about good practice in relation to alcohol and drugs. See www.swalcdrugs.com/.

National Treatment Agency for Substance Misuse (NTA)   The NTA is a Special Health Authority established by the UK government to increase the availability, capacity and effectiveness of treatment for drug misuse in England: see www.nta.nhs.uk.

Home Office: Research Development and Statistics Directorate (RDS)   This directorate produces a variety of publications on a wide range of Home Office issues, including drug misuse. Lists and downloads of their recent publications are available at www.homeoffice.gov.uk/rds.

Health Development Agency (HDA)   The HDA identifies the evidence of what works to improve people's health and reduce health inequalities. In partnership with professionals, policy-makers and practitioners, it develops guidance and works across sectors to get evidence into practice. See www. hda-online.org.uk/index.html.

Drugscope   Drugscope is an independent UK charity concerned with drug information and policy. The charity is a merger between the Institute for the Study of Drug Dependence (ISDD) and the Standing Conference on Drug Abuse (SCODA). The website contains information on UK trends and updates, an events calendar, information on European drug laws and access to drug prevention and education resources. There is also a drug search facility; a searchable drug encyclopaedia giving information on drug news, history, law, effects and risks. See www.drugscope.org.uk/.

FRANK   Supporting the joint Department of Health and Home Office communications campaign, FRANK, which was launched in May 2003, is a free helpline offering 24-hour, 365 days a year confidential advice, information and support to anyone concerned about drug and solvent/volatile substance misuse, including drug misusers, their families, friends or carers. See www. talktofrank.com/.

The Society for the Prevention of Solvent and Volatile Substance Abuse – Re-Solv   Re-Solv is a national charity solely dedicated to the prevention of solvent and volatile substance abuse (VSA). See www.re-solv.org.

Transform Drug Policy Foundation   The Transform Drug Policy Foundation is arguably the UK's leading think tank and campaign that exists to promote sustainable health and well-being by bringing about a just, effective and humane system to regulate and control drugs at local, national and international levels. While not about treatment, it is a useful resource on the debate surrounding prohibition, legalization and regulation of drugs. See www.tdpf. org.uk/.

The British Liver Trust   This Trust provides excellent information and advice on hepatitis and liver disease connected to drug and alcohol use. It is a very useful site for those who want to know more about hepatitis C and B. See www. britishlivertrust.org.uk/home.aspx.

Lifeline Lifeline is a drug information and treatment agency, best known for its 'cartoon' approach to drug information, based in Manchester, with offices in other parts of England. See www.lifeline.org.uk/.

The National Drugs Helpline The National Drugs Helpline is a helpline where calls are free, and trained telephone advisers provide confidential advice and information about drugs and available local drug services nationwide. Telephone 0800 776600 and can be found at www.urban75.com/Drugs/helpline.html.

Alcohol Concern Alcohol Concern is the leading national organization with issues surrounding alcohol use. The Alcohol Concern website contains a wealth of information about related issues and useful links to many other alcohol-related websites. See www.alcoholconcern.org.uk/.

Adfam Adfam is a national charity that works with families affected by someone's alcohol or drug use. It provides news and project updates, hosts a database of support services and provides some stories of people who have a loved one with a substance problem. See www.adfam.org.uk/.

Release Release provides confidential information and advice on the legal aspects of drug use. Telephone 0845 4500 215 and can be found at www.release.org.uk/.

HIT HIT is a drug-training and information agency based on Merseyside. Telephone 0844 4120972 and can be found at www.hit.org.uk/.

NICE (National Institute for Health and Clinical Excellence) NICE is the independent organization responsible for providing national guidance on the promotion of good health and the prevention and treatment of ill-health. NICE guidance has been developed by a number of independent advisory groups made up of health professionals, those working in the NHS, patients, their carers and the public. See www.nice.org.uk/.

International sources of information

Drugtext Drugtext has information on all aspects of drug use, from very basic to complex. Based in Holland; it has its own online library. See www.drugtext.org/.

The Drug Policy Alliance (DPA)   The DPA is based in the USA and publishes a range of materials, including reports and fact sheets on drug policy issues. They also have a large collection of online materials devoted to drugs and drug policy. See www.drugpolicy.org/.

EMCDDA (European Monitoring Centre for Drugs and Drug Addiction) The EMCDDA is the EU drugs agency. This is an excellent organization providing a host of good-quality information. The library holds most of their recent publications (in English). It provides the Community and its Member States with comparable information at European level concerning drugs and drug addiction and their consequences. It monitors the drugs situation and analyses the responses to this situation. The agency also plays a key role in implementing the EU joint action on new synthetic drugs as well as monitoring national and Community strategies and policies and their impact on the drug situation. See www.emcdda.europa.eu/.

UNODC (United Nations Office on Drugs and Crime)   The UNODC is a wide-ranging programme that includes publicity on the dangers of drug misuse, and statistics. See www.unodc.org/unodc/index.html.

Worldwide/miscellaneous

BBC World Drugs Site
www.news.bbc.co.uk/hi/english/static/in_depth/world/2000/drugs_trade/default.stm
Canadian Centre on Substance Abuse
www.ccsa.ca/Pages/Splash.htm
Center for Interpersonal Development
www.cid1.com/index.html
Cocaine Anonymous World Services Online
www.ca.org/
Doctor's Guide to the Internet – Doctor's Guide HomePage
www.docguide.com/dgc.nsf/ge/Unregistered.User.545434?OpenDocument
DRUGS, DRUG TESTING
www.streetdrugs.org/
Drug Wise: Newsletter on Psychotropic Drugs
www.home.vicnet.net.au/~drugwise/drugwise.htm
High Times
www.hightimes.com/
National Clearinghouse for Alcohol and Drug Information
www.ncadi.samhsa.gov/
National Institute on Drug Abuse
www.nida.nih.gov/

The Stanton Peele Addiction Website
www.peele.net/
Web of Addictions
www.well.com/user/woa/
Vienna NGO Committee on Narcotic Drugs
www.vngoc.org/

Notes

1 We acknowledge the problem of using the term 'social exclusion' to denote those on the margins of society (see Levitas, 1998; Williams, 1998; Munck, 2005).

2 Dominelli (2009) offers three schools or types of professional social work intervention: maintenance, therapeutic and emancipatory. Earlier Payne (1996) offered three very similar perspectives: Individual reformist, socialist collectivist and reflexive therapeutic. This 'siloing' of positions is quite crude – perhaps more relevant to what Froggett (2002) describes as 'old welfare' (see Stenner and Taylor, 2008 for reflections on 'psychosocial' work) – but quite helpful in highlighting the heated conflicts around values and principles surrounding social work. In Dominelli's defence her text is an 'introductory' one. See also Chapters 3 and 4 in Wilson *et al.* (2008).

3 While there are a number of views regarding what social work is, these are limited in comparison with opinions on what constitutes a 'drug'. This is explored in depth in Chapter 1. While the use of the term 'substance' is not without its problems (arguably too wide a term) but in order to achieve a degree of consistency henceforth we endeavour to use the term 'substance use' (encompassing legal, illegal and prescribed drugs or over the counter (OTC) drugs) other than when making a distinction between them or using the terms; for example, 'alcohol' and 'drugs' to illustrate a particular point. See Hammersley (2008) for an excellent discussion around 'What are drugs?'

4 DANOS – the Drugs and Alcohol National Occupational Standards – specify the standards of performance that people in the drugs and alcohol field should be working to. They also describe the knowledge and skills workers need in order to perform to the required standard. Used in a very straightforward way, DANOS standards allow *individual workers* to be perfectly clear about what is expected of them in their work. Workers can check that they are doing a good job. They can also identify any knowledge they need to acquire the skills they need to develop (www.alcohol-drugs.co.uk/DANOS/DANOS.html).

5 Regulation 5 of the Local Safeguarding Children Boards Regulations (LSCBs) 2006 requires LSCBs to undertake reviews of serious cases. These reviews are known as serious case reviews (SCRs).

6 This is not a peculiarly British problem. Evidence suggests that this is a common problem with social work education throughout the world.

7 There is a long and unsavoury history within Western culture linking 'men of colour' with drug-taking and more recently drug-dealing. From the 1920s and the Fu Manchu novels of Sax Rohmer – with their tales of innocent English virgins being seduced into crime and sexual perversion by an evil Chinese genius who lurked within the opium dens of Edwardian Britain – through to the Blaxploitation movies of the 1970s. See Berridge (1984) and Marsh and Melville (2009).

8 These are the two main illicit opium-producing areas. The Golden Triangle overlaps the mountains of four countries in Southeast Asia: Burma, Vietnam, Laos and Thailand. The Golden Crescent overlaps three nations, Afghanistan, Iran and Pakistan, whose mountainous peripheries define the crescent, though only Afghanistan and Pakistan produce opium, with Iran being a consumer and trans-shipment route.

9 Harm reduction is described and discussed in more detail in Chapter 2.

10 As we explained in the introductory chapter we endeavour to use the term substance use other than when referring to a particular drug or making a distinction between and/or using the terms 'alcohol' and 'drugs' to illustrate a particular point.

11 Drug action teams (DATs) or Drug and Alcohol Action Teams (DAATs) are the multi-agency partnerships working to implement the National Drug Strategy at a local level taking strategic decisions on expenditure and service delivery within the aims of the National Drugs Strategy. The DATs/DAATs ensure that the work of local agencies is brought together effectively and that cross-agency projects are coordinated successfully.

12 An alternative perspective on social perceptions of drug users has been provided by the work of the Manchester 'normalization' school of thought which was developed in the early 1990s. Parker et al.'s (1998) normalization thesis supports the US studies of Hirsch et al. (1990), Hathaway (1997) and Hallstone (2002) in suggesting that social attitudes to UK recreational drug users (as with US marijuana smokers) are changing from a focus on exclusion and outsiders, to acceptance and 'normalized' use. A key feature of normalization is that recreational use of drugs such as cannabis is becoming increasingly socially accepted and no longer the taboo that it once was, with prevalence of drug use increasing across the 1990s to peak in the millennium years with nearly half of young people experimenting with illegal drugs and up to one in ten going on to become regular users. As drug users reached their twenties and thirties, while the regularity of drug use may decline, the North West England longitudinal study found that occasional usage continued to feature and be fitted

around the changing demands of adult lives such as employment, parenting and housework (Aldridge *et al.*, 2011; Measham *et al.*, 2011). The key point of difference here is that it challenges Becker's (1963) analysis of marijuana-smoking jazz musicians and the processes of labelling by suggesting that drug users are no longer identified by oppositional values but are indistinguishable from non-drug users. Therefore drug users (if not drug use) can be considered 'normal', at least in terms of users being spread across the social spectrum and no longer identifiable simply by gender, ethnicity or social class.

13 The Diagnostic and Statistical Manual of Mental Disorders (DSM) is published by the American Psychiatric Association. It is used primarily in the USA by researchers and psychiatric drug regulation agencies. The DSM has attracted controversy since it was first published in 1952 and is now is in its fifth edition.

14 The human immunodeficiency virus (HIV) attacks the body's immune system. If your immune system is damaged by HIV, it increases the risk of developing a serious infection or disease, such as cancer. HIV is spread through the exchange of bodily fluids. There is no cure for HIV and no vaccine to stop you becoming infected. Acquired immune deficiency syndrome (AIDS) is a term that is used to describe the late stage of HIV. A recent House of Lords (2011) select committee reported that current efforts to prevent the spread of HIV and AIDS in Britain were 'woefully inadequate', amid rising infection rates and sharp increases in the cost of treating the disease. The number of patients treated for HIV/AIDS has trebled since 2000 and will pass 100 000 in 2012. Commenting on the report the chairman Lord Fowler said: 'Many feel themselves isolated because of their condition; there are frequent examples of discrimination, ranging from sufferers being ostracized in their communities to people losing their jobs following disclosure of their HIV status'.

15 Hepatitis C is a blood-borne virus (BBV) that predominantly infects the cells of the liver. It was identified in 1989 (DoH, 2002), with a test to establish its presence developed in early 1990 (Anti Discrimination Board of New South Wales, 2001). Hepatitis C is repeatedly described as a major concern to public health (Acejas and Rhodes, 2007; Winter *et al.*, 2008) as a 'global burden' (Lazarus *et al.*, 2007) with both an academic and policy focus on reducing the spread of the disease through testing treatment and education (DoH, 2004; DoH, 2002; Department of Health Social Services and Public Safety, 2007; Galindo *et al.*, 2007; Grebely *et al.*, 2008; Mateu-Gelabert *et al.*, 2007; Scottish Executive, 2006; The Scottish Government, 2008).

16 Gould (2006) presents a useful critique of randomized control trials.

17 A guide has been developed by the National Treatment Agency (NTA) (2010) in conjunction with the British Psychological Society that aims to help social workers make better use of 'talking therapies' to support substance misusers overcoming dependency.

18 The latest drug strategy (HM Government, 2010) suggested it was time to update *models of care for treatment of adult substance misusers* in the light of the

growing focus on 'recovery' (see Chapter 6). Currently, the NTA is consulting on the development of a new framework (see NTA, 2011).

19   DECLARE and SCARS are original models that have been devised by Trevor McCarthy. The SCARS model was originally presented to the New Directions in the Study of Alcohol Group annual conference in April 2002. (See McCarthy and Galvani, 2004.)

20   This point introduces ideas of 'risk' and a consideration as to whether a recovery model could ever be fully implemented. See the section on 'risk' (Chapter 6, p. 89).

21   This is the term we have chosen to use throughout the book.

22   Section 38 of the *Criminal Justice and Police Act 2001* would have extended Section 8 of the *Misuse of Drugs Act 1971* to include all illegal drugs. Fortunately, the government were persuaded that the extension of Section 8 could restrict the ability of social care agencies to deliver harm reduction (HR) services to some of the most vulnerable people and this provision was never implemented.

References

Acejas, C. and Rhodes, T. (2007) Global estimates of the prevalence of HCV infection among injecting drug users, *International Journal of Drug Policy*, 18: 352–58.

ACMD (2007) *Hidden Harm Three Years On: Realities, Challenges and Opportunities: Executive Summary*. Available online at www.homeoffice.gov.uk/publications/alcohol-drugs/drugs/acmd1/HiddenHarm20071.pdf?view=Binary (accessed 6 October 2011).

Adams, R., Dominelli, L. and Payne, M. (eds) (2009) *Practising Social Work in a Complex World*. Basingstoke: Palgrave Macmillan.

Advisory Council on the Misuse of Drugs (ACMD) (1988) *AIDS and Drug Misuse Report: Part 1*. London: Her Majesty's Stationery Office (HMSO).

Advisory Council on the Misuse of Drugs (2003) *Hidden Harm Responding to the Needs of Children of Problem Drug Users*. London: Home Office.

Advisory Council on the Misuse of Drugs (2006) *Pathways to Problems*. Available online at www.ias.org.uk/pathways/pathways.pdf (accessed 7 September 2011).

Advisory Council on the Misuse of Drugs (forthcoming) *Polysubstance Use*. London: Home Office.

Advisory Council on the Misuse of Drugs (2009) *The Primary Prevention of Hepatitis C Among Injecting Drug Users*. London: Home Office.

Aitken, C.K., Kerger, M. and Crofts, N. (2002) Peer-delivered hepatitis C testing and counselling: a means of improving the health of injecting drug users, *Drug and Alcohol Review*, 21: 33–7.

Akers, R. (2000) *Criminological Theories: Introduction and Evaluation*. Los Angeles: Roxbury.

Akhatar, S. and South, N. (2000) Hidden from heroin's history: heroin use and dealing within an English Asian community, in M. Hough and M. Natarajan (eds) *International Drug Markets: From Research to Policy, Crime Prevention Studies*, Vol. 11. New York: Criminal Justice Press.

Aldridge, J. (2008) Decline but no fall? New millennium trends in young people's use of illegal and illicit drugs in Britain, *Health Education*, 108(3): 189–206.

Aldridge, J., Measham, F. and Williams, L. (2011) *Illegal Leisure Revisited*. London: Routledge.

Aldridge, J., Parker, H. and Measham, F. (1999) *Drug Trying and Drug Use Across Adolescence: A Longitudinal Study of Young People's Drug Taking in Two Regions of Northern England*, Drugs Prevention Advisory Service Paper No.1. London: Home Office.

Aldridge, T. (1999) Family values: rethinking children's needs living with drug-using parents, *Drug Link*, 14(2): 8–11.

Allen, N. (2005) *Making Sense of the Children Act*. Chichester: John Wiley & Sons.

Allman, D., Myers, T., Schellenberg, J., Strike, C., Cockerill, R. and Cavalieri, W. (2007) Improving health and social care relationships for harm reduction, *International Journal of Drug Policy*, 18(3): 194–203.

Anglin, M.D. (1988) The efficacy of civil commitment in treating narcotic addiction, in C. Leukefeld and F. Tims (eds) *Compulsory Treatment of Drug Abuse: Research and Clinical Practice*, NIDA Research Monograph 86, DHHS Publication Number ADM 89–1578. Washington, DC: US Government Press.

Anti-Discrimination Board of New South Wales (2001) Appendix E: An epidemic of difference: a social analysis of hepatitis C-related discrimination, in *C-change. Report of the Enquiry into Hepatitis C Related Discrimination*. Sydney: Anti-Discrimination Board of New South Wales, pp. 136–47.

Antle, B.J., Wells, L.M., Goldie, R.S., DeMatteo, D. and King, S.M. (2001) Challenges of parenting for families living with HIV/AIDS, *Social Work*, 46(2): 159–69.

Association of Chief Police Officers (ACPO) (2009) *Guidance on Cannabis Possession for Personal Use: Revised Intervention Framework*. London: ACPO.

Bandura, A. (1977) *Social Learning Theory*. New York: Englewood Cliffs.

Barber, J.G. (1995) *Social Work with Addictions*. London: Macmillan.

Barber, J.G. (2002) *Social Work with Addictions* (2nd edn). Basingstoke: Palgrave Macmillan.

Barber, J.P., Luborsky, L., Gallop, R., Crits-Christoph, P., Frank, A., Weiss, R.D., Thase, M.E., Connolly, M.B., Gladis, M., Foltz, C. and Siqueland, L. (2001) Therapeutic alliance as a predictor of outcome and retention in The National Institute On Drug Abuse Collaborative Cocaine Treatment Study, *Journal of Consulting and Clinical Psychology*, 69: 119–24.

Bean, P. (2002) *Drugs and Crime*. Cullompton: Willan Publishing.

Bean, P. (2004) *Drugs and Crime* (2nd edn). Cullompton: Willan Publishing.

Beck, A.T. (1993) *Cognitive Therapy of Substance Abuse*. New York: Guilford Press.

Becker, H. (1963) *Outsiders; Studies in the Sociology of Deviance*. London: Free Press.

Beckett, C. and Maynard, A. (2005) *Values and Ethics in Social Work: An Introduction*. London: Sage Publications.

Bennett, L. and O'Brien, P. (2007) Effects of co-ordinated services for drug abusing women who are victims of intimate partner violence, *Violence Against Women*, 13: 395–411.

Benson, K. and Hartz, A. (2000) A comparison of observational studies and randomized, controlled trials, *New England Journal of Medicine*, 342: 1878–86.

Beresford, P. (2002) Thinking about 'mental health': towards a social model, *Journal of Mental Health*, 11(6): 581–84.

Beresford, P. (2005) 'Service user': regressive or libertory terminology? *Disablity and Society*, 4(20): 469–77.

Berg, I.K. and Shafer, K.C. (2004) Working with mandated substance abusers – the language of solutions, in S.L.A. Straussner (ed.) *Clinical Work with Substance-abusing Clients* (2nd edn.). New York: Guilford Press.

Berger, B.E., Estwing Ferrans, C. and Lashley, F.R. (2001) Measuring stigma in people with HIV: psychometric assessment of the HIV stigma scale, *Research in Nursing and Health Volume*, 24(6): 518–29.

Berridge, V. (1979) Morality and medical science: concepts of narcotic addiction in Britain, 1820–1926, *Annals of Science*, 36: 67–85.

Berridge, V. (1984) Drugs and social policy: the establishment of drug control in Britain 1900–30, *British Journal of Addiction*, 79(1): 17–29.

Berridge, V. (1996) *AIDS in the UK: The Making of Policy 1981–1984*. London: Oxford University Press.

Best, D., Groshkova, T. and McTague, P. (2009) The politics of recovery, *Druglink*, 24(4): 14–19.

Best, D., Noble, A., Finch, E., Gossop, M., Sidwell, C. and Strang, J. (1999) Accuracy of perceptions of hepatitis B and C status: cross sectional investigation of opiate addicts in treatment, *British Medical Journal*, 319: 290–91.

Best, D., Loaring, J., Ghufran, S. and Day, E. (2008) Different roads, *Drink and Drugs News*, 19 May, pp. 6–7.

Beutler, L.E., Zetzer, H. and Yost, E. (1997) Tailoring Interventions to clients: effects on engagement and retention, in L.S. Onken, J.D. Blaine and J.J. Boren (eds) *Beyond the Therapeutic Alliance: Keeping the Drug-dependent Individual in Treatment*, NIDA Monograph Number 165. Rockville, MD: National Institute on Drug Abuse.

Bien, T.H., Miller, W.R. and Tonigan, J.S. (1993) Brief interventions for alcohol problems: a review, *Addiction*, 88(3): 315–36.

Bonner, A. and Luscombe, C. (2009) *The Seeds of Exclusion 2009*. The Salvation Army with the University of Kent and Cardiff University. Available online at www1.salvationarmy.org.uk/seeds (accessed 6 Sepember 2011).

Bor, R. and Elford, J. (1998) *The Family and HIV Today: Recent Research and Practice*. London: Cassell & Co. Ltd.

Bordin, E.S. (1979) The generalizability of the psychoanalytic concept of the working alliance, *Psychotherapy: Theory, Research & Practice*, 16: 252–60.

Bordin, E.S. (1994) Theory and research on the therapeutic working alliance: new directions, in A.O. Horvath and L.S. Greenberg (eds) *The Working Alliance: Theory, Research and Practice*. New York: John Wiley & Sons, Inc.

Bradshaw, W., Armour, M.P. and Roseborough, D. (2007) Finding a place in the world: the experience of recovery from severe mental illness, *Qualitative Social Work*, 6(1): 27–47.

Brandon, M., Howe, A., Dagley, D., Salter, C. and Warren, C. (2006) What appears to be helping or hindering practitioners in implementing the common assessment framework and lead professional working? *Child Abuse Review*, 15: 369–413.

Brandt, S., Sumnall, H., Measham, F. and Cole, J. (2010) Analyses of second-generation 'legal highs' in the UK: initial findings, *Drug Testing and Analysis*, 2(8): 377–82.

British Association of Social Workers (BASW) (2002) *The Code of Ethics for Social Work*. Birmingham: BASW.

Brown, J.H. and Horowitz, J.E. (1993) Deviance and deviants: why adolescents substance use prevention programs do not work, *Evaluation Review*, 17: 529–55.

Buchanan, J. (2006) Understanding problematic drug use: a medical matter or a social issue? *British Journal of Community Justice*, 4(2): 387–97.

Buchanan, J. and Young, L. (1998) Failing to grasp the nettle: UK drug policy, *Probation Journal*, 45(2): 220–22.

Burke, B.L., Arkowitz, L.H. and Dunn, C. (2002) The efficacy of motivational interviewing and its adaptations, in W.R. Miller and S. Rollnick (eds) *Motivational Interviewing: Preparing People to Change*. New York: Guilford Press.

Burman, S. (1997) The challenge of sobriety: natural recovery without treatment and self-help groups, *Journal of Substance Abuse*, 9: 41–61.

Bussema, E.F. and Bussema, K.E. (2007) Gilead revisited: faith and recovery, *Psychiatric Rehabilitation Journal*, 30(4): 301–05.

Butt, G., Patterson, B.L. and Mcguiness, L.K. (2008) Living with the stigma of hepatitis C, *Western Journal of Nursing Research*, 30: 204–21.

Cabinet Office (1999) *Modernising Government*. London: Stationery Office, Cm 4310. http://www.cabinet-office.gov.uk/moderngov/whtpaper/index.htm

Care Services Improvement Partnership (CSIP) (2006) *The Social Work Contribution to Mental Health Services the Future Direction: Report of Responses to the Discussion Paper*. Available online at www.gscc.org.uk/NR/rdonlyres/69AB43E0–8AAD-4A23–8234-860546208EAD/0/swdiscussionpaperreportfinal.pdf (accessed 8 June 2009).

Carey, M. (2009) The order of chaos: exploring agency care managers' construction of social order within fragmented worlds of state social work, *British Journal of Social Work*, 39(3): 556–73.

Carr, S. (2007) Participation, power, conflict and change: theorising dynamics of service user participation in the social care system of England and Wales, *Critical Social Policy*, 27(2): 266–76.

Cave, J., Hunt, P., Ismail, S., Levitt, R., Pacula, R., Rabinovich, L., Rubin, J. and Weed, K. (2009) *Tackling Problem Drug Use*. Brussels: RAND Europe.

Chatterton, P. and Hollands, R. (2003) *Urban Nightscapes: Youth Cultures, Pleasure Spaces and Corporate Power*. London: Routledge.

Children in Scotland (2002) *Good Practice Guidelines for Practitioners: Working with Children and Young People whose Parent or Carer is HIV Positive*. Available online at www.childreninscotland.org.uk/docs/pubs/HIVguidelines.pdf (accessed 19 July 2011).

Cigno, K. (2002) *Cognitive-behavioural Practice*, in R. Adams, L. Dominelli and M. Payne (2002) (eds) *Social Work: Themes, Issues and Critical Debates*. Basingstoke: Palgrave Macmillan.

Cleaver, H., Unell, I. and Aldegate, A. (1999) *Children's Needs Parenting Capacity: The Impact of Parental Mental Olness, Problem Alcohol and Drug Use, and Domestic Violence on Children's Development*. London: The Stationery Office.

Cleaver, H., Walker, S. and Meadow P. (2003) *Assessing Children' Needs and Circumstances: The Impact of Assessment Framework*. London: Jessica Kingsley Publishers.

Cleaver, H., Nicholson, D., Tarr, S. and Cleaver, D. (2007) *Child Protection, Domestic Violence and Parental Substance Misuse: Family Experiences and Effective Practice*. London: Jessica Kingsley Publishers.

Cloninger C. (1999) Genetics of substance abuse, in M. Galanter and H.D. Kleber (1999) (eds) *Textbook of Substance Abuse Treatment* (2nd edn.). Washington, DC: American Psychiatric Press.

Coffey, E., Young, D. and Gerada, C. (2005) Injecting drug use and harm reduction, in C. Gerada (ed.) *RCGP Guide to The Management of Substance Misuse in Primary Care*. London: Royal College of Practitioners, pp. 225–42.

Cohen, B.-Z. (1985) A cognitive approach to the treatment of offenders, *British Journal of Social Work*, 15: 619–33.

Commission for Social Care Inspection (CSCI) (2006) *Supporting Parents, Safe-Guarding Children: CSCI Special Study Report*. London: CSCI.

Compas, B.E., Hinden, B.R. and Gerhardt, C.A. (1995) Adolescent development: pathways and processes of risk and resilience, *Annual Review of Psychology*, 46: 265–93.

Concato, J., Shah, N. and Horwitz, R. (2000) Randomized, controlled trials, observational studies, and the hierarchy of research designs, *New England Journal of Medicine*, 342: 1887–92.

Coulshed, V. and Orme, J. (2006) *Social Work Practice* (4th edn). Basingstoke: Palgrave Macmillan.

Cournoyer, B. (2004) *Evidence-based Practice: Skills Book*. New York: Allyn & Bacon.

Cournoyer, L.-G., Brochu, S., Landry, M. and Bergeron, J. (2007) Therapeutic alliance, patient behaviour and dropout in a drug rehabilitation programme: the moderating effect of clinical subpopulations, *Addiction*, 102: 1960–70.

Crawford, M.J., Rutter, D., Manley, C., Weaver, T., Bhui, K., Fulop, N. and Tyrer, P. (2002) Systematic review of involving patients in the planning and development of health care, *British Medical Journal*, 325: 1263–67.

Cree, V.E., Kay, H., Tisdall, K. and Wallace, J. (2004) Stigma and parental HIV, *Qualitative Social Work*, 3(1): 7–25.

Croft, S. and Beresford, P. (2008) Service users' perspectives, in M. Davies (2008) (ed.) *The Blackwell Companion to Social Work*. Oxford: Blackwell Publishing.

Crofts, N., Louie, R. and Loff, B. (1997) The next plague: stigmatisation and discrimination related to the hepatitis C virus infection in Australia, *Health and Human Rights*, 2: 87–97.

Crome, I., Chambers, P. with Frisher, M., Bloor, R. and Roberts, D. (2009) *The Relationship between Dual Diagnosis: Substance Misuse and Dealing with Mental Health Issues*, SCIE Briefing No. 30. Available online at www.scie.org.uk/publications/briefings/files/briefing30.pdf (accessed 24 March 2010).

Daddow, R. and Broome, S. (2010) *Whole Person Recovery: A User Centred Approach to Problem Drug Use*. London: RSA Projects.

Davies, J.B. ([1992] 1997) *The Myth of Addiction* (2nd edn). Amsterdam: Harwood.

Day, C., Ross, J. and Dolan, K. (2003) Hepatitis C discrimination among heroin users in Sydney: drug user or hepatitis C discrimination, *Drug and Alcohol Review*, 22: 317–21.

De, P., Cox, J., Boivin, J.F., Platt, R.W. and Jolly, A.M. (2007) The importance of social networks in their association to drug equipment sharing among injection drug users: a review, *Addiction*, 102(11): 1730–39.

De, P., Roy, E., Boivin, J.F., Cox, J. and Morissette, C. (2008) Risk of hepatitis C virus transmission through drug preparation equipment: a systematic and methodological review, *Journal of Viral Hepatitis*, 15(4): 279–92.

De Dios, M., Anderson, B., Herman, D., Hagerty, C., Caviness, C., Budney, A. and Stein, M. (2010) Marijuana use subtypes in a community sample of young adult women, *Women's Health Issues*, 20(3): 201–10.

Deci, E.L. and Ryan, R.M. (1985) *Intrinsic Motivation and Self-determination in Human Behaviour*. New York: Plenum.

Deehan, A. and Saville, E. (2003) *Calculating The Risk: Recreational Drug Use Among Clubbers in the South East of England*, Home Office Online Report 43/03. London: Home Office.

De Leon, G. and Jainchill, N. (1986) Circumstance, motivation, readiness and suitability as correlates of treatment tenure, *Journal of Psychoactive Drugs*, 18(3): 203–09.

De Leon, G., Melnick, G. and Kressell, D. (1994) Circumstances, motivation, readiness, and suitability (the CMRS scales): predicting retention in therapeutic community treatment, *American Journal of Drug and Alcohol Abuse*, 20(4): 495–515.

Denzin, N.K. (1987) *Treating Alcoholism: An Alcoholics Anonymous Approach*. London: Sage Publications.

Department for Children, Schools and Families (DCSF) (2009) Department of Health (DoH) and National Treatment Agency for Substance Misuse (NTA) (2009) *Joint Guidance on Development of Local Protocols between Drug and Alcohol Treatment Services and Local Safeguarding and Family Services*. Available online at www.nta.nhs.uk/uploads/yp_drug_alcohol_treatment_protocol_1109.pdf (accessed 6 September 2011).

Department for Education (2011) *The Munro Review of Child Protection: Final Report – A Child-centred System*. Cm 8062. London: Department for Education. Available online at www.education.gov.uk/munroreview/downloads/8875_DfE_Munro_Report_TAGGED.pdf (accessed 6 September 2011).

Department for Education and Skills (DFES) (2004) *Every Child Matters: Change for Children*. London: DFES.

Department for Education and Skills (2005a) *Every Child Matters: Change for Children: Young People and Drugs*. London: DFES.

Department for Education and Skills (2005b) *Youth Matters*. London: DFES.

Department of Health (1999a) *Framework for the Assessment of Children in Need and their Families Consultation Document*. London: HMSO.

Department of Health (DoH) (1999b) *Working Together to Safeguard Children: A Guide to Inter-agency Working to Safeguard and Promote the Welfare of Children*. London: Her Majesty's Stationery Office (HMSO).

Department of Health (2001a) *The Journey to Recovery: The Government's Vision for Mental Health Care*. London: Department of Health Publications.

Department of Health (2001b) *The Expert Patient: A New Approach to Chronic Disease Management for the 21st Century*. London: Department of Health Publications.

Department of Health (2002) *Hepatitis C Strategy for England*. London: DoH. Available online at www.dh.gov.uk/dr_consum_dh/groups/dh_digitatassets/@dh/@en/documents/digitalasset/dh_4103282.pdf (accessed 1 August 2009).

Department of Health (2003) *Mental Health Policy Implementation Guide: Support, Time and Recovery (STR) Workers*. London: Department of Health Publications.

Department of Health (2004) *The National Service Framework for Mental Health – Five Years On*. London: Department of Health Publications.

Department of Health (2005) *The National Service for Long-term Conditions*. London: Department of Health Publications.

Department of Health (2006a) *Reviewing the Care Programme Approach 2006: A Consultation Document*. London: Department of Health Publications.

Department of Health (2006b) *Supporting People with Long Term Conditions to Self Care*. London: Department of Health.

Department of Health (2007) *Best Practice in Managing Risk: Principles and Evidence for Best Practice in the Assessment and Management of Risk to Self and Others in Mental Health Services*. London: Department of Health Publications.

Department of Health Social Services and Public Safety (2007) *Action Plan for the Prevention, Management and Control of Hepatitis C*. London: Department of Health Publications.

Dixon, J. (2006) Developing collaborative relationships in interagency child protection work edition book review, *Child and Family Social Work*, 11: 183–86.

Dobkin, P.L., Civita, M.D., Paraherakis, A. and Gill, K. (2002) *The Role of Functional Social Support in Treatment Retention and Outcomes among Outpatient Adult Substance Abusers Addiction*. Oxford: Blackwell Publishing Limited.

Dodds, C., Keogh, P., Chime, O., Haruper, T., Nabulya, B., Ssanyu Sseruma, W. and Weatherburn, P. (2004) *Outsider Status: Stigma and Discrimination Experienced by Gay Men and African People with HIV*. Available online at www.researchasylum. org.uk/?lid=104.

Doel, M. (2002) Task-centred work, in R. Adams, L. Dominelli and M. Payne (eds) *Social Work: Themes, Issues and Critical Debates* (2nd edn). Basingstoke: Palgrave Macmillan.

Dolan, M. (1998) *The Hepatitis C Handbook: Revised Edition*. London: Catalyst Press.

Dominelli, L. (2009) *Introducing Social Work*. Cambridge: Polity Press.

DrugScope (2009) *Awareness of Hepatitis C Transmission Risks Low as New Campaign Launched*. London: DrugScope.

Duffy, D. and Cuddy, K. (2008) *Merseyside DIP Clients: A Comparison of Client Characteristics for Under and Over 25 Year Olds*. Liverpool: Centre for Public Health, JMU.

Duke, K. (2006) Out of crime and into treatment?: The criminalization of contemporary drug policy since tackling drugs together, *Drugs: Education, Prevention and Policy*, 13(5): 409–15.

Dundon, W.D., Pettinati, H.M., Lynch, K.G., Xie, H., Varillo, K.M., Makadon, C. and Oslin, D.W. (2008) The therapeutic alliance in medical-based interventions impacts outcome in treating alcohol dependence, *Drug And Alcohol Dependence*, 95: 230–36.

Eaton, G, Seymour, H. and Mahmood, R. (1998) The development of services for drug misusers on Mersey, *Drugs: Education, Prevention and Policy*, 5(3): 305–18.

Edwards, G. (1989) What drives British Drug policies? *British Journal of Addiction*, 84: 219–26.

Edwards, G. and Grant, M. (1977) *Alcoholism: New Knowledge and New Responses*. London: Croom Helm.

Edwards, G., Grattoni, F., Hensman, C. and Peter, J. (1976) Drinking problems in prison populations, in G. Edwards *et al.* (eds) *Alcohol Dependence and Smoking Behaviour*. New York: Saxton House.

Emmelkamp, P.M.G. and Vedel, E. (2006) *Evidence-based Treatment for Alcohol and Drug Abuse: A Practitioner's Guide to Theory, Methods, and Practice*. New York: Routledge.

Erickson, P. and Cheung, Y. (1999) Harm reduction among cocaine users: reflections on individual intervention and community social capital, *International Journal of Drug Policy*, 10(3): 235–46.

Ettorre, E. (1992) *Women and Substance Use*. Basingstoke: Palgrave Macmillan.

Ettorre, E. (2007) *Revisioning Women and Drug Use: Gender, Power and the Body*. Basingstoke: Palgrave Macmillan.

European Monitoring Centre for Drugs and Drug Addiction (2009) *Polydrug Use: Patterns and Responses*. Lisbon: EMCDDA.

European Monitoring Centre for Drugs and Drug Addiction (2011) *Annual Report: The State of the Drugs Problem in Europe*. Lisbon: EMCDDA.

Fallot, R.D. (2007) Spirituality and religion in recovery: some current issues, *Psychiatric Rehabilitation Journal*, 30(4): 261–70.

Farabee, D., Shen, H. and Sanchez, S. (2002) Perceived coercion and treatment need among mentally ill parolees, *Criminal Justice and Behavior*, 29(1): 76–86.

Farrell Brodie, J. and Redfield, M. (2002), *High Anxieties: Cultural Studies in Addiction*. Berkeley: University of California.

Fiorentine, R., Nakashima, J. and Anglin, M.D. (1999) Client engagement in drug treatment, *Journal of Substance Abuse Treatment*, 17: 199–206.

Fischer, J. and Neale, J. (2008) Involving drug users in treatment decisions: an exploration of potential problems, *Drugs: Education, Prevention and Policy*, 2: 161–75.

Fischer, J., Jenkins, N., Bloor, M., Neale, J. and Berney, L. (2007) *Drug User Involvement in Treatment Decisions*. York: Joseph Rowntree Foundation.

Fischer, J., Neale, J., Bloor, M. and Jenkins, N. (2008) Conflict and user involvement in drug misuse treatment decision-making: a qualitative study, *Substance Abuse Treatment, Prevention and Policy*, 3: 21.

Flatley, J., Kershaw, C., Smith, K., Chaplin, R. and Moon, D. (2010) *Crime in England and Wales 2009/10: Findings from the British Crime Survey and Police Recorded Crime*, Home Office Statistical Bulletin 12/10. London: Home Office.

Flores-Macias, F. and Lawson, C. (2008) Effects of interviewer gender on survey responses: findings from a household survey in Mexico, *International Journal of Public Opinion Research*, 20(1): 100.

Forrester, D. (2000) Parental substance misuse and child protection in a British sample: a survey of children on the Child Protection Register in an Inner London District Office, *Child Abuse Review*, 9(4): 235–46.

Forrester, D. (2004) Social work assessments when parents misuse drugs and alcohol, in R. Philips (ed.) *Children Exposed to Parental Substance Misuse: Implications for Family Placement*. London: BAAF.

Forrester, D. and Harwin, J. (2011) *Parents who Misuse Drugs and Alcohol*. Chichester: Wiley Blackwell.

Forrester, D., McCambridge, J., Waissbein, C., Emlyn-Jones and Rollnick, S. (2008) Child risk and parental resistance: can motivational interviewing improve the practice of child and family social workers in working with parental alcohol misuse, *British Journal of Social Work*, 38(7): 1302–19.

Foster, G. (2007) *Symptoms of Chronic Infection with Hepatitis C*. The Hepatitis C Trust. Available online at www.hepctrust.org.uk/hepatitis-c/Symptoms+of+chronic+infection+with+hepatitis+C.htm (accessed 3 March 2009).

Foster, G. (2008) Injecting drug users with chronic hepatitis C: should they be offered antiviral therapy? *Addiction*, 103: 1412–13.

Fraser, H. (2009) Trying to complete socially just, politically sensitive social work research, *Journal of Social Work*, 9(1): 87–98.

Fraser, S. (2004) 'It's your life!': injecting drug users, individual responsibility and hepatitis C prevention', *Health: An interdisciplinary Journal for the Social Study of Health, Illness and Medicine*, 8(2): 199–221.

Fraser, S. and Moore, D. (2008) Dazzled by unity? Order and chaos in public discourse on illicit drug use, *Social Science and Medicine*, 66(3): 740–52.

Fraser, S. and Treloar, C. (2006) 'Spoiled identity' in hepatitis C infection: the binary logic of despair, *Critical Public Health*, 16: 99–110.

Froggett, L. (2002) *Love, Hate and Social Welfare: Psychosocial Approaches to Policy and Practice*. Bristol: Policy Press.

Galindo, L.M.T., Wallace, G., Hansen, A. and Sylvestre, D. (2007) Education by peers is the key to success, *International Journal of Drug Policy*, 18: 411–16.

Galvani, S. (2006) *Safeguarding Children: Working with Parental Alcohol Problems and Domestic Abuse*. One briefing in a series for the Alcohol and Parenting Project, Alcohol Concern. Available online at www.alcoholconcern.org.uk/servlets/doc/1123.

Galvani, S. (2007) Refusing to listen: are we failing the needs of people with alcohol and drug problems? *Social Work Education*, 26(7): 697–707.

Galvani, S. (2008) Alcohol or Drug Problems in Davies, M. (2008) (ed.) *The Blackwell Companion to Social Work*. Oxford: Blackwell Publishing.

Galvani, S. (2009) *Living with Domestic Abuse and Substance Use*. Factsheet for family members produced for the national charity ADFAM. Available online at www.adfam.org.uk/docs/livingwith_dv.pdf.

Galvani, S. and Forrester, D. (2008) *What Works In Training Social Workers About Drug And Alcohol Use*, University Of Bedforshire. Available online at www.Beds.ac.uk/Departments/Appliedsocialstudies/Staff/Sarah-Galvani/Galvani-Forrester-Horeport 2008pdf.

Galvani, S. and Forrester, D. (2011) 'Guest editorial' practice, *Social Work in Action*, 23(4): 177–82.

Garret, D. and Foster, J. (2005) Fumbling in the dark, *Druglink*, May/June: 12.

General Social Care Council (GSCC) (2002) *Code of Practice for Social Care Workers and Employers*. London: GSCC.

General Social Care Council (2007) *Roles and Tasks of Social Work in England*. London: GSCC.

Gilman, M. (1991) Beyond opiates . . . and into the '90s, *Druglink*, 6(6): 16–18.

Godfrey, C., Eaton, G., McDougall, C. and Culyer, A. (2002) *The Economic and Social Costs of Class A Drug Use in England and Wales*, 2000, Home Office Research Study 249, London: Home Office.

Goffman, E. (1963) *Behavior in Public Places: Notes on the Social Organization of Gatherings*. Glencoe, IL: Free Press.

Golden, J., Conroy, R.M., O'Dwyer, A., Golden, D. and Hardouin, J. (2006) Illness related stigma, mood and adjustments to illness in persons with Hepatitis C, *Social Science and Medicine*, 63: 3188–98.

Goldsmith, R. (2008) The demon druggies, *Druglink*, 23(3): 20–21.

Goldstein, P. (1985) The drugs/violence nexus: a tripartite conceptual framework, *Journal of Drug Issues*, 39: 143–74.

Gorwood, P., Aissi, F., Batel, P., Ades, J., Cohen-Salmon, C., Harmon, M., Boni, C. and Lanfurmey, L. (2002) Reappraisal of the serotonin 5 HT (IB) receptor gene in alcoholism: of mice and men, *Brain Research Bulletin*, 57: 103–7.

Gossop, M. (2006a) Classification of illegal and harmful drugs: the UK's confusing and inadequate ABC system is ready for an urgent overhaul, *British Medical Journal*, 333: 272–73.

Gossop, M. (2006b) *Treating Drug Misuse Problems: Evidence of Effectiveness*. London: National Treatment Agency (NTA).

Gottfredson, M. and Hirschi, T. (1990) *A General Theory of Crime*. Stanford: Stanford University Press.

Gray, E., McCambridge, J. and Strang, J. (2005) The effectiveness of motivational interviewing delivered by youth workers in reducing drinking, cigarette and cannabis smoking among young people: quasi-experimental pilot study, *Alcohol and Alcoholism*, 40(6): 535–39.

Greater London Authority (GLA) (2005) *Domestic Violence and Substance Use: Overlapping Issues in Separate Services?* Available online at www.legacy.london. gov.uk/mayor/strategies/dom_violence/docs/dom_vi_sub.pdf.

Grebely, J., Genoway, K.A., Raffa, J.D., Dhadwal, G., Rajan, T., Showler, G., Kalousek, K., Duncan, F., Tyndall, M.W., Fraser, C., Conway, B. and Fischer, B. (2008) Barriers associated with the treatment of hepatitis C virus infection among illicit drug users, *Drug And Alcohol Dependence*, 93: 141–47.

Griffin, C., Bengry-Howell, A., Hackley, C., Mistral, W. and Szmigin, I. (2009) 'Every time I do it I absolutely annihilate myself': loss of (self-)consciousness and loss of memory in young people's drinking narratives, *Sociology*, 43(3): 457–76.

Griffiths, R. and Pearson, B. (1988) *Working with Drug Users*. Aldershot: Wildwood House.

Gould, N. (2006) An inclusive approach to knowledge for mental health social work practice and policy, *British Journal of Social Work*, 36: 109–25.

Grow, J.M. and Christopher, S.A. (2008) Breaking the silence surrounding hepatitis C by promoting self-efficacy: hepatitis C public service announcements, *Qualitative Health Research*, 18(10): 1401–12.

Grund, J.P.C., Blanken, P., Adriaans, N.F.P., Kaplan, C.D., Barendregt, C. and Meeuwsen, M. (1992) Reaching the unreached – an outreach model for 'on the spot' AIDS prevention among active, out-of-treatment drug addicts, in P.A. O'Hare, R. Newcombe, A. Matthews and E.C. Buning (eds) *The Reduction of Drug-related Harm*. London: Routledge, pp. 172–80.

Gupta, A. and Blewett, J. (2007) Challenges and opportunities for the social work-force, *Child and Family Social Work*, 112: 172–81.

Hall, C.J. (1999) Integrating services for children and families: the way forward? *Children and Society*, 13: 216–22.

Hallstone, M. (2002) Updating Howard Becker's theory of using marijuana for pleasure, *Contemporary Drug Problems*, 29(Winter): 821–45.

Hammersley, R. (2008) *Drugs and Crime*. Cambridge: Polity Press.

Hammersley, R., Forsyth, A., Morrison, V. and Davies, J. (2006) The relationship between crime and opioid use, *British Journal of Addiction*, 84(9): 1029–43.

Hammersley, R., Marsland, L. and Reid, M. (2003) *Substance Use by Young Offenders: the Impact of the Normalisation of Drug Use in the Early Years of the 21st Century*, Home Office Research Study *261*, London: Home Office.

Hanson, M. and El-Bassel, N. (2004) Motivating substance-abusing clients through the helping process, in S.L.A. Straussner (ed.) *Clinical Work with Substance-abusing Clients* (2nd edn). New York: Guilford Press.

Harbin, F. (2006) The rollercoaster of change: the process of parental change from a child's perspective, in F. Harbin, and M. Murphy (eds) *Secret Lives: Growing with Substance*. Lyme Regis: Russell House Publishing, pp. 81–94.

Harbin, F. and Murphy, M. (2006) Developing whole family treatment services, in F. Harbin and M. Murphy (eds) *Secret Lives: Growing with Substance*. Lyme Regis: Russell House Publishing, pp. 95–109.

Harlow, E. (2003) New managerialism, social service departments and social work practice today, *Practice*, 15(2): 29–44.

Harris, M. (2005) Living with hepatitis C: the medical encounter, *New Zealand Sociology*, 20: 4–19.

Harris, P. (2007) *Empathy for the Devil: How to Help People Overcome Drug and Alcohol Problems*. Lyme Regis: Russell House Publishing.

Hathaway, A. (1997) Marijuana and lifestyle: exploring tolerable deviance, *Deviant Behaviour*, 18(3): 213–32.

Hathaway, A. (2000) Shortcomings of harm reduction: toward a morally invested drug reform strategy, *International Journal Drug Policy*, 12(2): 125–37.

Health Protection Agency (2005) *Shooting Up: Infections among Injecting Drug Users in the UK 2004: An Update*. London: Health Protection Agency.

Health Protection Agency (2008) *Hepatitis C in the UK: The Health Protection Agency Annual Report*. London: Health Protection Agency Centre For Infections.

Heather, N. (2000) Psychosocial treatment approaches and the findings of project match, in M. Plant and D. Cameron (eds) *The Alcohol Report*. London: Free Press.

Henderson, S. (1999) Drugs and culture: the question of gender, in N. South (ed.) *Drugs: Cultures, Controls and Everyday Life*. London: Sage Publications, pp. 36–48.

Henry, W.P. and Strupp, H.H. (1994) The therapeutic alliance as interpersonal process, in A.O. Horvath and L.S. Greenberg (eds) *The Working Alliance: Theory, Research and Practice*. New York: John Wiley & Sons, Inc.

Hibell, B., Guttormsson, U., Ahlström, S., Balakireva, O., Bjarnason, T., Kokkevi, A. and Kraus, L. (2009) *The 2007 ESPAD Report: Substance Use among Students in 35 European Countries*. Stockholm: The Swedish Council for Information on Alcohol and Other Drugs.

Higham, P. (2006) *Social Work: Introducing Professional Practice*. London: Sage Publications.

Hiller, M.L., Knight, K., Leukefeld, C. and Simpson, D.D. (2002) Motivation as a predictor of therapeutic engagement in mandated residential substance abuse treatment, in D. Farabee (ed.) *Criminal Justice and Behavior*, 29(1): 56–70.

HM Government (2010) *Drugs Strategy 2010. Reducing Demand, Restricting Supply, Building Recovery: Supporting People to Live a Drug Free Life*. London: Home Office.

Hoare, J. and Moon, D. (2010) *Drug Misuse Declared: Findings from the 2009/10 British Crime Survey England and Wales*, Home Office Statistical Bulletin 13/10. London: Home Office. Available online at www.homeoffice.gov.uk/rds/pdfs10/hosb1310.pdf.

Hobart, J. and Frankel, C. (2005) *Child Protection*. Cheltenham: Nelson Thornes.

Hodge, S. (2005) Participation, discourse and power: a case study in service user involvement, *Critical Social Policy*, 52(2): 164–79.

Hodgson, R. (2002) Brief interventions, brief interaction, in T. Petersen and A. Mc Bride (eds) *Working with Substance Misusers: A Guide to Theory and Practice*. London: Routledge.

Home Office (2006) *Review of the UK's Drugs Classification System: A Public Consultation*, Home Office Crime and Drug Strategy Directorate. London: Home Office (draft released 2010 under Freedom of Information legislation).

Home Office (2008) *Drugs: Protecting Families and Communities 2008–2018*. London: Home Office.

Hopwood, M. and Treloar, C. (2003) *The 3D Project: Diagnosis, Disclosure and Discrimination – Living with Hepatitis C*. Sydney: University of New South Wales.

Horton, R. and Das, P. (2010) Rescuing people with HIV who use drugs, *The Lancet*, 376(9737): 07–208.

Hougaard, E. (1994) The therapeutic alliance – a conceptual analysis, *Scandinavian Journal of Psychology*, 35(1): 67–85.

House of Commons Science and Technology Committee (2006) *Drug Classification: Making a Hash of It?* Fifth Report of Session 2005–06, HC 1031. London: The Stationery Office.

House of Lords (2011) *Select Committee on HIV and AIDS*. Available online at www.parliament.uk/business/committees/committees-a-z/lords-select/hiv-select-committee/news/report-publication/.

Howarth, J. and Morrison, T. (2007) Collaboration, integration and change in children's services: critical issues and key ingredients, *Child Abuse and Neglect*, 31: 55–69.

Howe, D. (2008) Relating theory to practice, in M. Davies (2008) (ed.) *The Blackwell Companion to Social Work*. Oxford: Blackwell Publishing.

Howe, D., Dooley, T. and Hinings, D. (2000) Assessment and decision making in a case of child neglect and abuse using an attachment perspective, *Child and Family Social Work*, 5.

Hugman, R. (2007) The place of values in social work education, in M. Lymbery and K. Postle (eds) *Social Work: A Companion to Learning*. London: Sage Publications.

Hugman, R. (2008) An ethical perspective on social work, in M. Davies (ed.) *The Blackwell Companion to Social Work*. Oxford: Blackwell Publishing.

Humphreys, C. and Stanley, N. (2006) *Domestic Violence and Child Protection: Directions for Good Practice*. London: Jessica Kingsley Publishers.

Humphreys, C., Regan, L., River, D. and Thiara, R.K. (2005) Domestic violence and substance use: tackling complexity, *British Journal of Social Work*, 35: 1303–20.

Hunt, G., Moloney, M. and Evans, K. (2010) *Youth, Drugs and Nightlife*. Abingdon: Routledge.

Hunt, N. and Stevens, A. (2004) Whose harm? Harm reduction and the shift to coercion in UK drug policy, *Social Policy and Society*, 3(4): 333–42.

Hutton, F. (2006) *Risky Pleasures? Club Cultures and Feminine Identities*. Aldershot: Ashgate.

Inciardi, J. (ed.) (1999) *The Drug Legalization Debate*. Thousand Oaks, CA: Sage Publications.

Jacobson, N. (2003) Defining recovery: an interactionist analysis of mental health policy development, Wisconsin 1996–1999, *Qualitative Health Research*, 13: 378–93.

Jenner, A. and Scott, A. (2007) Circulating beliefs, resilient metaphors and faith in biomedicine: hepatitis C patients and interferon combination therapy, *Sociology of Health & Illness*, 30: 197–216.

Jewell, C. and Bero, L. (2008) Developing good taste in evidence: facilitators of and hindrances to evidence-informed health policymaking in state government, *Milbank Quarterly*, 86(2): 177–208.

Joe, G.W., Broome, K.M., Rowan-Szal, G.A. and Simpson, D.D. (2002) Measuring patient attributes and engagement in treatment, *Journal of Substance Abuse Treatment*, 22: 183–96.

Joe, G.W., Simpson, D.D., Dansereau, D.F. and Rowan-szal, G.A. (2001) Relationships between counseling rapport and drug abuse treatment outcomes, *Psychiatry Services*, 9(52): 1223–29.

Johnson, I. (2000) Alcohol problems in old age: a review of recent epidemiological research, *International Journal of Geriatric Psychiatry*, 15: 575–81.

Jones, L., Holmes, R. and Powell, J. (2005) *Early Childhood Studies: A Multiprofessional Perspective*. Maidenhead: Open University Press.

Jowitt, M. and O'Loughlin, S. (2005) *Social Work with Children and Families*. Exeter: Learning Matters.

Judd, A., Hutchinson, S., Wadd, S., Hickman, M., Taylor, A., Jones, S., Parry, J.V., Cameron, S., Rhodes, T., Ahmed, S., Bird, S., Fox, R., Renton, A. and Stimson, G.V. (2005) Prevalence of, and risk factors for, hepatitis C virus infection among recent initiates to injecting in London and Glasgow: cross sectional analysis, *Journal of Viral Hepatitis*, 12(6): 655–62.

Kavanagh, A.M. and Broom, D.H. (1998) Embodied risk: my body, myself? *Social Science Medicine*, 46(3): 427–44.

Kay, H., Cree, V.E., Tisdall, K. and Wallace, J. (2002) *Listening to Children and Young People Whose Parent or Carer is HIV Positive*. Edinburgh: Children in Scotland.

Keane, H. (2002) Critiques of harm reduction, morality and the promise of human rights, *International Journal of Drug Policy*, 14(3): 227–32.

Keene, J. (1997) *Drug Misuse: Prevention, Harm Minimisation and Treatment*. London: Chapman & Hall.

Keene, J. (2001) An international social work perspective on drug misuse problems and solutions – reviewing implications for practice, *Journal of Social Work*, 1(2): 187–99.

Kirkpatrick, S., Barlow, J., Stewart-Brown, S. and Davis, H. (2007) Working in partnership: user perceptions of intensive home visiting, *Child Abuse Review*, 16: 32–46.

Klag, S., O'Callaghan, F. & Creed, P. (2005) The use of legal coercion in the treatment of substance abusers: an overview and critical analysis of thirty years of research, *Substance Use & Misuse*, 12(40): 1777–95.

Klee, H., Faugier, C., Hayes, C. and Morris, J. (1991) Risk reduction among injecting drug users: changes in the sharing of injecting equipment and in condom use, *Aids Care*, 3(1): 63–73.

Klee, H., Jackson, M. and Lewis, S. (eds) (2002) *Drug Misuse and Motherhood*. London: Routledge.

Klein, A. (2008) *Drugs and the World*. London: Reaktion.

Knight, A., Aggleton, P. and Candappa, M. (1999) *Social Care Services for Children and Families affected by HIV in London: A Review*. London: University of London, Thomas Coram Research Unit.

Knight, K., Hiller, M.L., Broome, K.M. and Simpson, D.D. (2000) Legal pressure, treatment readiness, and engagement in long-term residential programs, *Journal of Offender Rehabilitation*, 31(1–2): 101–15.

Koester, S., Glanz, J. and Barón, A. (2005) Drug sharing among heroin networks: implications for HIV and hepatitis B and C prevention, *AIDS and Behaviour*, 9(1): 27–40.

Krane, J. and Davies, L. (2000) Rethinking risk assessment in mothering and child protection practice, *Child and Family Social Work*, 5(1): 35–45.

Kroll, B. (2004) Living with an elephant: growing up with parental substance misuse, *Child & Family Social Work*, 9(2): 129–40.

Kroll, B. (2007) A family affair? Kinship care and parental misuse: some dilemmas explored, *Child and Family Social Work*, 12: 84–93.

Kroll, B. and Taylor, A. (2003) *Parental Substance Misuse and Child Welfare*. London: Jessica Kingsley Publishers.

Kurtz, E. (2008) *The Complete Ernie Kurtz*. Bloomington, IN: iUniverse.

Labouvie, E. and Pinsky, I. (2001) Substance use and driving: the coexistence of risky and safe behaviors, *Addiction*, 96: 473–84.

Lawson, A. (1994) Identification of and responses to problem drinking among social service users, *British Journal of Social Work*, 24: 325–42.

Lazarus, J.L., Shete, P.B, Eramova, I., Merkinaite, S. and Matic, S. (2007) HIV/ hepatitis coinfection in eastern Europe and new Pan-European approaches to hepatitis C prevention and management, *International Journal of Drug Policy*, 18: 426–32.

Levine, H. (2003) Global drug prohibition: its uses and crises, *International Journal of Drug Policy*, 14: 145–53.

Levitas, R. (1998) *The Inclusive Society? Social Exclusion and New Labour*. Basingstoke: Palgrave Macmillan.

Lewis, E. (2001) *Afraid to Say: The Needs and Views of Young People Living with HIV/ AIDS*. London: National Children's Bureau.

Lindstrom, L. (1992) *Managing Alcoholism: Matching Clients to Treatment*. New York: Oxford University Press.

Link, B.G. and Phelan, J. (2001) Conceptualising stigma, *Annual Review of Sociology*, 27: 363–85.

Lloyd, C. (2010) *Sinning and Sinned Against: The Stigmatisation of Problem Drug Users*. York: UK Drug Policy Commission.

Longshore, D., Prendergast, M. and Farabee, D. (2004) Coerced treatment for drug-using criminal offenders, in P. Bean and T. Nemitz (eds) *Drug Treatment: What Works*. London: Routledge.

López Viets, V., Walker, D.D. and Miller, W.R. (eds) (2002) *What is Motivation to Change? A Scientific Analysis*. Chichester: John Wiley & Sons.

Luborsky, L., Barber, J. P., Siqueland, L., Mclellan, T.A. and Woody, G. (1997) Establishing a therapeutic alliance with substance abusers, *NIDA Monograph*, 165: 233–44.

MacDonald, R. and Marsh, J. (2002) Crossing the Rubicon: youth transitions, poverty, drugs and social exclusion, *International Journal of Drug Policy*, 13(1): 27–38.

Mack, H. (2007) *Evaluating Harm Reduction Responses to Hepatitis C*. University of East Anglia: Social Work Monographs School of Social Work and Psychological Studies.

Macleod, J. and Hickman, M. (2010) How ideology shapes the evidence and the policy: what do we know about cannabis use and what should we do? *Addiction*, 105: 1326–30.

Maddux, J.F. (1988) Clinical experience with civil commitment, in C. Leukefeld and F. Tims (eds) *Compulsory Treatment of Drug Abuse: Research and Clinical Practice*, NIDA Research Monograph 86, DHHS Publication Number ADM 89–1578. Washington, DC: US Government Press.

Maher, L. (1997) *Sexed Work: Gender, Race, and Resistance in a Brooklyn Drug Market*. Oxford: Clarendon.

Maher, L., Chant, K., Jalaludin, B. and Sargent, P. (2004) Risk behaviors and antibody hepatitis B and C prevalence among injecting drug users in south-western Sydney, Australia, *Journal of Gastroenterology and Hepatology*, 19(10): 1114–20.

Maher, L., Li, J., Jalaludin, B., Chant, K.G. and Kaldor, J.M. (2007) High hepatitis C incidence in new injecting drug users: a policy failure? *Australian and New Zealand Journal of Public Health*, 31(1): 30–5.

Manderson, D. (1995) The semiotics of the title: a comparative and historical analysis of drug legislation, *Law/Text/Culture*, 2: 160–77.

Mantle, G., Williams, I. with Leslie, J., Parsons, S. and Shaffer, R. (2008) Beyond assessment: social work intervention in family court enquiries, *British Journal of Social Work*, 38(3): 431–43.

Marlatt, G. and George, W. (1984) Relapse prevention: introduction and overview of the model, *British Journal of Addiction*, 79: 261–73.

Marlatt, G. and Gordon, J. (1980) Determinants of relapse: implications for the maintenance of behavioural change, in P. Davidson and S. Davidson (eds) *Behavioural Medicine: Changing Health Lifestyles*. New York: Bruner/Mazel.

Marlatt, G. and Gordon, J. (eds) (1985) *Relapse Prevention*. New York: Guilford Press.

Marlowe, D.B., Kirby, K.C., Bonieskie, L.M., Glass, D.J., Dodd, L.D., Husband, S.O., Platt, J.J. and Festinger, D.S. (1996) Assessment of coercive and noncoercive pressures to enter drug abuse treatment, *Drug and Alcohol Dependence*, 42(2): 77–84.

Marsh, I. and Melville, G. (2009) *Crime, Justice and the Media*. Abingdon: Routledge.

Marsh, P. (2002) Task-centred work, in M. Davies (ed.) *The Blackwell Companion to Social Work* (2nd edn.). Oxford: Blackwell.

Martinic, M. and Measham, F. (2008) (eds) *Swimming with Crocodiles: The Culture of Extreme Drinking*. New York and Abingdon: Routledge.

Mason, J. (2006) The Climbie inquiry: context and critique, *Law and Society*, 33(2): 221–43.

Masterson, S. and Owen, S. (2006) Mental health service user's social and individual empowerment: using theories of power to elucidate far-reaching strategies, *Journal of Mental Health*, 15(1): 19–34.

Mateu-Gelabert, P., Treloar, C., Calataud, V.A., Sandoval, M., Valderrama Zurian, J.C., Maher, L., Rhodes, T. and Friedman, S.R. (2007) How can hepatitis C be prevented in the long term? *International Journal of Drug Policy*, 18: 338–40.

Mathei, C., Shkedy, Z., Denis, B., Kabali, C., Aerts, M., Molenberghs, G., Van Damme, P. and Buntinx, F. (2006) Evidence for a substantial role of sharing of injecting paraphernalia other than syringe/needles to the spread of hepatitis C among injecting drug users, *Journal of Viral Hepatitis*, 13(8): 560–70.

McCambridge, J. and Strang, J. (2004) The efficacy of single-session motivational interviewing in reducing drug consumption and perceptions of drug-related risk and harm among young people: results from a multi-site cluster randomized trial, *Addiction*, 99(1): 39–52.

McCarthy, T. and Galvani, S. (2004) Scars: a new model for social work with substance users, *Practice*, 2: 85–97.

McCrystal, P. (2009) *The Belfast Youth Development Study: A Longitudinal Study of the Onset and Development of Adolescent Drug Use*. Paper presented at a One Day

Symposium: Cohort Studies and Substance Use: Implications for Analysis, Theory and Intervention. Nuffield College, University of Oxford.

McGuire, J. (ed.) (1995) *What Works: Reduce Offending*. London: Wiley.

McIntosh, J. and McKeganey, N. (2001) Identity and recovery from dependent drug use: the addict's perspective, *Drugs: Education, Prevention and Policy*, 8(1): 47–59.

McIntosh, J. and McKeganey, N. (2002) *Beating the Dragon*. Harlow: Prentice Hall.

McIntosh, J. and Saville, E. (2006) The challenges associated with drug treatment in prison, *Probation Journal*, 53: 230–47.

McIntosh, J., MacDonald, F. and McKeganey, N. (2005) The reasons why children in their pre- and early teenage years do or do not use illegal drugs, *International Journal of Drug Policy*, 16: 254–61.

McKeganey, N. (2005) Where's the morality in UK drug policy? *Druglink*, 20(5): 18–20.

McKeganey, N. (2007) The challenge to UK drug policy, *Drugs: Education, Prevention and Policy*, 14(6): 559–71.

McKeganey, N. and Barnard, M. (2007) *Meeting the Needs of Children whose Parents have a Serious Problem*. Bristol: Polity Press.

McKeown, C. and Gibson, F. (2007) Determining the political influence of nurses who work in the field of hepatitis C: a Delphi survey, *Journal of Clinical Nursing*, 16(7): 1210–21.

McLaughlin, D.F., Taggart, L., Quinn, B. and Milligan, V. (2007) The experiences of professionals who care for people with intellectual disability who have substance related problems, *Journal of Substance Use*, 12(2): 133–43.

McLellan, A.T. (2006) What we need is a system: creating a responsive and effective substance abuse treatment system, in W.R. Miller and K.M. Carroll (eds) *Rethinking Substance Abuse: What the Science Shows and What we Should Do About It*. New York: Guilford Press, pp. 275–92.

McPherson, B. (2010) *People Management in a Harsh Financial Climate: Developing your Managers on a Tight Budget*. Lyme Regis: Russell House Publishing.

McSweeney, T. and Turnbull, P. (2007) *Exploring User Perceptions of Occasional and Controlled Heroin Use: A Follow-up Study*. York: Joseph Rowntree Foundation.

McSweeney, T., Stevens, A., Hunt, N. and Turnbull, P. (2007) Twisting arms or a helping hand? Assessing the impact of 'coerced' and comparable 'voluntary' drug treatment options, *British Journal of Criminology*, 47(3): 470–90.

McVie, S. and Bradshaw, S. (2005) *Adolescent Smoking, Drinking and Drug Use: Edinburgh Study of Youth Transitions and Crime Number 7*. Edinburgh: University of Edinburgh.

Measham, F. (2002) 'Doing gender' – 'doing drugs': conceptualising the gendering of drugs cultures, *Contemporary Drug Problems*, 29(2): 335–73.

Measham, F. (2004) Drug and alcohol research: The case for cultural criminology, in J. Ferrell, K. Hayward, W. Morrison and M. Presdee (eds) *Cultural Criminology Unleashed*. London: GlassHouse, pp. 207–18.

Measham, F., Aldridge, J. and Parker, H. (2001) *Dancing on Drugs: Risk, Health and Hedonism in the British Club Scene*. London: Free Association Books.

Measham, F. and Brain, K. (2005) 'Binge' drinking, British alcohol policy and the new culture of intoxication, *Crime, Media, Culture: An International Journal*, 1(3): 263–84.

Measham, F. and Moore, K. (2008) The criminalisation of intoxication, in P. Squires (ed.), *ASBO Nation: The Criminalisation of Nuisance*. Bristol: Policy, pp. 273–88.

Measham, F. and Moore, K. (2009) Repertoires of distinction: exploring patterns of weekend polydrug use within local leisure scenes across the English night time economy, *Criminology and Criminal Justice*, 9(4): 437–64.

Measham, F., Moore, K., Newcombe, R. and Welch, Z. (2010) Tweaking, bombing, dabbing and stockpiling: the emergence of mephedrone and the perversity of prohibition, *Drugs and Alcohol Today*, 10(1), 14–21.

Measham, F., Newcombe, R. and Parker, H. (1993) The post-heroin generation, *Druglink*, 8(3): 16–17.

Measham, F., Wood, D., Dargan, P. and Moore, K. (2011) The rise in legal highs: prevalence and patterns in the use of illegal drugs and first and second generation 'legal highs' in south London gay dance clubs, *Journal of Substance Use*, 16(4): 263–72.

Meier, P.S., Barrowclough, C. and Donmall, M.C. (2005a) The role of the therapeutic alliance in the treatment of substance misuse: a critical review of the literature, *Addiction*, 100: 304–16.

Meier, P. S., Donmall, M.C., Barrowclough, C., Mcelduff, P. and Heller, R.F. (2005b) Predicting the early therapeutic alliance in the treatment of drug misuse, *Addiction*, 100: 500–11.

Meier, P.S., Donmall, M.C., Mcelduff, P., Barrowclough, C. and Heller, R.F. (2006) The role of the early therapeutic alliance in predicting drug treatment dropout, *Drug and Alcohol Dependence*, 83: 57–64.

Miah, J., Waugh, S., Divac, A., Turner, R., Colyer, E., Conway, M. and Walters, C. (2004) *Talking with Children, Young People and Families about Chronic Illness and Living with HIV*. London: National Children's Bureau.

Millar, J. (2010) Stop and search in England: a reformed tactic, or business as usual, *British Journal of Criminology*, 50(5): 954–74.

Milbourne, L., Macrea, S. and Maguire, M. (2003) Collaborative solutions or new policy problems: exploring multi-agency partnerships in education and health work, *Journal of Education Policy*, 18(1): 19–35.

Miller, W.R. (1985) Motivation for treatment: a review with special emphasis on alcoholism, *Psychological Bulletin*, 1(98): 84–107.

Miller, W.R (1998) Enhancing motivation for change, in W.R. Miller and N. Heather (eds) *Treating Addictive Behaviours* (2nd edn). New York: Plenum Press.

Miller, W.R. and Rollnick, S. (1991) *Motivational Interviewing: Preparing People to Change Addictive Behaviours* (1st edn). New York: Guilford Press.

Miller, W.R. and Rollnick, S. (2002) *Motivational Interviewing: Preparing People to Change Addictive Behaviours* (2nd edn). New York: Guilford Press.

Miller, W.R. and Tonigan, J.S. (1996) Assessing drinkers' motivation for change: the stages of change readiness and treatment eagerness scale (SOCRATES), *Psychology of Addictive Behaviors*, 10(2): 81–9.

Montagne, M. (2002) Appreciating the user's perspective: listening to the 'methadonians', *Substance Use and Misuse*, 4: 565–70.

Moran, P., Jacobs, C., Bunn, A. and Bifulco, A. (2006) Multi-agency working: implications for an early intervention social work team, *Child and Family Social Work*, 11: 1–9.

Morgan, C.J.A., Curran, H.V. and the Independent Scientific Committee on Drugs (ISCD) (2012) Ketamine use: a review, *Addiction*, 107: 27–38.

MORI Social Research Institute and Police Foundation (2002) *Policing the Possession of Cannabis: Residents' Views on the Lambeth Experiment*: London: Police Foundation.

Morin, S. and Collins, C. (2000) Substance abuse prevention: moving from science to policy, *Addictive Behaviors*, 25: 975–83.

Mulia, N. (2002) Ironies in the pursuit of well-being: the perspectives of low-income, substance-using women on service institutions, *Contemporary Drug Problems*, 29(Winter): 711–48.

Munck, R. (2005) *Globalization and Social Exclusion: A Transformationalist Perspective*. Bloomfield, CT: Kumarian Press.

Murphy, M. (2004) *Developing Collaborative Practice Relationships in Interagency Child Protection Work* (2nd edn). London: Jessica Kingsley.

Murphy, M. and Harbin, F. (2000) Background and current context of substance misuse and child care, in F. Harbin and M. Murphy (eds) *Substance Misuse and Child Care*. Lyme Regis: Russell House Publishing.

Murphy, M. and Harbin, F. (2006) What do we know about children and young people who grow up in substance misusing households, in F. Harbin and M. Murphy (eds) *Secret Lives: Growing with Substance*. Lyme Regis: Russell House Publishing.

Murphy, M. and Oulds, G. (2000) Establishing and developing co-operative links between substance misuse and child protection systems, in F. Harbin and M. Murphy (eds) *Substance Misuse and Child Care*. Lyme Regis: Russell House Publishing.

National Treatment Agency (NTA) (2006a) *Models of Care for the Treatment of Adult Drug Misusers: Update 2006*. London: NTA. Available online at www.nta.nhs.uk/uploads/nta_modelsofcare_update_2006_moc3.pdf (accessed 7 October 2011).

NTA (2006b) *Care Planning Practice Guide*. London: NTA.

NTA (2006c) *NTA Guidance For Local Partnerships on User and Carer Involvement*. London: NTA.

NTA (2010) *Psychosocial Interventions in Drug Misuse: A Framework and Toolkit for Implementing NICE-recommended Treatment Interventions*. Available online at www.nta.nhs.uk/uploads/psychosocial_toolkit_june10.pdf (accessed 6 September 2011).

NTA (2011) *Healthcare Professionals: Building Recovery, Building Recovery Consultation*. Available online at www.nta.nhs.uk/recovery-consultation.aspx (accessed 6 September 2011).

Neale, J. (2002) *Drug Users in Society*. New York: Palgrave Macmillan.

Neale, J. (2006) Feel Good Factor, *Druglink*, January/February: 20–21.

Newcombe, R. (1990) Drug use and drug policy in Merseyside, in W. Schneider (ed.), *First Conference of European Cities at the Centre of the Illegal Drug Trade*. Conference City Reader, Frankfurt.

Newcombe, R. (1992) The reduction of drug-related harm: a conceptual framework for theory, practice and research, in P.A. O'Hare, R. Newcombe, A. Mathews, E.C. Bunning and E. Drunker (eds) *The Reduction of Drug-related Harm*. London: Routledge.

Newcombe, R. (1995) *Summary of UK Drugs Prevalence Surveys 1964–94*. Liverpool: 3D Research Bureau.

Newcombe, R. (2005) Injecting new life into harm reduction, *Druglink*, 20(5): 10–11.

Newcombe, R. (2007) *Details of 10 Specific Rights of Drug Users*. Available online at www.lifeline.org.uk/docs/SB_RightsDetails.htm (accessed 8 September 2011).

Nutt, D. (2009a) Equasy: an overlooked addiction with implications for the current debate on drug harms, *Journal of Psychopharmacology*, 23: 3–5.

Nutt, D. (2009b) Government versus science over drug and alcohol policy, *The Lancet*, 374(9703): 1731–33.

Nutt, D., King, L. and Phillips, L. (2010) Drug harms in the UK: a multicriteria decision analysis, *The Lancet*, 376(9752): 1558–65.

Nutt, D., King, L., Sausbury, W. and Blakemore, C. (2007) Development of a rational scale to assess the harm of drugs of potential misuse, *The Lancet*, 369(9566): 1047–53.

Office of National Statistics (ONS) (2008) *National Statistics Online – Focus on Older People*. Available online at www.statistics.gov.uk/focuson/olderpeople/.

OPSI (2001) *Health and Social Care Act 2001*. Available online at www.legislation. gov.uk/ukpga/2001/115/pdfs/ukpga_20010015.

Østergaard, J. (2009) Learning to become an alcohol user: adolescents taking risks and parents living with uncertainty, *Addiction Research and Theory*, 17(1): 30–53.

Padesky, C., Greenberger, D. (1995) *Clinicians Guide to Mind over Mood*. New York: Guilford Press.

Parker, H. (2005) Normalization as a barometer: recreational drug use and the consumption of leisure by younger Britons, *Addiction Research and Theory*, 13(3): 205–15.

Parker, H. and Williams, L. (2004) Intoxicated weekends: young adults' work hard-play hard lifestyles, public health and public disorder, *Drugs: Education, Prevention and Policy*, 10: 345–67.

Parker, H., Aldridge J. and Measham, F. (1998) *Illegal Leisure: The Normalization of Adolescent Recreational Drug Use*. London: Routledge.

Parker, H., Bakx, K. and Newcombe, R. (1988) *Living with Heroin: The Impact of a Drugs 'Epidemic' on an English Community*. Maidenhead: Oxford University Press.

Parker, H., Egginton, R. and Elson, N. (2001) Unreachable? The new young heroin users, in H. Parker, J. Aldridge and R. Egginton (eds) (2001) *UK Drugs Unlimited: New Research and Policy Lessons on Illicit Drug Use*. Basingstoke: Palgrave Macmillan, pp. 98–127.

Parker, H., Williams, L. and Aldridge, J. (2002) The normalisation of 'sensible' recreational drug use: further evidence from the north west England longitudinal study, *Sociology*, 36(4): 941–64.

Parker, J. (2008) Assessment, intervention and review, in M. Davies (2008) (ed.) *The Blackwell Companion to Social Work*. Oxford: Blackwell Publishing.

Parker, R. and Aggleton, P. (2003) HIV- and AIDS-related stigma and discrimination: a conceptual framework and implications for action, *Social Science and Medicine*, 57(1): 13–24.

Patel, K. (2000) The missing drugs users: minority ethnic drug users and their children, in F. Harbin and M. Murphy (eds) *Substance Misuse and Child Care*. Lyme Regis: Russell House Publishing.

Paternoster, R. (1989) Decisions to participate in and desist from four types of common delinquency: deterrence and rational choice perspective, *Law and Society Review*, 23: 7–40.

Paterson, B.I., Backmund, M., Hirsch, G. and Yim, C. (2007) The depiction of stigmatisation in research about hepatitis C, *International Journal of Drug Policy*, 18: 364–73.

Paylor, I. (2008) Social work and drug use, in K. Wilson, G. Ruch, M. Lymbery, A. Cooper, with S. Becker, A. Brammer, R. Cawson, B. Littlechild, I. Paylor and R. Smith *Social Work: An Introduction to Contemporary Practice*. Harlow: Pearson Longman.

Paylor, I. (2009) 'Be healthy': tackling children's drug and alcohol issues, in K. Broadhurst, C. Grover, J. Jamieson and J. Mason (eds) *Safeguarding Children: Critical Perspectives*. Oxford: Blackwell.

Paylor, I. and Mack, H. (2010) Gazing into the scarlet crystal ball: social work and hepatitis C, *British Journal of Social Work*, 40(7): 2291–307.

Paylor, I. and Orgel, M. (2004) Sleepwalking through an epidemic: Why social work should wake up to the threat of hepatitis C, *British Journal of Social Work*, 34: 897–906.

Payne, M. (1991) *Modern Social Work Theory: A Critical Introduction*. London: Macmillan.

Payne, M. (1996) *What is Professional Social Work?* Birmingham: Venture.

Pearson, G. (1999) Drugs at the end of the century, *The British Journal of Criminology*, 39(4): 477–87.

Peay, J. (2004) Law and stigma – present, future and futuristic solutions, in A. Crisp (ed.) *Every Family in the Land: Understanding Prejudice and Discrimination Against People with Mental Illness*. London: Royal Society of Medicine Press, pp. 367–72.

Phillips, M. (2007) A private past, yes, but Cameron sends out all the wrong signals on drugs. *Daily Mail* website article published 12 February.

Phillips, R. (2004) *Children Exposed to Parental Substance Misuse: Implications for Family Placement.* London: BAAF Fostering and Adoption.

Pilgrim, D. (2008) 'Recovery' and current mental health policy, *Chronic Illness*, 4: 295–304.

Platt, D. (2006) Congruence and co-operation in social worker's assessments of children, *Child and Family Social Work*, 12: 326–35.

Police Foundation (2000) *Drugs and the Law: Report of the Independent Inquiry into the Misuse of Drugs Act 1971.* London: The Police Foundation (also known as the Runciman Report). Available online at www.druglibrary.org/schaffer/Library/studies/runciman/default.htm.

Powell, B.J., Landon, J.F., Cantrell, P.J., Penick, E.C., Nickel, E.J., Liskow, B.I., Coddington, T.M., Campbell, J.L., Dale, T.M., Vance, M.D. and Rice, A.S. (1998) Prediction of drinking outcomes for male alcoholics after 10 to 14 years, *Alcoholism: Clinical And Experimental Research*, 3(22): 559–66.

Prendergast, M.L., Farabee, D., Cartier, J. and Henkin, S. (2002) Involuntary treatment within a prison setting: impact on psychosocial change during treatment, *Criminal Justice and Behaviour*, 29(1): 5–27.

Preston, A., Derricott, J. and Hunt, N. (undated) *Harm Reduction, No 7. What and Why?* Guide Produced by DrugScope. Published by Exchange Publications/Department of Health.

Prime Minister's Strategy Unit (PMSU) (2007) *Building on Progress: Security, Crime and Justice.* London: Prime Minister's Strategy Unit, Cabinet Office.

Prochaska, J.O. and DiClemente, C.C. (2009) Towards a comprehensive model of change, in W.R. Miller and N. Heather (eds) *Treating Addictive Behaviours: Processes of Change* (2nd edn). New York: Plenum.

Project MATCH Research Group (1993) Project MATCH: rationale and methods for a multisite clinical trial matching patients to alcoholism treatment, *Alcoholism: Clinical and Experimental Research*, 17: 1130–45.

Project MATCH Research Group (1997) Matching alcoholism treatments to client heterogeneity: Project MATCH post treatment drinking outcomes, *Journal of Studies on Alcohol*, 58: 7–29.

Raine, P. (2001) *Women's Perspectives on Drugs and Alcohol: The Vicious Circle.* Aldershot: Ashgate.

Raistrick, D., Hodgson, R. and Ritson, B. (eds) (1999) *Tackling Alcohol Together.* London: Free Association Books.

Ramsey, J., Dargan, P., Smyllie, M., Davies, S., Button, J., Holt, D. and Wood, D. (2010) Buying 'legal' recreational drugs does not mean that you are not breaking the law, *Quarterly Journal of Medicine*, 103(10): 777–83.

Rasmussen, S. (2000) *Addiction Treatment: Theory and Practice.* Thousand Oaks, CA: Sage Publications.

Rassool, G.H. (2009) *Alcohol and Drug Misuse: A Handbook for Students and Health Professionals*. Abingdon: Routledge.

Rassool, G.H. (ed.) (1998) *Substance Use and Misuse: Nature, Context and Clinical Interventions*. Oxford: Blackwell Science Ltd.

Reidpath, D.D. and Chan, K.Y. (2005) A method for the quantitative analysis of the layering of HIV-related stigma, *AIDS Care*, 17(4) 425–32.

Reinarman, C., Cohen, P. and Kaal, H. (2004) The limited relevance of drug policy: cannabis in Amsterdam and in San Francisco, *American Journal of Public Health*, 94(5): 836–42.

Reuter, P. and Stevens, A. (2007) *An Analysis of UK Drug Policy: A Monograph Prepared for the UK Drug Policy Commission*. London: UK Drug Policy Commission.

Reuter, P. and Stevens, A. (2008) Assessing UK drug policy from a crime control perspective, *Criminology and Criminal Justice*, 8(4): 461–82.

Rhodes, T. (2002) The risk environment: a frame work for understanding and reducing drug-related harm, *International Journal of Drug Policy*, 3(2): 85–94.

Rhodes, T. and Treloar, C. (2008) The social production of hepatitis C risk among injecting drug users: a qualitative synthesis, *Addiction*, 103(10): 1593–603.

Rhodes, T., Davis, M. and Judd, A. (2004) Hepatitis C and its risk management among drug injectors in London: renewing harm reduction in the context of uncertainty, *Addiction*, 99(5): 621–33.

Richardson, M. (2003) A personal reflective account: the impact of the collation and sharing of information during the course of a child protection investigation, *Child and Family Social Work*, 8: 123–32.

Roberts, G. and Wolfson, P. (2004) The rediscovery of recovery: open to all, *Advances in Psychiatric Treatment*, 10: 37–49.

Roberts, M. (2010) *Young People's Drug and Alcohol Treatment at the Crossroads*. London: DrugScope.

Roe, S. and Mann, L. (2006) *Drug Misuse Declared: Findings from the 2005/06 British Crime Survey, England and Wales*, Home Office Statistical Bulletin 15/06. London: Home Office.

Rogers, C. (1951) *Client-centred Therapy*. London: Constable.

Rolles, S. and Measham, F. (2011) Questioning the method and utility of ranking drug harms in drug policy, *International Journal of Drug Policy*, 22: 243–6.

Ronen, T. (2008) Cognitive-behavioural therapy, in M. Davies (ed.) *The Blackwell Companion to Social Work* (3rd edn). Oxford: Blackwell Publishing.

Room, R. (1989) The U.S. general population's experiences of responding to alcohol problems, *British Journal of Addiction*, 84: 1291–304.

Rothman, A.J. and Salowey, P. (1997) Shaping perceptions to motivate healthy behavior: the role of message framing, *Psychological Bulletin*, 121: 3–19.

Royal College of General Practitioners (RCGP) (2007) *Guidance on the Prevention Testing Treatment and Management of Hepatitis C in Primary Care*. Available online at www.smmgp.org.uk/download/guidance/guidance.003.pdf (accessed 6 October 2011).

Royal Society of Arts Drugs Commission (2007) *Drugs – Facing Facts: The Report of the RSA Commission on Illegal Drugs, Communities and Public Policy*. London: RSA.

Ruch, G. (2005) Relationship-based and reflective practice in contemporary child care social work, *Child and Family Social Work*, 4(2): 111–24.

Ruggerio, V. (1999) Drugs as a password and the law as a drug: discussing the legalisation of illicit substances, in N. South (ed.) *Drugs: Cultures, Controls and Everyday Life*. London: Sage.

Ruggiero, V. (2010) Unintended consequences: changes in organised drug supply in the UK, *Trends in Organised Crime*, 13(1): 46–59.

Russinova, Z. and Cash, D. (2007) Personal Perspectives about the meaning of religion and spirituality among persons with serious mental illnesses, *Psychiatric Rehabilitation Journal*, 30(4): 271–84.

Sampson, S. (2008) Access all areas, *Druglink*, 23(3): 12–15.

Scambler, G. (1998) Stigma and disease: changing paradigms, *The Lancet*, 352(9133): 1054–55.

Schur, E.M. (1965) *Crimes without Victims: Deviant Behaviour and Public Policy – Abortion, Homosexuality, Drug Addiction*. Upper Saddle River, NJ: Prentice-Hall.

Scottish Executive (2006) *Hepatitis C Action Plan For Scotland: Phase I; September 2006–August 2008*. Edinburgh: Scottish Executive.

Scottish Executive (2007) *Getting our Priorities Right: Policy and Practice Guidelines for Working with Children and Families Affected by Problem Drug Use*. Edinburgh: Scottish Executive.

Seddon, T. (2000) Explaining the drug-crime link: theoretical, policy and research issues, *Journal of Social Policy*, 29(1): 95–107.

Seddon, T. (2007) The regulation of heroin: drug policy and social change in early twentieth-century Britain, *International Journal of the Sociology of Law*, 35: 143–56.

Shapiro, H. (1999) Dances with drugs: pop music, drugs and youth culture, in N. South (ed.) *Drugs: Cultures, Controls and Everyday Life*. London: Sage Publications, pp. 17–35.

Shapiro, H. (2005) Nothing about us, without us: user involvement, past, present and future, *Druglink*, 20(3): 10–11.

Simmill-Binning, C., Paylor, I. and Wilson, A. (2009) Alcohol and older people, *Drug and Alcohol Today*, 9(2): 13–18.

Simmonds, L. and Coomber, R. (2009) Injecting drug users: a stigmatised and stigmatising population, *International Journal of Drug Policy*, 20: 121–30.

Simpson, D.D. and Joe, G.W. (1993) Motivation as a predictor of early dropout from drug abuse treatment, *Psychotherapy: Theory, Research, Practice, Training*, 2(30): 357–68.

Simpson, D.D., Joe, G.W., Rowan-Szal, G. and Greener, J. (1995) Client engagement and change during drug abuse treatment, *Journal of Substance Abuse*, 1(7): 117–34.

Simpson, D.D., Joe, G.W. and Rowan-Szal, G.A. (1997a) Drug abuse treatment retention and process effects on follow-up outcomes, *Drug and Alcohol Dependence*, 47: 227–35.

Simpson, D.D., Joe, G.W., Rowan-Szal, G.A. and Greener, J.M. (1997b) Drug abuse treatment process components that improve retention, *Journal of Substance Abuse Treatment*, 14: 565–72.

Simpson, M. (2003) The relationship between drug use and crime: a puzzle inside an enigma, *International Journal of Drug Policy*, 14: 307–19.

Smith, D., Paylor, I. and Mitchell, P. (1993) Partnerships between the independent sector and the probation service, *The Howard Journal of Criminal Justice*, 32(1): 25–38.

Smith, K. (2010) Research, policy and funding – academic treadmills and the squeeze on intellectual spaces, *The British Journal of Sociology*, 61(1): 176–95.

Smyth, B.P., Barry, J. and Keenan, E. (2005) Irish injecting drug users and hepatitis C: the importance of the social context of injecting, *International Journal of Epidemiology*, 34(1): 166–79.

Snyder, V. (1997) Aging, alcoholism and reactions to loss, *Social Work*, 22(3): 232–33.

Social Care Institute for Excellence (SCIE) (2007) *A Common Purpose: Recovery in Future Mental Health Services*. London: SCIE.

Social Work Task Force (2009) *Building a Safe, Confident Future*. Final report of the Social Work Task Force. Available online at www.education.gov.uk/publications/eOrderingDownload/01114-2009DOM-EN.pdf (accessed 6 September 2011).

Spandler, H., Secker, J., Kent, L., Hacking, S. and Shenton, J. (2007) Catching life: the contribution of arts initiatives to recovery approaches in mental health, *Journal of Psychiatric and Mental Health Nursing*, 14: 791–99.

Stall, R., Paul, J., Greenwood, G., Pollack, L., Bein, E., Crosby, G., Mills, T., Binson, D., Coates, T. and Catania, J. (2001) Alcohol use, drug use and alcohol-related problems among men who have sex with men: the urban men's health study, *Addiction*, 96: 1589–1601.

Stanley, N. (2007) Exploring the relationship between children's and adult services, *Child Abuse Review*, 16: 279–82.

Steadman Jones, G. ([1971] 1984) *Outcast London: A Study in the Relationship Between Classes in Victorian Society*. Harmondsworth: Peregrine.

Stein, M.D., Weinstock, M.C., Herman, D.S., Anderson, B.J., Anthony J.L. and Niaura, R. (2006) A smoking cessation intervention for the methadone-maintained, *Addiction*, 101(4): 599–607.

Steinberg, M., Hobbs, J. and Mathewson, K. (2004) *Dangerous Harvest: Drug Plants and the Transformation of Indigenous Landscapes*. New York: Open University Press.

Stenner, P. And Taylor, D. (2008) Psychosocial welfare: reflections on an emerging field, *Critical Social Policy*, 28(4): 415–37.

Stern, T. with Clough, R. (eds) (1996) *Knowing Yourself: A Foundation for Professional Practice*. Lancaster: Lancaster University.

Stevens, A. (2011) *Drugs Crime and Public Health: The Political Economy of Drug Policy*. London: Routledge.

Stevens, A., Berto, D., Heckmann, W., Kerschl, V., Oeuvray, K., Van Ooyan, M., Steffan, E. and Uchtenhagen, A. (2005) Quasi-compulsory treatment of drug dependent offenders: an international literature review, *Substance Use and Misuse*, 40: 269–83.

Stevens, A., Berto, D., Frick, U., Hunt, N., Kerschl, V., Mcsweeney, T., Oeuvray, K., Puppo, I., Maria, A.S., Schaaf, S., Trinkl, B., Uchtenhagen, A. and Werdenich, W. (2006) The relationship between legal status, perceived pressure and motivation in treatment for drug dependence: results from a European study of quasi-compulsory treatment, *European Addiction Research*, 12: 197–209.

Stimson, G. (1992) Public health and health behaviour in the prevention of IDV infection, in P.A. O'Hare, R. Newcombe, A. Matthews, E.C. Bunning and E. Drunker (eds) *Reduction of Drug-related Harm*. London: Routledge, pp. 39–48.

Stimson, G. (1995) Aids and injecting drug use in the United Kingdom, 1987–1993: the policy response and the prevention of the epidemic, *Social Science and Medicine*, 41(5): 699–716.

Stimson, G. (2001) 'Blair declares war': the unhealthy state of British drug policy, *International Journal of Drug Policy*, 11(4): 259–64.

Straussner, S.L.A. (2004) Assessment and treatment of clients with alcohol and other drug abuse problems, in S.L.A. Straussner (ed.) *Clinical Work with Substance-abusing Clients* (2nd edn). New York: Guilford Press.

Sukul, D. (2000) Complementary therapies for the treatment of alcohol dependence, in M. Plant and D. Cameron (eds) *The Alcohol Report*. London: Free Association Books.

Szmigin, I., Griffin, C., Mistral, W., Bengry-Howell, A., Weale, L. and Hackley, C. (2008) Reframing 'binge drinking' as calculated hedonism: empirical evidence from the UK, *International Journal of Drug Policy*, 19(5): 359–66.

Tanenbaum, S.J. (2006) The role of 'evidence' in recovery from mental illness, *Health Care Analysis*, 14: 195–201.

Taylor, A. and Kroll, B. (2004) Working with parental substance misuse: dilemmas for practice, *British Journal of Social Work*, 34: 1115–32.

Temple-Smith, M., Jenkinson, K., Lavery, J., Gifford, S.M. and Morgan, M. (2006) Discrimination or discretion? Exploring dentists' views on treating people with hepatitis C, *Australian Dental Journal*, 51: 318–23.

The NHS Information Centre (2009) *Statistics on Alcohol: England, 2009*. London: The Health and Social Care Information Centre.

The Observer (2010) All parties must see that the drugs war has failed, Editorial, Sunday 19 December. Available online at www.guardian.co.uk/commentis-free/2010/dec/19/observe-editorial-drugs-policy-reform-needed (accessed 9 September 2011).

The Scottish Government (2008) *Hepatitis C Action Plan For Scotland: Phase II; May 2008–March 2011*. Edinburgh: The Scottish Government.

Thevos, A.K., Thomas, S.E. and Randall, C.L. (2001) Social support in alcohol dependence and social phobia: treatment comparisons, *Research on Social Work Practice*, 11(4): 458–72.

Thiede, H., Valleroy, L.A., MacKellar, D.A., Celentano, D.D., Ford, W.L., Hagan, H., Koblin, B.A., LaLota, M., McFarland, W., Shehan, D.A. and Torian, L.V. (2003) Regional patterns and correlates of substance use among young men who have sex with men in 7 US urban areas, *American Journal of Public Health*, 93(11): 1915–21.

Thom, B., Sales, R. and Pearce, J.J. (eds) (2007) *Growing Up with Risk*. Bristol: Policy Press.

Thompson, N. (2008) Anti-discriminatory practice, in M. Davies (2008) (ed.) *The Blackwell Companion to Social Work*. Oxford: Blackwell Publishing.

Thompson, N. (2009) *Understanding Social Work: Preparing for Practice*. Basingstoke: Palgrave Macmillan.

Training Organisation for the Personal Social Services (TOPSS) (2002) *The National Occupational Standards for Social Work*. Leeds: TOPSS.

Trinder, L. (ed.) (2000) *Evidence Based Practice: a Critical Appraisal*. Oxford: Blackwell Science.

Trotter, C. (1999) *Working with Involuntary Clients*. London: Sage Publications.

Tunstill, J., Aldegatem J. and Hughes, M. (2007) *Improving Children's Services Networks: Lessons from Family Centres*. London: Jessica Kingsley Publishers.

UK Drug Policy Commission (2008) *Recovery Consensus Group: A Vision of Recovery*. Available online London: UKDPC.

UKATT Research Team (2001) United Kingdom Alcohol Treatment Trial (UKATT): hypotheses, design and methods, *Alcohol and Alcoholism*, 36(1): 11–21.

UKATT Research Team (2005) Effectiveness of Treatment for Alcohol Problems: Findings of the Randomized UK Alcohol Treatment Trial, *British Medical Journal*, 331: 544–48.

UKHRA (2011) *UKHRA Definition of Harm Reduction*. Available online at www.ukhra.org/harm_reduction_definition.html (accessed 6 October 2011).

Van Bilsen, H. (1991) Motivational interviewing: perspectives from the Netherlands, with particular emphasis on heroin-dependent clients, in W.R. Miller and S. Rollnick (eds) *Motivational Interviewing: Preparing People to Change Addictive Behaviour*. New York: Guilford Press.

Van Bilsen, H. and Van Ernst, A. (1990) Motivating heroin users for change, in G. Bennett (ed.) *Treating Drug Abusers*. London: Routledge.

Van Den Berg, C., Smit, C., Van Brussel, G., Coutinho, R. and Prins, M. (2007) Full participation in harm reduction programmes is associated with decreased risk for human immunodeficiency virus and hepatitis C virus: evidence from the Amsterdam Cohort Studies among drug users, *Addiction*, 102(9): 1454–62.

van Ree, E. (1999) Drugs as a human right, *International Journal of Drug Policy*, 10: 89–98.

Vervaeke, H., Benschop, A. and Korf, D. (2008) Fear, rationality and opportunity: reasons and motives for not trying ecstasy, *Drugs: Education, Prevention and Policy*, 15(4): 350–64.

Wahab, S. (2005) Motivational interviewing and social work practice, *Journal of Social Work*, 5(1): 45–60.

Waller, T. (2005) *An introduction to Early Childhood: A Multidisciplinary Approach*. London: Paul Chapman Publishing.

Walsh, C. (2010) Drugs and human rights: private palliatives, sacramental freedoms and cognitive liberty, *International Journal of Human Rights*, 14(3): 425–41.

Wanigaratne, S., Davis, P., Pryce, K. and Brotchie, J. (2005) The effectiveness of psychological therapies on drug misusing clients, *Research Briefing*: 11, London, National Treatment Agency (NTA).

Warburton, H., May, T. and Hough, M. (2005a) Looking the other way: the impact of reclassifying cannabis on police warnings, arrests and informal action in England and Wales, *British Journal of Criminology*, 45(2): 113–28.

Warburton, H., Turnbull, P. and Hough, M. (2005b) *Occasional and Controlled Heroin Use: Not a Problem?* York: Joseph Rowntree Foundation. Available online at www.jrf.org.uk/knowledge/findings/socialpolicy/0695.asp.

Warrin, J. (2007) Joined-up services for young children and their families: papering over the cracks or reconstructing foundations? *Children and Society*, 21: 87–97.

Watson, E. (2010) A clear diagnosis, *Children and Young People Now*, 13–19 April 2010, p. 13.

Waugh, S. (2003) Parental views on disclosure of diagnosis to their HIV positive children, *AIDS Care*, 15(2): 169–76.

Webb, S. (2006) *Social Work in a Risk Society: Social and Political Perspectives*. Basingstoke: Palgrave Macmillan.

Webster, R. (2002) *Safer Clubbing: A Guide for Licensing Authorities, Club Managers and Promoters*. Home Office and London Drugs Policy Forum in partnership with Release at www.drugs.homeoffice. www.gov.uk/publication-search/young-people/safer-clubbingguide.pd:q13/11/07.

Weil, A. and Rosen, W. (1993) *From Chocolate to Morphine: Everything You Need to Know about Mind-altering Drugs*. Boston, MA: Houghton Mifflin.

Weinstein, J., Whittington, C. and Leiba, T. (2003) *Collaboration in Social Work Practice*. London: Jessica Kingsley Publishers.

White, W. and Kurtz, E. (2005) *The Varieties of Recovery Experience*. Chicago, IL: Great Lakes Addictions Technology Transfer Center.

Wild, T.C. (2006) Social control and coercion in addiction treatment: towards evidence-based policy and practice, *Addiction*, 101(1): 40–9.

Wild, T.C and Enzle, M.E. (2004) Social contagion of motivational orientations, in E.L. and R.M. Ryan (eds) *Handbook of Self-determination Research*. Rochester: University of Rochester Press.

Wild, T.C., Newton-Taylor, B. and Alletto, R. (1998) Perceived coercion among clients entering substance abuse treatment: structural and psychological determinants, *Addictive Behaviors*, 1(23): 81–95.

Wilson, K., Ruch, G., Lymbery, M., Cooper, A., with Becker, S., Brammer, A., Cawson, R., Littlechild, B., Paylor, I. and Smith, R. (2011) *Social Work: An Introduction to Contemporary Practice* (2nd edn). Harlow: Pearson Longman.

Winstock, A., Mitcheson, L., Ramsey, J., Davies, S., Puchnarewicz, M. and Marsden, J. (2011) Mephedrone: use, subjective effects and health risks, *Addiction*, 106: 1991–6.

Winter, R., Nguyen, O., Higgs, P., Armstrong, S., Duong, D., Thach, M.L., Aitken, C. and Hellard, M. (2008) Integrating Hepatitis C testing and counselling in research, *International Journal of Drug Policy*, 19: 66–70.

Wodak, A., Reinarman, C. and Cohen, P. (2002) Cannabis control: costs outweigh the benefits, *British Medical Journal*, 324: 105–8.

Wood, E. (2010) *Evidence Based Policy for Illicit Drugs*. Available online at 341:c3374 doi: 10.1136/bmj.c3374 (published 1 July 2010); (accessed 9 August 2011).

Wood, D., Warren-Gash, C., Ashraf, T., Greene, S., Shather, Z., Trivedy, C., Clarke, S., Ramsey, J., Holt, D. and Dargan, P. (2008) Medical and legal confusion surrounding gamma-hydroxybutyrate (GHB) and its precursors gamma-butyrolactone (GBL) and 1,4-butanediol (1,4BD), *QJM*, 101(1): 23–29.

Wright, N.M.J., Tompkins, C.N.E. and Jones, L. (2005) Exploring risk perception and behaviour of homeless injecting drug users diagnosed with hepatitis C, *Health and Social Care in the Community*, 13(1): 75–83.

Yates, R. (2002) A brief history of British drug policy, 1950–2001, *Drugs: Education, Prevention and Policy*, 9(2): 113–24.

Young, J. (1971) *The Drugtakers: The Social Meaning of Drug Use*. London: Paladin.

Zinberg, N.E. (1984) *Drug, Set, and Setting*. New Haven: Yale University Press.

Index

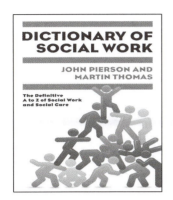

DICTIONARY OF SOCIAL WORK
The Definitive A to Z of Social Work and Social Care

John Pierson and Martin Thomas

9780335238811 (Paperback)
September 2010

eBook also available

With over 1500 entries, this popular dictionary provides concise and up to date explanations of the theories, approaches and terminology that define front-line social work and social care. These entries explain, in jargon-free language, how key concepts can be used to improve practice. Clear explanations outline significant developments such as Every Child Matters and the personalization of adult services.

Key features:

- Entries are helpfully cross referenced and are evidence based
- Written by specialists in the field
- Specific focus on the most recent legislation and policy guidance from government

www.openup.co.uk

OPEN UNIVERSITY PRESS
McGraw - Hill Education

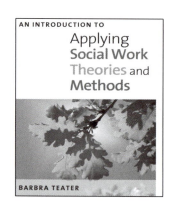

AN INTRODUCTION TO APPLYING SOCIAL WORK THEORIES AND METHODS

Barbra Teater

9780335237784 (Paperback)
July 2010

eBook also available

This practical book provides a basic introduction to the most commonly used theories and methods in social work practice. The book explores the concept of a theory and a method, the difference between the two and the ways in which they are connected. Teater also discusses the social worker-client relationship and offers a handy overview of anti-oppressive practice.

Key features:

- Each chapter explores a single theory or method in depth
- Uses a variety of interactive tools to encourage exploration of thoughts and beliefs
- Step-by-step illustrations show how to apply the theory/method to a social work case

www.openup.co.uk

OPEN UNIVERSITY PRESS
McGraw - Hill Education

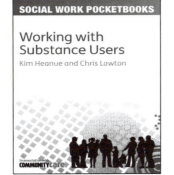

Working with Substance Users

Kim Heanue and Chris Lawton

9780335245192 (Paperback)
2012

eBook also available

This book, part of the Pocketbook series, will be a useful tool not only for experienced professionals but also newly qualified social workers and students. It deals with topics such as why people take substances and the risks involved as well as suggesting ways to deal with challenging situations.

Key features:

- A practical desk guide for social workers to refer to on a day-to-day basis.

www.openup.co.uk

OPEN UNIVERSITY PRESS
McGraw - Hill Education